D0687244

MEN, WOMEN AND TENORS

Portrait by Halmi

PORTRAIT OF MADAME ALDA
Metropolitan Opera House, 1926

FRANCES ALDA

MEN
WOMEN
and
TENORS

with illustrations

AMS PRESS
NEW YORK

Reprinted from the edition of 1937, Boston

First AMS EDITION published 1971

Manufactured in the United States of America

International Standard Book Number :0-404-00306-0

Library of Congress Number :75-149653

All AMS books are printed on acid-free paper that meets the guidelines
for performance and durability of the Committee on Production
Guidelines for Book Longevity of the Council on Library Resources.

AMS PRESS INC.
NEW YORK, N.Y.10003

TO
THE MEMORY OF
MY MOTHER

CONTENTS

ILLUSTRATIONS

PART

I

A DÉBUT AND A DASH OF COLD WATER

Elle ne savait pas
Dans sa candeur naïve . . .
MIGNON

I

DIRECTLY I announced my intention of leaving the Metropolitan Opera in 1930, after twenty-two seasons with the company, it seemed as though every other person I met said to me:

'I suppose you will write a book.'

Then the idea of writing about myself and my experiences at New York's famous opera house through its most brilliant and successful years, both as a singer and as the wife of its director, Giulio Gatti-Casazza, appealed to me about as much as the suggestion that I fly over the moon. For one thing, I had always made fun of the autobiographies of opera singers. If you've ever had one of those pompous, gilded volumes given you for a Christmas present you know what they are like.... 'When I sang this, or that, or the other ... the audience applauded ... cheered ... bravoed ... wept.... The critics praised ... raved ... went into ecstasies.... *My* Violetta ... *My* Manon ... *My* Marguerite ...' Never a mention, you'll notice, of any of the other artists who, likely as not, had something to do with the success of those performances.

Who, I ask you, would want another book of that sort?

I am saying all this at once before my reader has really caught his breath (at least I hope it's *his* breath. I hope men are going to read this book. I think they'll like it. Perhaps more than women will. Just as more men than women have liked me). I am saying all this for the same reason that the management pastes up playbills outside the theatre. Let the public know the best and the worst before the queue forms before the box office.

Therefore, let me announce: I am not writing as a singer; though, naturally, I can't keep from saying a good deal about singing and singers. I am writing as a woman.

For fifty years (everyone from the radio announcer to the Motor License Bureau knows my age, so why try to hide it from you?) — for fifty-one years, to be exact — I have been enjoying tremendously the adventure of being alive. I have had success and failure; and, perhaps, more than my share of fame in an art that I love passionately and into which, for more than thirty years, I have put every day hours of hard, concentrated study and work. I have known love and ecstasy; deep hurt and bitterness and loss; and some strong, sustaining friendships. And whether I owe this to an irrepressible sense of humor or to an almost equally irrepressible pride, I can't say; there has grown up in me a tolerance for the extraordinary, sometimes ridiculous, often exasperating creatures that are men and women. Many of those I have known are what the world calls famous. Not all of them singers or musicians. There have been half a dozen kings, and several queens; princes, great ladies, ballet girls; bank presidents and tenors; movie stars, ambassadors, and crooners; débutantes, admirals, advertising men, politicians, lawyers and other thieves.

But all of them interesting.

I refuse to know bores. My world is active and amusing; sometimes exciting; never dull.

That is the world I mean to write about.

Naturally, as is true of everybody's world, mine revolves around me. So I can't leave myself out, entirely. You will have to get used to seeing me and my world through my eyes.

There! Now you know what the play is about.

Does it seem to you worth the price of admission?

If you decide to come in, hurry, please. The overture is finished. The lights are dimming. The curtain is about to rise.

WHEN does a life begin? At the instant of birth, with that first protesting cry against being alive at all? Or in some later moment of sharp self-consciousness? Some moment when every fibre of your body and mind — perhaps of your soul, too — is suddenly intensely aware of its livingness?

At the later, I think.

Such a moment, deeply realized, shapes the life forever after.

Accordingly, my life story begins not in the New Zealand city where I was born, and about which I remember nothing at all, but twenty-three years later, on the rainy night of December 7, 1908, which was the night when I faced my first American audience.

RIGOLETTO — with a new 'Gilda,' Mlle. Frances Alda. With Caruso, Amato, Didur, and Madame Homer.

That was how the papers had announced my début.

Not that Gilda and I were new to each other. I had sung the rôle of the hunchback's daughter many times — at La Monnaie in Brussels, at Covent Garden (also with Caruso — strange prophecy!), in Warsaw, in Buenos Aires, and — highest honor of them all — in Parma, at the annual Verdi festival.

But what set this performance apart from all others before and after it was that the Metropolitan and I were meeting for the first time. I hadn't the ghost of an idea of it then, but in the twenty-two years ahead of me its draughty stage was to become as familiar as my own drawing-room. Its affairs, from the chronic toothache of the eldest stage hand and the squeaky high note of the trombone player to the weakness of certain of its trustees for certain types of singers and première danseuses, were to form my horizon. All the feuds, jealousies, successes, failures, envies, ambitions, and despairs that can breed in the fertile soil of the world's biggest company of operatic temperaments were to season my daily life with joy, tragedy, bitterness, or humor

None of that, of course, was known to me then.

In the international world of grand opera there are three stages where every singer dreams of triumphing some day. These are La Scala in Milan, London's Covent Garden, and New York's Metropolitan. I had already achieved success in two of these. That night was to be my final and severest test as a singer. By my success or failure, at the Metropolitan, all the rest of my career — and I was just twenty-three — would stand or fall.

All this filled my mind as the ripple of violins in the Second Act overture died away. The house went dark; the stage lights came on. The great crimson velvet curtains swung impressively backward and upward, revealing the walled garden of Rigoletto's house in Mantua, and I, his daughter, making my first bow to the richest, most powerful, most-difficult-to-please audience in the world.

Was I scared?

No one who doesn't know from actual experience of it what stage fright can do to one could possibly know *how* scared. I have never gone on the stage without that awful terror gripping me somewhere in the middle. In that I am no different from most singers. I remember Caruso telling me that he had never sung a single performance that he wasn't nervous, and miserable and afraid.

But stage fright is being afraid that you won't do the best that you know you are capable of doing. It is not concerned with anyone or anything but yourself. This fear that set every nerve in my body to quivering lay outside my own emotions. It had a basis of proved reality. It even had a face, and a name.

That morning every music critic in New York had received an anonymous letter. The letters were all alike. Gatti had brought one of them to my dressing-room as I was making up for the performance.

What I read was a scurrilous attack on my ability as a singer, and on my personal life and character. The writer went so far as to say that I was not the Frances Alda I represented myself as being, but one of the Barrison sisters, well known in the English music halls, and a person totally unfitted to appear before the Metropolitan's audience. The letter concluded with the request that the critics turn thumbs down on my performance that evening.

There had been little doubt in Gatti's mind as to the intent of the letters.

'It is an attack at me, as Director, through you,' he said.

'But why?'

The dresser was setting my wig in place. I could not turn my head, but Gatti's sombre face was reflected in the mirror. I watched it.

'You know how I found things when I came to take charge a few months ago. I wrote you at the time. In signing my contract I had understood that I was to have full power. As I had at La Scala. And as Conried, my predecessor here, had. Instead of which, I arrive here to find that the Board has engaged a co-director to divide the duties and the authority with me. So there are two of us. And who is that other director? Andreas Dippel. A member of the company. A tenor. You know what I think of tenors! It is an impossible situation. The company is split into factions, cliques, jealousies. The Germans hate the Italians...'

'But why do they attack me? I am not Italian. I am English.'

He lifted his shoulders.

'*Cosa vuoi fare?* You were singing at La Scala when I was Director there. Everyone knows that the Board engaged Toscanini and you and me...'

'They engaged me first.' I said. 'I had signed my contract with the Metropolitan and the contract for Buenos Aires *before* you, or Toscanini either, had been engaged to come to America. No one can say it was you brought me here.'

He made that gesture of the hands I was to come to know so well.

'They know that I am in love with you. That is enough to give birth to a cabal. And that you are going to marry me ...'

My hair is red. That means something as to temper. I could feel mine rising. I burst out:

'I have told you a hundred times, Giulio, that I won't marry you. Must I tell all New York that, too?'

Down the corridor the call-boy was sing-songing, 'Second Act!'

'Patience, *cara*,' Gatti implored me. 'Try to keep calm ...'

By that time I was boiling mad. I swept my skirts by him without a word and went onto the stage.

Standing in the wings while the overture began, I recalled with sudden illuminating vividness something that had happened at rehearsal the day before. There had been but one. I had arrived in New York, my sailing delayed by concert engagements and by a motor accident in Paris that had resulted for me in a broken arm, just a week before. At the rehearsal, whilst I was singing, I saw a woman member of the company who had no part in that opera come into the house and, followed by her husband, seat herself in the second row.

That is something that is never done in the theatre. No members of the company, however important, are supposed to attend the rehearsal of other singers.

Toscanini, who was standing with Gatti in the wings (Spetrino was conducting), spoke to me in Italian: 'Sing it half voice.'

I obeyed, and went through the rest of the opera in so light a tone that the prima donna, who had sung Gilda many times, and who was now too old for the rôle, could not possibly judge of my voice. Presently I saw her gather her furs about her. Attended by her husband, she swept out in disgust.

Could she, or her husband, be the author of those anonymous letters? If so, what a cruel revenge for one artist to take against a younger one who could not help becoming her rival! She had as press agent, so Gatti had told me, a man who was musical critic for one of the big New York dailies. It so happened that his sister had occupied the apartment above my own on the Avenue Bugeaud in Paris. Before I sailed for my New York début she had offered me a letter to her brother in America. With the arrogant self-sufficiency of my youth I had not accepted it. I was so confident of success that one critic had seemed to me beneath my notice.

Had I thereby made an enemy? And one who was in a position to wreck my career before it was begun?

Then the curtains parted. I heard my cue. I went forward into the floodlights.

Spetrino, the conductor, was eyeing me sternly. (Oh, *why* hadn't they given me Toscanini, whom I knew from the days at La Scala and whose baton was an admonitory, but friendly, finger?) All the while Amato's fruity baritone was bidding me be an obedient daughter and not ask to see more of the world than I could glimpse over the top of my prayer book, all the while I was singing my dutiful responses, it seemed as though icy fingers were playing the score up and down my backbone.

Beyond the orchestra the house was filled with misty darkness. In those rows of red plush-covered seats, in the gilded boxes of the famous Diamond Horseshoe, in the packed overhanging balconies, thousands of New Yorkers leaned forward to see and to hear the Metropolitan's new soprano.

What were they thinking?

What could I expect from those critics who had received the condemnatory letters?

If I could win the audience, the critics would have to come round. I had won other audiences. The Belgians had forgiven my bad French, and the Milanese my shaky Italian for the sake of a voice that was fresh and young and true, and for my plump youth and red hair and *simpatica* smiles. Would those lean-cheeked, hawk-nosed Americans sitting back in the boxes with their high-corseted, brocaded, and jewelled wives, and their lovely, tall, cool débutante daughters, approve me? Desperately I hoped they would. Other audiences I had played with, flirted with. None of them, till now, had I taken *au grand sérieux*.

That had been my weak spot. The great Melba, sitting in the box with Marchesi (who had taught her, and me) when I made my début at the Opéra Comique in Paris, had put her finger on it. And Marchesi, shrewd and theatre-wise as she was, had reported it to me later.

'She takes it too casually,' Melba had said. 'Greatness doesn't come that way.'

So I had, then. But there was nothing casual about my attitude now.

The act went on. Rigoletto went away, and through the door in the wall came the Duke, my lover. Caruso! As always, something warm and vibrant happened to the house when he came on the stage.

'*Coraggio, cara,*' he whispered, and squeezed my arm, while his melting, lover-like tones flowed round me and out to the rapt audience.

The curtain fell. Applause. We took our calls, Caruso generously giving me first place. The great tenor was the finest artist, the truest friend, the kindest person I ever knew in the theatre. We sang together hundreds of times. I never knew him to be other than generous and encouraging, and as interested in another's success as in his own. 'Why not try it this way?' he would often suggest, and then show his ideas how a phrase should be sung, or a bit of business played. And his ideas were always good. He was actor and artist to his fingertips. Many times, later on, while we ate spaghetti and ravioli and zabaglione in out-of-the-way Italian restaurants he was always 'discovering,' and dragging Scotti and Gatti and me off to (to prove to us that the cooking there was every bit as good as in Naples), we laughed together over that uneasy début of mine.

Perhaps he could sympathize with me because of what he had gone through on the season's opening night after the publicity of the 'monkey-house scandal, several years before.' (The in-

I always loved Caruso's boyishness

cident that provoked that storm of publicity grew out of Caruso's liking to visit zoos. He had an enthusiastic and child-like love of wild animals, especially monkeys. One day he was walking about the Central Park monkey house, where a number of persons recognized him. One of these, a young woman and not ill-favored, proceeded to follow the famous tenor around, staring at him. Finally, Caruso responded to her evident interest in him and showed his appreciation of her charms, in a fashion customary in Italy. Probably no woman has ever gone through Italy without getting a pinch or two. But this young woman was American and was promptly and loudly 'insulted'). The opera that night was *Bohème*. When the curtain rose Caruso was on the stage, his back to the audience. There were several moments before he turned and sang, moments in which the sweat ran down his face for agony of not knowing whether applause or hisses would meet him when he showed himself to the public. The atmosphere on the stage was full of apprehension as the cue came. He turned, and from the waiting house came the most tremendous ovation it had ever given him.

The relief of it almost rendered him unable to go on.

Our Third Act went better. At its close, when I sang the touching confession of my shame, I could feel the wall of ice that had been between me and the audience melt. Something warm and human flowed over the footlights to me.

Then, curtain. And back to my dressing-room to change to the boy's doublet and hose for the last act. I loved that costume. It had won for me the hearts of the critical audience at the Verdi festival in Parma, who were so used to middle-aged Gildas with thick calves and bulging thighs that had to be concealed by careful draperies, that they cheered my trim figure in the smooth, skin-tight black hose, before I sang a note.

Well, even in the Metropolitan, legs counted. I was to have proof of this long afterward when we gave *Marouf*. Someone questioned why I should sing the part of the Princess, who dons boy's attire for her escapades. The question brought the retort from James Huneker:

'There are two excellent reasons why Alda should sing the rôle. Her right and left legs.'

Now I set the cap with its perky feather on my red curls, swung the short velvet cape from one shoulder, and studied my reflection in the mirror.

My spirits were rising.

A knock at the dressing-room door. It was Andreas Dippel, co-Director with Gatti. He came, he said, to congratulate me.

'No new singer at the Metropolitan in recent years has met with such success.'

I thanked him, and he went away. I had almost forgotten those anonymous letters. My nervous fears had abated. I went through the last act, with the great aria '*Donna e mobile*,' which whenever Caruso sang it brought wild applause, almost debonairely.

It was over.

Half a dozen curtain calls; Caruso and Amato and Madame Homer (who had sung Maddalena), giving place to me. I could see the people standing in the aisles with opera glasses raised the better to see what I looked like.

If only I could see into their minds and know what they were thinking!

Then suddenly I was tired, exhausted. 'No, no, I can't see anyone,' I said to the repeated knocks at the dressing-room door. Emilie, the maid I had brought with me from Paris, was waiting with a long fur cloak. She wrapped me in it and I went quickly out the stage door to the waiting cab, and drove to the Ansonia Hotel.

While New Yorkers were having supper at Jack's and the Café Martin and discussing that night's opera and its débutante, I dropped off to sleep, too utterly weary to wonder what any of them might be saying, or to care for anything but the blessedness of oblivion.

BUT next morning....

I sat up in bed and went through one newspaper after another, caring for nothing but the reviews of *Rigoletto* at the Metropolitan. I sent Emilie downstairs for more papers, and still later editions. The bed was covered with crumpled sheets of newsprint.

The reviews were all terrible.

I had no voice.... I showed myself too untrained for the Metropolitan.... If I was a sample of what Signor Gatti-Casazza meant to introduce to New York, things were just too bad....

And, finally:

'The young singer who made her début last evening comes from the land of the sheep, and she bleated like one of them....'

Was I down in the blues?

My heart ached and my throat was sore. I shivered all over. I hated America.

'I'll never sing in your old opera house again,' I stormed at Gatti when he came to see me. 'I'll take the next boat back to Europe.'

He shook his beard at me gloomily.

'You can't. You are billed to sing *Le Villi* ten days from today.'

'I tell you I shall. Instantaneously. I'll break the contract...'

At that moment Emilie came into the sitting-room. She carried a huge basket of roses. I reached for the card and read:

MADAME LILLIAN NORDICA

and this message:

> There was never a young singer who appeared at the Metropolitan who wasn't severely criticized on her début. Melba, Sembrich, Farrar, myself... all of us have gone through what you are going through today. Have courage. Affectionate good wishes.

To the end of my days I shall never forget Nordica's generous gesture toward a newcomer whom she had never met, and to whom she had no particular reason for being kind. Years later I was able to repay part of the debt I felt I owed her, by prompting Gatti to arrange for her several gala performances at the Metropolitan. And always, if I have needed any urge to be cordial to young singers, I have had the remembrance of Nordica's roses and message, and what they meant to me on that dark morning-after.

'*Va bene.*' I said to Gatti. 'I shall not break the contract. Not immediately. I shall sing on the seventeenth. But meanwhile I must see a doctor. My throat is sore.'

He sent me to Doctor Clarence Rice.

That visit turned out to be the first of many visits. For more than twenty years, until his death, Doctor Rice took care of me and kept me in condition to sing sometimes three performances a week.

On that first morning Doctor Rice looked at my throat, and then he looked at me. Presumably, he had also looked at the morning papers.

'Here is my prescription,' he said. 'Forget about your throat. Go down to the Library in Astor Place, ask for the newspaper files, and read the reviews of Emma Eames's, of Farrar's, of Jean de Reszké's first performance. If your throat still bothers you tomorrow, come back and let me look at it.'

I followed his advice. In the Library I pored over the old newspapers. The same critic who had complained of my 'bleat' had been offended by Caruso's 'Italianate mannerisms.' They had looked down their noses at the glorious de Reszké. Farrar, then, in 1908, at the height of her popularity, had seemed to the reviewers of her début '*peu de chose.*'

I gave the files back to the librarian and went out. The streets were thronged with Christmas shoppers. Salvation Army Santa Clauses tinkled bells on every corner. In front of Grace Church a street band played 'Silent Night.' I hailed a hansom, and told the driver to take me up Fifth Avenue — past Madison Square, folded in the winter's first snowfall; past the Waldorf Astoria, in whose successor I now make my home; past the banks and the clubs and the brownstone fronts of the Metropolitan's box-holders. Past the pile of masonry on the corner of Forty-Second Street where the new Public Library was in process of building.

Suddenly I felt the energy, the vitality, the thrill that *is* New York. I leaned over the hansom's apron and shook my fist at the city.

'I'm going to conquer you,' I whispered fiercely. 'See if I don't.'

PART
II

I WANT TO SING

Tout un monde enchanté
Semble naître à mes yeux;
Tout me fête et m'enivre,
Et mon âme ravie
S'élance dans la vie
Comme un oiseau s'envole aux cieux.

ROMÉO ET JULIETTE

II

NEW YORK, Winter, 1908.
Roosevelt going out, Taft coming in.

Everywhere orchestras playing the waltz from *The Merry Widow*. Prohibition undreamed of. Women in long sheath skirts and enormous feather or fur boas, and cartwheel hats sprouting flowers, ribbons, buckles, plumes.... Rustling taffeta petticoats. High, laced-up shoes.

Men still talking about last year's panic.

Everybody saying, 'Ain't it awful, Mabel!'

'Why?' I demanded. 'What does it mean?'

But nobody could tell me.

Everybody whistling or humming the new songs: 'I Hear You Calling Me' and 'Every Little Movement Has a Meaning All its Own.' Everybody wondering what would happen to society now that Mrs. Astor had died. Everybody talking about Mrs. Stuyvesant Fish's parties which Harry Lehr made 'too amusing.'

Over on Broadway, Maude Adams playing *What Every Woman Knows*, Ethel Barrymore starring in *Lady Frederick*, John Drew packing houses in *Jack Straw*.

New York with *two* opera companies, playing simultaneously. No other city in the world offered such grand opera. During the week that I made my début music-lovers had choice of:

At the Metropolitan: Mon. *Rigoletto*, with Alda, Homer, Caruso, Amato, Didur (Spetrino conducting). Wed. *Aïda*, with Eames, Homer, Caruso, Scotti, Didur (Toscanini conducting). Thurs. *Goetterdaemmerung*, with Fremstad, Homer, Schmedes, Hinckley. Fri. *Bohème*, with Sembrich, Bonci Amato, Didur. Sat. Matinée *Carmen*, with Farrar, Gay,

Caruso (Toscanini conducting). Sat. eve. *Tosca* with Eames, Scotti (Spetrino conducting).

At the Manhattan Opera House (Companini conducting): *Le Jongleur de Notre Dame*, with Mary Garden; *Lucia de Lammermoor*, with Tetrazzini; *Thaïs*, with Mary Garden; *La Traviata*, with Tetrazzini and John McCormack.

Oh, I know I am not the first to sing the glories of yesterday's snows. But where are the operatic personalities today to stand beside these I have mentioned?

'You can't give opera without personalities,' I told Eddy Johnson when he took over the Metropolitan.

And where are the singers?

There is but one. Kirsten Flagstad. Last winter Mary Garden and I went together to hear her. Never in all my years at the Metropolitan have I heard anyone look, play, sing, interpret Isolde as this woman does. She *is* Isolde. I looked at Mary Garden. She was motionless and enrapt, and great tears were running down her face. My own heart was in my mouth from the beauty of the performance.

Mary Garden — gifted artist, beautiful woman. She was the sensation of New York that winter of 1908-1909. Stories went round about her wit. At one dinner she had as *vis-à-vis* Chauncey Depew. His eyes fixed themselves on Mary's gown, very décolleté. She asked him what he was looking at. 'I am wondering, Miss Garden,' he said, 'what keeps that gown up.'

Mary flashed him one of her enchanting smiles: 'Two things, Mr. Depew, your age and my discretion.'

I had known Garden in Paris when we were both singing at the Opéra Comique. And now, after thirty years, we are warm friends. No American artist has given more and none deserves more from the public. Her Mélisande, which Debussy taught her, and which she sang for the first time in New York that winter, remains immortal. She was so still. Just that one little phrase: '*Il fait froid ici*,' as it came from her lips, and you shivered under the chill winds that blow between the worlds of

Where are the operatic personalities today?
There is but one. Kirsten Flagstad

the real and the unreal. Contrasted with it, Bori's rendering of the line sounded like a schoolgirl who steps out of bed without her slippers.

Conried, who had preceded Gatti as Director of the Metropolitan, had been an ill man for some time before his resignation, else he would not have allowed the production rights to Massenet's works as well as all Debussy's to be bought by Hammerstein, who proceeded to make his Manhattan Opera House the Metropolitan's rival. Hammerstein was a brilliant producer, but he lacked the shrewd business acumen that Gatti possessed. Gatti never lost sight of the box-office receipts in the cause of ART. He never forgot what Verdi had said to him when he went to La Scala: 'An opera house exists to be filled.'

Several years later when Hammerstein failed, the production rights to many of the French operas were taken up by the Metropolitan, and a number of the singers joined our company at the Metropolitan.

Tetrazzini sang one performance at the Metropolitan that first winter I was in New York. Lina Cavalieri, then one of the stars in the Hammerstein firmament, had made her début at the Metropolitan in 1906 — *Fedora* with Caruso. She sang there a season. A beautiful woman with a good voice.

The Metropolitan Opera Company glittered with stars. Sembrich was going out that year. She sang her farewell performance in February. It was an amazing display of her musical versatility. She sang acts from three different operas and played a violin obligato with the orchestra. Eames, too, left the company that season. In her autobiography she recounts her triumphs at the Metropolitan, but she does not mention that a certain little Italian tenor named Caruso was singing with her, and that he may have had a share in winning those enthusiastic audiences. I have been told that long after Eames left the Metropolitan she was at a luncheon one day at the Duchesse de Richelieu's and gave, freely and somewhat acrimoniously, her opinion of the various artists — Farrar, Jeritza, Bori, Alda...

'Oh, Alda? What do I think about her? All right for the chorus.'

Fremstad and Gadski stayed on with the company for a number of years. Fremstad sang magnificently. Her interpretation of Kundry, the enchantress in *Parsifal*, was memorable. It was a characteristic trait of Gatti's character that made him insist that Fremstad, who had sometimes been temperamental and difficult for him to deal with, should sing her farewell as Elizabeth in *Tannhäuser*. It was, of all her rôles, the one in which she shone least. He did the same thing when Farrar made her farewell. She wanted to sing *Butterfly*, in which she had triumphed so signally. But he insisted that she sing *Zaza* that afternoon.

When I joined the company Scotti had been singing with it for several seasons. Amato made his Metropolitan début that same year. So did Herbert Witherspoon.

But the great treasure of the Metropolitan was Caruso. On nights when he was singing, every seat in the house was sold out.

Gatti paid Caruso twenty-five hundred dollars a performance. He was worth every penny of it in box-office receipts.

Caruso and I quickly became friends. We had met before. I had sung with him at Covent Garden two years earlier. I always loved his boyishness, and the irresistible sense of humor that made him play pranks with everyone, on and off the stage.

SUCH was the New York I had set myself to conquer. Now, what about me?

I was born at Christ Church, New Zealand, and christened Frances Jeanné Davies. My father was British, but he was gone from my life before I was old enough to remember him at all. My young mother took my brother and me and returned from New Zealand to Melbourne, where her parents were living. She had a charming voice and had been trained to sing, light rôles and in concerts. She was determined to make a career for herself and to support her children. When she was twenty-four she came to America, to California, bringing us with her.

I never see it snowing that I don't think of my mother.

I am four years old, my brother Alby is six. We stand at the window with our noses pressed to the pane, watching the white flakes come down over San Francisco. It is twilight, but the snowflakes make a dusty pattern against the dark.

We are waiting for our mother to come home.

The door behind us opens. We turn eagerly ...

'Mama!'

She stands there a moment in her long coat of sealskin, and the tiny sealskin cap on her bright hair. The snow is powdered thickly over her shoulders and makes a little drift in the fold of the cap's crown.

Suddenly she sways, and falls forward ...

Someone comes, running. There is confusion, hushed voices, a sense of anxiety.

Two days later she is dead, of pneumonia. Her young American husband, our stepfather, to whom she had been married only a few weeks, stares at Alby and me in bewilderment.

Our grandfather made the long journey from Melbourne to fetch the two orphans home. I have no recollections of him then, or of the voyage. My next memory-picture is of a room in a strange house, of someone lifting me into a high-chair, of someone asking:

'Are you hungry, dear? Do you want something to eat?'

'No, I want to sing,' I replied.

And sing I did, a song which began and ended too, as far as I remember now:

'Naughty boy, naughty boy,
Naughty boy, naughty boy ...'

If my mother's children needed any extra grace to win the heart of my mother's mother, that song did it. Grandmother adored and spoiled us both, as conscientiously as Grandfather disciplined us. Grandmother was French, and of the nobility. Grandfather was German. He had been violinist at the court of Bavaria in the extravagant days of Ludwig the Mad and his mistress, Lola Montez. When the revolution broke Grandfather went to France, where he met and fell madly in love with my grandmother. She ran away from home, her church, her titles to marry the impecunious violinist. They went to Italy, where he organized an Italian opera company, which he booked, grandly, for a tour of the world.

They went in sailing vessels to South America. They crossed the mountains in mule carts heaped with scenery, costume trunks, and musical instruments. They gave *The Barber of Seville* and *Don Giovanni* and *Robert the Devil* to audiences of Spanish grandees and *mestizos* and unkempt Indian herdsmen in tattered serapes. Grandmother, exquisite little aristocrat to her fingertips, copied music, sewed spangles on costumes, sang rôles no other member of the company could or would sing, and had a baby in each one of half a dozen cities. My mother was born in Montevideo. She was christened Leonora, which might mean that the company had added *Trovatore* to its repertory. Two boys could claim Lima and Mexico City as birthplaces. Another daughter (years later, as Madame Frances Saville she was a member of the Hofoper in Vienna, and a guest artist at the Metropolitan in New York) was born in San Francisco.

The family already numbered nine when the opera company arrived in Australia. Grandfather bought a house in St. Kilda, a suburb of Melbourne, then, in the late sixties, a raw, gangling town. But he had faith in the country's future, and in its appetite for Italian opera. He took over the management of an opera house and sent companies on tour of the provinces. His own family settled down and Grandmother had four more children. The last, a boy, was born after my mother had married and had given birth to her son. This uncle, younger than Alby, older than I, was our playmate when we went back to St. Kilda to live.

L ITTLE Francie Davies had a temper as fiery as her hair. She was stage-struck. She gave herself airs. But in spite of all this — or was it because of it? — our croquet lawn was the most popular playground in St. Kilda. The theatre which Alby built for me out of lath and old burlap under the eucalyptus trees against the orchard wall played to capacity.

My fiancés formed the major part of the audience. Next door to my grandmother's house was a boys' school. Across the road from it was another. Before I was ten I was engaged to half the boys in each school.

What is it that makes small boys single out one little girl and flock round her, with no eyes or ears for the others, who may be prettier than she? What is it in one woman that makes men drift to her as inevitably as water runs downhill? Everyone who has ever written an opera, a play, or a novel has tried to answer that question in his own way. One person's guess is as good as another's. Call it charm, call it sex appeal, call it vitality — what you will — that current, strong in one, weak in another, is what determines a woman's destiny.

The theatre on the croquet lawn was the scene of my first triumphs. My fiancés cheered any song, any bit of tragedy, I gave them. In response I was as haughty as I fancied a prima donna should be.

My haughtiness was not allowed to show itself inside the house, where children were expected to be promptly obedient, industrious ('Find some work to do, *chérie,*' Grandmother would admonish me whenever I showed a tendency to idleness), and to speak French or German at table. Under this rule Alby, my young uncle, and I evolved a form of conversation that was our own: *'Comment est-ce qu'on dit* "Pass me the butter"?' — *'Comment est-ce qu'on dit* "Are you going to play tennis this afternoon"?' — *'Comment est-ce qu'on dit* "How about a bathe after tea"?'

I cannot remember a time when I couldn't beat my boy playmates at tennis, or swim as far and as fast as they could. All through the long Australian summers we ran on the beach and were in and out of the water half a dozen times a day.

The house at St. Kilda was wide and roomy, with a hall running straight through it. On one side was the salon, kept locked, and not to be entered by children. Across from it was the Green Room where the piano was, and where I was expected to practise three hours a day at the piano, and two hours at the violin. At any moment Grandfather's head, bald on top with a ring of white curls around the bald spot, might thrust itself between the curtains, and Grandfather's peremptory voice demand corrections and repetitions. After all, he would remind me when I showed signs of rebellion, I myself had chosen to study music. That was true. On my fifth birthday, when they asked what I wanted for a present, I had said:

'A piano. And piano lessons.'

Two years later, in the same way, I asked for a violin.

The piano and the violin have remained my good friends through all the years since those childish birthdays. I gave up the latter when I began to study singing with Madame Marchesi in Paris. She told me to try to do one thing, and that thing well. Not to sing a little, play a little, fiddle a little. But Grandfather's strict discipline bore this good fruit — I can play any piece of music at sight. That is something I have been grateful for many a time when professional accompanists have failed to appear, or have balked at sight of some piece of music.

Which reminds me:

Last winter, at Palm Beach, my friend Mrs. Donahue asked me to sing at her house. The concert was impromptu.

I put a song of César Franck's, with which I intended to begin the concert, on the piano. The accompanist took one look at it, turned pale, and stood up.

'I can only play in three keys,' he objected.

'That's just too bad,' I said. 'Where does that leave me? What am I going to do?' And a good deal more.

'Now, Alda, don't get excited,' Jessie Donahue kept telling me. 'We'll get you an accompanist. We'll get B——. You know who he is. One of the two-piano team at the —— Club. He's the best musician in Palm Beach.'

'Fine and dandy,' I said.

Presently B—— appeared. He sat at the piano and music began to trickle out from under his fingers. I gave him the Franck song.

'I can't play that,' he said, pointing to a long run. 'I can't read.'

The guests were beginning to arrive. There was nothing for it but for me to sit down and play my own accompaniments while Palm Beach's best musician stood by.

But singing into a piano is no fun. After several songs I turned to B——. 'Surely you can play something I sing. *Butterfly*? *Manon*? *Bohème*?'

His face brightened.

'I can play *Bohème*.'

He took my place at the piano, I stood up, and we began Mimi's tender 'Farewell' — two or three bars. Then, suddenly, improvisations of jazz:

BOOP — BOOP — A — DOOP
YO — HO — HO — HO — HO

I grabbed his shoulder.

'*Don't* do that,' I said. 'Play it the way it's written.'

He stared up at me.

'But it's so *badly* written.'

'Well, I suppose it's all as you see it.'

IN MY childhood I never had a singing lesson. That did not deter me from singing, however — and all the time. As I practised, as I played croquet and cricket with the boys, as I sat with Grandmother, dutifully learning how to darn and mend fine laces, and how to tell rose point from point de Venise — something she believed every woman should know — I sang.

Grandmother would clap her hands over her ears and beg me to be still.

'For just a quarter of an hour.'

With one eye on the clock and one on my needle, I would obey. Meanwhile she would tell me of some of the great singers she had heard in Europe, the singers who had brought the art of *bel canto* to life once more. Grisi, Persiani, Trebelli, Alboni, Jenny Lind and Patti, and Madame Viardot and her brother Manuel Garcia, the greatest teacher of singing in all Europe. He had taught Jenny Lind and Mathilde Marchesi, with whom my own aunt, Frances Saville, was then studying.

I never smell lavender that I do not see Grandmother's bedroom on the first floor of the house behind the Green Room. It is cool and shaded, with the Venetian blinds drawn against the bright sun outside. There is the high, wide black walnut bed, and the sofa against the foot of it where Grandmother rested every afternoon in a white lawn negligée with her curly dark hair loose about her plump white shoulders. There is the wardrobe, the biggest one I ever saw anywhere, where the linen was kept. . . . And Grandmother unlocking the drawers to take out piles of snowy, sweet-smelling sheets for Bertha, her maid, to carry upstairs. . . .

It was a sweet, simple, wholesome existence for any child to grow up in.

Perhaps it is too simple to be worth telling now. Yet all those things — the hours in the Green Room, Grandfather's afternoon naps when he would lie on the sofa and I would be called to stand behind his head and gently rub his bald spot (how I hated that!) until sleep came to him and set me free; Grandmother's stories about my mother, and the scrapbooks of press clippings that told of my mother's concert career that I pored over for hours; the day Alby, playing French Revolution, assembled all my dolls in my own little garden and shot them down with a toy cannon, thereby ending dolls as playthings for me forever; running very fast up the hill to the day school where I went when I was quite young; and running faster and faster down again with the wind from the sea in my face — all these things are a background from which I, as I am today, emerge. It is not too fanciful to believe that without all of them I should not have been I.

Grandmother had her own ideas about the proper behavior and dress for little girls. Most of these seemed to me ignominiously old-fashioned. I was a fat little girl. That was bad enough. To go dressed in shapeless white linen frocks, cotton stockings, round plain hats, and with my curly hair in long ringlets which Grandmother or Bertha brushed twice a day over a polished curling-stick, seemed more than I could endure. When I looked in the glass, my appearance had none of that allure that I felt belonged to one destined for greatness. I teased Grandmother, I pleaded, I wept. Finally she relented. I was told that I might go into Melbourne, to the largest shop, and choose for myself a dress and a hat.

'Alone?'

'Alone,' Grandmother agreed.

I refused to see the misgivings in her face.

I went on my adventure. When the box containing the purchases was delivered I carried it to my room. I tore it open, scattered the tissue paper, and took out the beautiful garments. I put them on and paraded before my mirror. At last I was dressed as befitted my talents!

The dress was of very bright blue velvet. It had a tight bodice that strained over my breasts. The skirt was ruffled and looped and puffed and piped. A row of large pearl buttons fastened it down the back. The hat matched it perfectly — a dashing affair of blue velvet that had to be skewered to my head with two long pearl pins.

The costume might have been designed for the first purchase of a woman whose husband had struck it right in the mines. Or for a barmaid's trousseau. But I was sublimely happy in it.

I presented myself, all smiles, before Grandmother.

A stricken look came over her face.

'Francie!'

'Isn't it beautiful?' I demanded.

But already she was ringing for Bertha to bring her bonnet.

'Take those things off at once,' she commanded. 'Do them up in the box. I will go into town and ask the shop to take them back. And I will bring you back a nice, plain, white frock...'

And she did.

In time I forgave Grandmother for the loss of the blue velvet dress. But the cotton stockings rankled for years. Otherwise I would not have done what I did do, immediately after Grandmother's death (when I was sixteen): I went into Melbourne and ordered six dozen pairs of silk stockings.

They were the first purchases I ever made for myself after the affair of the blue velvet.

THE year I was twelve I was sent to boarding-school. Miss Brown's was the most select school in Australia. Leaving me there, Grandmother exacted of Miss Brown one solemn promise. On no account was I to be allowed to sing. Grandmother knew well how a child, straining her voice, as all children do, could impair it forever.

Of course, I disobeyed. And was reprimanded, and punished.

'Why shouldn't I sing?'

'Because your Grandmamma said that you were not to.'

'But I'm going to be an opera singer. How can I ever be a singer if I don't *sing?*'

Miss Brown refused to be impressed by my ambitions. When, one spring morning, the sunshine, the prospect of holidays, and my own natural high spirits overcame me, and I suddenly carolled

'Ta, ra, ra, ra
BOOM de ay'

out loud, during prayers, she dropped her glasses and her prayer-book and said 'Amen,' hastily, two pages too soon.

Poor Miss Brown! I was a trial to her proper, schoolmistress soul. When I went to school, Grandmother had had made for me a brown cashmere wrapper, in the Kate Greenaway mode. It was my first long skirted garment, and I adored it. No sooner was I unpacked and Grandmother out of sight than the wrapper became a 'dress.' I wore it when we went to walk. I also 'improved' my hair by braiding it at night in several tight braids, which I brushed out in the morning.

Miss Brown looked at the frowzy-haired child in the brown cashmere wrapper and stopped the procession.

'Francie, are you sure your Grandmamma allows you to wear that dress on the street?'

'Oh, yes, Miss Brown,' demurely, and with no regard for truth.

SHE was vaguely troubled, too, by my adoration of the beautiful red-haired American actress Mrs. Brown-Potter, then touring Australia with her leading man, Kyrle Bellew. Most of my allowance went to buy photographs of my idol. I tacked them up over my bed and around my dressing table.

Cora Brown-Potter as Ophelia. As Desdemona. As herself. In every sort of attitude and dress. And enchanting in all of them. I looked ardently at each one of them every night before going to bed.

That was before the days of Freud and psychiatry. Miss Brown had never heard of complexes. She did not consider my 'crush' alarming, but only in bad taste.

Still, anyone would prefer to be considered shocking to being dismissed as 'silly.'

Only my roommate knew that I had sent Mrs. Brown-Potter a box of roses with a note expressing my admiration. Only she knew when the reply came. She *had* to know. She could see me slip it under my pillow each night.

Then the holidays came. I was at home, at St. Kilda. Mrs. Brown-Potter was playing in Melbourne. I borrowed from Alby's allowance enough to pay for a gallery seat at a matinée.

That afternoon I was in heaven. The play was melodrama and maudlinly sentimental, but I didn't know it. Nor should I have cared, had I known. Not Duse, whom I was to know years later, not Bernhardt, not Ellen Terry, never Melba or Destinn or Farrar thrilled me as did Cora Brown-Potter.

Next day I made further inroads on Alby's good nature and his pocket-money to send another box of flowers with a note of ecstatic admiration. By return post came a gracious card of thanks and an invitation for me to come to her hotel to tea.

Her maid opened the door to the Presence. She was lying on a chaise longue drawn up before the open window. She wore a tea gown of grey chiffon bordered with sable and with the very long sleeves affected by Sarah Bernhardt. Her glorious shining hair was unbound, like one of Rossetti's ladies, and framed exotically her camellia-white face. Her mouth was sweet and full and red.

The short, plump little girl in the white linen frock like a pillowcase stood speechless and awed. The awkward shyness of a child may be too much for even a charming woman to overcome. But Cora Brown, the New Orleans belle who had captivated New York and London society before she went on the stage, who was the protegée and intimate friend of Edward VII, had not forgotten her own childhood. It was she who asked me tactfully if I played the piano. Would I play for her?

'What shall I play?'

'What you like best.'

So I played Chopin and looking at her soulfully, the 'Rosemonde' of Schubert. Not too badly either, as I was clever enough to know. Emboldened by her obvious respect for this ability of mine, I sang. I remember I chose a song of Isidor de Lara's that I had heard my Grandmother sing:

> 'In my garden of sleep
> Where the poppies do grow...'

Isidor de Lara was just a name to me. I didn't know, what all Europe at that time was smiling over, that he was the lover of a French princess. One morning the guests in a certain Riviera hotel read, across the door of the Princess' suite: '*Ici dort de Lara.*' Years later, when I heard the story, I recalled the glint of roguish amusement in Cora Brown-Potter's eyes when I announced that as my favorite song.

Afterward she gave me tea, I sitting on a hassock at her feet and chattering about myself and my ambitions. No shyness now. When it was time to go she took my face in her two hands and kissed me on the mouth.

'When you come to England, Francie dear, you must let me know and come and stay with me.'

That evening I was too exalted to bowl to Alby on the cricket pitch. Instead, I unlocked the forbidden salon, went in, and sat alone in the dark on one of the little damask-covered rosewood sofas. Not for me the rough and tumble of the everyday world. That day I had stood in high places, and I was changed.

WHEN the next holidays came round I was to feel the nearness of something greater still.

That was Death.

A languorous summer evening, Grandmother and I alone in the Green Room with the sweetness of the daphne drifting in the windows. Grandmother saying she was tired, and going into her own room while I sat on at the piano playing snatches of Mozart and Gounod, composers she loved. Singing Gounod's Lullaby:

> *'Dormez, dormez, ma belle,*
> *Dormez, dormez toujours ...'*

then tiptoeing to the door to see if she slept ...

An hour or so later, Alby, coming home from a party and whistling as he turned in at the gate, heard a sound of sobbing in the dark garden. I ran to him, felt his arms about me. I tried to tell him:

'Grandmother is dead.'

But that didn't tell it, really. Nothing ever expressed for me what happened within me that summer night until years later, as Marguerite, I knelt beside Valentin's bier and poured out in song a young girl's first experience of death.

Grandmother was buried, as she had requested long before, with the score of Gounod's *Faust* in her coffin.

I never went back to Miss Brown's. There was no one to make me. With Grandmother gone, the household at St. Kilda fell apart like a house of cards. Grandfather had never inspired love in his own children or in his grandchildren. Now he retired within himself, bitter and inconsolable. Six months after Grandmother's death he shot himself. They found his body tumbled over on his desk. The bullet that had pierced his temples had gone through the photograph of his wife, which he held in his left hand.

I was christened Frances Jeanné
Davies

My mother, young and gentle

Grandmother, exquisite aristocrat

Mathilde Marchesi — what a
czarina she was

SHORTLY after that happened, I went into Melbourne, rapped on the door of the office of Williamson and Musgrove's Light Opera Company, and said to the astonished Mr. Williamson:

'I can sing as well as any of the singers in your company. Why don't you engage me?'

I shouldn't recommend those tactics to any of my own pupils seeking a chance on the stage or in Hollywood. Even though in my case, they worked.

Williamson and Musgrove were the Klaw and Erlanger of Australia.

The company toured the provinces, playing Gilbert and Sullivan operas. It was neither better nor worse than the usual travelling stock company. There was a peaked, bleached blonde soprano with sharp red elbows and sharp high notes. She held herself haughtily aloof from the rest of us. I learned, on the first day of my engagement, that she had an 'angel,' a rich shipping man in Sydney. The contralto was buxom and friendly with the manager of every theatre we played on tour, and sympathetic with the stage hands and shifters and carpenters about their neuralgia or their wives or their hangovers. The comedian had a wife who sang in the chorus. She was avidly jealous of her husband, perhaps with cause. Anyway, she would jerk herself out of her last act costume and into her street clothes to get to his dressing-room before he had removed all his make-up to keep him from taking any of the other girls out to supper.

After all, this too was education, though far removed from Miss Brown's standards.

I sang in *The Mikado*, and *The Gondoliers* and *Iolanthe*. I was seventeen and already a prima donna. I was, to myself and to Alby, who was studying medicine and boasted of his sister on the stage to all his fellow students, a success. I had bouquets from admirers — big, red-faced ranchers and mining men who would drive forty miles to town for one evening at the theatre, and the chance to take an actress out to supper. At Christmas, the company came back to Melbourne and played old-fashioned pantomime. I, as the youngest member of the company, played the Princess. Alby and his friends filled the boxes and applauded wildly and pelted me with flowers.

THE photographs of my mother show her young and gentle, but with great firmness of character. Before she went to America, she had insured her life for the benefit of her two children. The premium, invested carefully, was to be divided between Alby and me when I reached the age of eighteen.

We sat across the green baize-covered table facing the solemn-faced lawyer as he explained all this to us. So many pounds sterling invested for so many years at such a rate of interest, accrued, amounted to — ten thousand pounds.

He coughed drily, and laid a cheque for that amount before us.

Ten thousand pounds!

To us the sum seemed enormous. I doubt if either of us had ever had more than ten pounds in his possession at any one time. We had no training or experience in saving money, or in spending it. We were to get plenty of the latter, soon enough.

We were decided on one thing; we would go to England. Alby would take a degree at St. Andrews University in Edinburgh. I would go on at the Gaiety Theatre in London.

We caught the next steamer. Arrived in London, at the Walsingham Hotel, opposite Devonshire House and the forerunner of the Ritz, we engaged the largest, most elegant and correspondingly expensive suite. We set up our own carriage and coachman. Had there been automobiles to hire in those days, we should have rented the largest Rolls in England.

I had forgotten most of the details of that youthful splurge. But we had come to conquer London, and we set about it with vigor. We went shopping, a regular orgy, up and down Bond Street. London is a man's town, and Alby was tempted by every shop window and fell into every temptation. I chafed for Paris, but managed to content myself with fifteen new hats and a corresponding number of parasols.

Heaven knows what they thought of us at the sedate Walsingham.

On our first night we went to Covent Garden to hear Melba. She was singing *Bohème*. That was the first time I had heard the opera and felt the poignant spell of Mimi, the rôle I love best of all the forty and more rôles that I have sung. Mimi is all feminine. In her gaiety, her frailty, her complete abandonment to love. But there was something rigid in Melba, glorious as her voice was. She couldn't lose herself in the little grisette.

At that performance, I remember, Fritzi Scheff sang Musette. In the Second Act, in the Latin Quarter scene, her vivacious acting, as well as her singing, won her quick applause. When the curtain went down she received many calls.

And the curtain stayed down. An unconscionable time. Presently Forsythe, the Director, announced that Miss Scheff had been taken ill and could not continue. In order that the audience should not be disappointed, Mme. Melba would sing the mad scene from *Lucia*.

Which she did. Marvellously.

I heard later what had really happened that night behind the scenes was that Melba was so furious at the applause given Fritzi Scheff that she had a tantrum and refused to go on with the performance of *Bohème*. Fritzi Scheff's illness was an invention of the Director's to help himself out of an awkward dilemma.

Having satisfied the demands of art and loyalty to Australia, Alby and I pleased ourselves the next evening by going to the Gaiety. Not in stalls, or up in the gallery where we belonged.

In deference to my designs on the company, we took a box. We sat well forward and wore our best clothes and laughed and applauded, and afterwards had a champagne supper, and went to bed a little tipsy.

A girl of eighteen and a boy of twenty weren't sophisticated to the point of boredom in that day.

Very soon I went to see the manager of the Gaiety. He heard me sing, made some vague non-committal remarks about keeping my name and address, in case he should need a singer later on, and bowed me out.

There went ambition No. 1!

My disappointment was keen, but my hopes of a stage career in England were not dashed. After all, there were other theatres and other managers. Then too, to console me, there was the letter, a reply to one of my own, from Mrs. Brown-Potter. I had not forgotten she had told me I might go and see her if ever I went to England. I had written to her shortly after our arrival. Now she replied, asking me down to her home at Maidenhead for the week-end.

That was my first experience of an English country-house party. England was in the Edwardian era; society was elegant and leisurely and, if naughty, amusingly so. Mrs. Brown-Potter was one of the famous hostesses. That week-end she had among her guests Whistler, Lavery (plain Mr., not yet Sir John), Marcel Journet, the basso from the company at Covent Garden; Messager, conductor at the Opéra Comique and the author of *Madame Chrysanthème*, and Miss Frances Davies of New Zealand.

Truth to tell, I was too deeply impressed with Miss Davies, and all that was happening and might happen to her, to be more than dimly aware that I was playing croquet with the two greatest portrait painters of the time. Messager seemed to me much more important. And Journet, who teased me, and was gay and full of entertaining quips, even more so. He sang for us after dinner. And when he had finished, Mrs. Brown-Potter asked me to sing. They were all kind and complimentary and even enthusiastic about my voice, untrained as it was. Journet gave me a photograph of himself as Mephistopheles. Across it he wrote:

> To Mademoiselle Frances, the new Marguerite, with the sure confidence of being her Mefisto within a year.

Is there a fatalistic power in the spoken and written word? It would seem to be so. Journet's prophecy, given so gaily, is only one of several in my life that I have known to come true. In the spring of 1906, after I had been singing at La Monnaie in Brussels, I was engaged by Harry Higgins, Director of Covent Garden, to sing with his company during the season then opening. According to my contract, I was to go to London in June to sing Gilda in *Rigoletto* with the famous tenor from New York's Metropolitan, Caruso. Several weeks before that, and while I was still in Brussels, I received a telegram. It was from Higgins. He wired that Melba, who was to sing Marguerite in *Faust* the next night, was suddenly ill. Could I, would I, cross the Channel and take her place? I wired that I would, and next day made the journey, arriving in London just in time to drive to Covent Garden, and to go to my dressing-room to dress for the performance. I had no knowledge with whom I was to sing that night, and of course there was no time for a rehearsal. But I had sung Marguerite many times and I had no worries on that score.

When I went on the stage it was to discover, clothed in the black and scarlet devil's dress of Mefisto, the face and form of Marcel Journet. His prophecy had come true.

WHEN the other guests left on Monday, Mrs. Brown-Potter asked me to stay on. I remained with her for about a fortnight. Alby had gone to Edinburgh to see about the university requirements, and I was glad to be in the country.

The house and garden at Maidenhead were at their loveliest in perfect June weather. The Thames ran close to the house — a lazy stream where I tried punting, in a long-skirted, tight-waisted chiffon frock and a floppy lingerie hat of lace and ribbons. Every week-end saw new guests coming down from London, all of them smart and amusing, and many of them famous.

Does Derby Day still mean a picnic luncheon of cold salmon and green peas and champagne? It did then. It was my first Derby, and I remember we drove out to Epsom on a coach, too gay to care for the showers that sprinkled our finery. England was a little country then. Everybody seemed to know everybody else. They all called each other by nicknames, and there were a great many private jokes, awfully funny apparently to those who understood them, and quite incomprehensible to anyone else.

Our box was not far from the royal enclosure. We could see the King in his beautiful grey top hat, and Queen Alexandra, lovely and distinguished-looking in pale mauve. It was my first glimpse of royalty and I kept my glasses turned in that direction more than on the course, even though I had placed a fiver on the favorite. Presently, one of the equerries came and said His Majesty invited Mrs. Brown-Potter and her guests to come to his box.

So I had my first presentation to royalty. Mrs. Brown-Potter presented me as an Australian, and a young singer who might some day rival Melba, one of those social exaggerations. The King asked me to sing at a benefit one of the regiments was holding a few days off. I still have — and how highly I prize it! — the oval silver box he gave me on that occasion. Two years later I was to meet King Edward again at Marienbad, where he was taking a cure. He remembered me — indeed, he had the most marvellous and truly royal memory, a gift which his grandson Edward, Duke of Windsor, has inherited. At Marienbad, the King used to drink the waters each morning and later breakfast at his table in the gardens. Nearly every morning I was one of his breakfast guests, with Lady Cunard, Mrs. Hall-Walker, and other intimate friends. We sat where we could see the people pass, and I remember the King had the greatest curiosity about who this one or that one was, and all about them. I had been singing for a season then at the Royal Theatre in Brussels, and how he pumped me for gossip concerning old King Leopold (his own cousin) and the dancer Cléo de Mérode! She was a beautiful woman, and she wore her hair parted in the severe classic style and brushed flat down on either side of her face. Gossips said she wore it that way because *one of her lovers had bitten off her ears!*

It was King Edward, also at Marienbad, who induced me to try to play golf. He was an enthusiastic golfer, and sometimes invited me to walk round the course with him. 'Try it,' he commanded one day, and put one of his clubs in my hand.

I took a resounding thwack at the ball and hit the turf so hard the niblick snapped in two.

'Damn it to hell!' I exploded, entirely forgetting that in the presence of royalty profanity is royalty's prerogative.

I can hear the King laughing yet. A big, jolly outburst. He told the story at breakfast next morning, and used to tease me about it ever after. He had a strong German accent and rolled his r's. 'Frrrancess!' he called me.

I have tried to play golf several times since then. I even took lessons from Gil Nichols. He said in time he would make a good golfer out of me. But after a few trials in which I found my arm too short and my bust too big for me to develop the proper swing, I decided God hadn't built me the right shape for action on a golf course, and I gave up!

ALAS for Alby's plans! St. Andrews wouldn't recognize for a degree all of the work he had done at the University in Australia. I went up to London, met him, and we had an hour of dismay as we went over our accounts.

Alby had spent five hundred pounds in about three weeks. I had trunks full of hats and frocks, and a shadow of my former letter of credit as well as the remembrance of the Gaiety manager's indifference to my voice and charms.

And, so far, we had seen only London.

'Let's go to Paris,' Alby suggested. 'We might as well before all the money is spent.'

So we went.

The corner seat, opposite to mine, in the first-class carriage on the Dover train was marked 'Reserved.' At the last minute a man came rapidly down the platform, the guard jerked open the door, slammed it after him, and the train started. After a minute the stranger caught his breath and took a look around. His eye lighted on me.

It was Messager.

He talked to Alby and me all the way to Dover. It was he who urged me, when I was in Paris, to go to see Mathilde Marchesi, who had taught Melba and who, he said, knew more about the female voice and how to train it than anyone else in the world.

I told him that my aunt had been one of Marchesi's pupils. He knew Frances Saville, then in Vienna singing at the Hofoper. Before we saw the white chalk cliffs of Calais I had made up my mind to waste no time in finding my aunt and asking her advice. Again, on the boat train to Paris, Messager sought us out.

'Don't forget, mademoiselle; go to Marchesi. There is no one like her.'

Paris for a few dazzling days, then Vienna. That city took hold of me by the heart strings. Everywhere you went there was music, *tzigane* orchestras playing under the chestnut trees in the

gardens, beautiful women and, to my eye, even more beautiful
officers in resplendent uniforms who were not averse to trying to
impress an English miss who possessed that youthful capacity
for enjoyment the Viennese call *'fesh.'*

Aunt Frances had a charming apartment. She was a person of
consequence in Vienna, and a strikingly beautiful woman. Her
career had taken her all over Europe, and she had sung several
seasons at the Metropolitan, with the great tenor Van Dyck. He
had been madly in love with her. I knew him later, and when he
found that I was Frances Saville's niece, he talked to me of her
with the reminiscent tenderness of an elderly man for the youth
and love that are gone.

Then, in Vienna, Aunt Frances was anything but encouraging
or cordial to me. Perhaps she felt that the arrival of an unknown
niece with strong operatic aspirations was considerable of a
nuisance. Anyway, I quickly made up my mind that my best
course was to go back to Paris, on my own, and see Madame
Marchesi, as Messager had advised. I did not see Aunt Frances
again for many years. Then, in Venice, during the summer of
1912 Gatti and I were riding in a gondola on the Grand Canal.
Another gondola passed us.

'Che bella donna!' Gatti exclaimed.

I looked at the woman who leaned back against the scarlet
cushions.

It was my Aunt Frances.

Well, a stage-struck young girl, and the wife of the Director of
the greatest opera company in the world, are two different
kettles of fish. The cordiality that had been so noticeably lacking in Vienna overflowed in Venice. We saw her often at the
Lido that summer. But either the memory of that first meeting
still rankled in me, or our temperaments were too dissimilar for
us ever to be really friends.

MATHILDE MARCHESI was already past eighty years of age. She had been teaching singing for sixty years. Her house, No. 88 Rue Jouffroy, was the musical centre of Paris. Her soirées were frequented by Massenet, Debussy, Ambroise Thomas, Saint-Saens, and Delibes, the author of *Lakmé*. She had taught Sybil Sanderson, Emma Nevada, Emma Eames, Melba, and Calvé, to mention only singers who have had brilliant careers in America. She never would accept a man as a pupil. She claimed no woman could understand or successfully place a male voice. She had refused, too, to teach Mary Garden. That was because she did not think the young American girl was sufficiently respectful of her ideas and criticism.

And what a czarina she was! Upright and stiff as a ramrod, with snapping black eyes and stern, tightly compressed mouth. She seated herself regally in her chair at that first interview and motioned me to the piano.

'I will hear you sing, mademoiselle. Then I will say what I think of your voice and whether I will accept you as a pupil.'

What flare of schoolgirl pique prompted me to choose to sing not one of the classic songs, I knew, but Francis Allison's 'Song of Thanksgiving'? Perhaps because this gave me opportunity to open my throat and pour out all the voice I had. I stole a look at Marchesi. Her mouth was grim, but was there a twinkle in her eye?

I finished. My hands dropped from the keys to my lap. I awaited the verdict...

Marchesi rose stiffly from her chair. She did not give me a glance. She walked across the salon to the closed double doors leading into the hall, and threw them wide. Her voice rang out commandingly:

'*Salvatore, viens. J'ai trouvé la nouvelle Melba.*'

MARCHESI altered the entire course of my life. Having taken me as a pupil, she assumed direction of all my activities for the ten months I studied with her before I made my début. Even after that, I continued to study with her whenever I was in Paris. But at the beginning, she decided for my good everything connected with my career. It was she who selected the hotel where I was to live — in the Avenue Friedland. It was expensively quiet and correct and proper for a young girl living alone. Alby had gone back to Australia. I was not to see him for twenty-four years. Then it was difficult to recognize in the busy doctor the brother of those youthful adventures.

Every morning at nine I presented myself in the rue Jouffroy for my lesson. I was expected to stay on to hear all the other pupils in order to learn as much and as quickly as possible. This was Marchesi's method of teaching, and it is the method I use today with my pupils. Beside the singing lessons, I was studying French and Italian, and later, when I began to prepare myself in operatic rôles, Marchesi arranged for me to study *mise-en-scène* with the famous tenor Victor Capoul, late of the Opera. He was an old man then, past seventy. But he had sung with all the greatest opera companies all over the world, including the Metropolitan in New York, and he had the memory and the tradition of the great singers of *bel canto*. Marchesi had immense faith in his judgment.

Nearly every day I lunched with Marchesi and her aged husband the Marquis de Castrone. Frequently, their daughter Blanche was there, too. Guests, many of them musicians, all of them music-lovers, came and went. The conversation was all Music: who was singing this or that rôle with this or that opera company and how she had been received. . . . Recollections of Verdi, who had died only a short time before, and whom Marchesi and her husband had known well. . . . News of the new French operas that Albert Carré, Director of the Opéra Comique, was producing beautifully. *Pelléas and Mélisande* had its première there that year. All Paris was raving about Mary Garden, who had created the rôle, to the chagrin, people said, of Georgette Leblanc, Maeterlinck's mistress, who had wanted to sing it.

Marchesi, herself, had begun her career as a singer in Germany. Mendelssohn had obtained for her an engagement to sing at the Düsseldorf Festival. She had come to Paris to study singing under Manuel Garcia, then at the height of his fame, who taught Jenny Lind for the Swedish Government; and also dancing, acting, and harmony from Samson of the Théâtre Français, who had taught the great Rachel. (Rachel, she told me, had used to write her teacher love letters and leave them under the cushions on his sofa.) Very soon, however, Marchesi gave up her career as a singer for the work in which her genius was paramount — teaching. She had taught at the Vienna Conservatoire before coming to Paris. There her fame mounted instantaneously.

After all, there are three kinds of women. There is the woman who is all mother. There is the woman whose sole *métier* is love. And there is the worker. I am a worker. That doesn't mean that I don't care about young people; because I do. Nor does it mean that men have not meant a great deal in my life; because they have. But it means that I have in me the capacity for concentrated work, and that I actually derive a pleasure from this. That is, when I know it is getting me somewhere that I want to go. Never once have I laid my hand on my heart and talked sentimentally about 'MY ART.' 'MY WORK,' yes. in the twenty-two years I was at the Metropolitan I sang in forty-two different operas. Never through illness or carelessness did I miss a single performance.

It was my zest for work and my ability to stick to it that delighted Marchesi. I had the capacity to take as much as she would give; wherefore she gave generously. I think now the grand old lady felt I was her Benjamin, the last of a long line.

That doesn't mean she was not often arbitrary and temperamental and even ridiculous. There were plenty of times when her temper, always quick, flew away from her. Once she flung the music book at my head, and ordered me out of her sight.

'And don't come back. I will teach you no more.'

I took her at her word.

Next day Georges, her old valet, came round to the hotel with a note. She demanded to know why I had not presented myself that morning for my lesson as usual.

But she could be loving and even tender, too.

'*You know how much I love you, my dear Frances,*' she wrote me after I was singing in Brussels and was officially at least, no longer under her direction. '*I have proved it to you, and I love you like my own child. But there are times when it is necessary to tell the truth to those whom one loves . . .*' and she went on to give me stern and sound advice about my voice and my care of it.

'*Toujours la voix de tête,*' she would reiterate. 'Head tones, head tones.'

Lots of work all day, and in the evenings, fun. The theatres! Bernhardt was playing, and Duse. Never shall I forget the latter in Francesca da Rimini. My Italian wasn't up to understanding a single word, but that didn't matter. Duse *was* pure poetry and emotion. Her loveliness impregnated every scene and every line. Then one knew about her and d'Annunzio — a story in itself to rival Francesca's. Years later, in December, 1916, Gatti produced Zandonai's opera, *Francesca da Rimini*, at the Metropolitan, and I sang the title rôle. I remember when we were rehearsing I was terribly annoyed because the stage director had not provided a column for me to stand beside, leaning my hand against it, as Duse had done in the play.

'I can't possibly play Francesca without a column,' I objected, still with the memory of those performances I had seen in Paris.

Francesca without a column? As well try to play Santa Claus without a beard!

And I went on objecting until they wrote a column into the script and the stage carpenters manufactured one, and set it up where I could stand as Duse used to stand.

Yes, Paris then was rich in beautiful things to see and to hear. Like the concert given for *Les Enfants de la Presse*, at which Bernhardt and Réjane, with Coquelin and another great actor whose name now escapes me, danced a minuet; Tamagno sang; and Paderewski and Pouliot, with two other pianists, played a concerto for four pianos.

But the star of that concert program was Patti.

That was the first and the only time in my life that I ever heard her sing. She was old then — all of sixty-five, and her voice had lost some of its power. But it had not lost its marvellous velvet quality. Standing there on the Trocadéro stage, she was enchantingly lovely, with a wistful loveliness that tugged at your heart strings.

She sang — I remember it as though it all happened only last week — the Jewel Song from *Faust*, transposed down two keys to suit her register, and '*Voi che sapete*' from *La Nozze de Figaro*.

Her exquisite singing thrilled me so, I remember, I went home in a daze, unable to sleep all that night. Next morning when I went to Madame Marchesi for my lesson I burst out that it was no use my going on studying: 'I know I'll never sing like Patti.'

Marchesi steadied me wisely. Not with sympathy, but with sound advice about work.

Two years later, when I made my début at Covent Garden, at the close of the performance of *Rigoletto*, a gentle old man and a very exquisite old lady came round to my dressing-room to offer me their congratulations.

They were Paolo Tosti and Adelina Patti!

Not that all the good times in Paris were strictly cultural. One party, I remember, began with a theatre, then supper and dancing, then on to Les Halles for the fun of watching the country wagons come in with the market produce, and to eat onion soup — great brimming bowls of it — with the carters and night workers. One of the men had a Mercedes, scarlet and with much shining brass about it. Like a Tommy on parade. We piled in, I sitting on the top, which had been let down, and went for a ride in the Bois. But at the gate the gendarme stopped us. The car's lights were too weak to comply with the regulations. Someone thought of carnival lanterns. Someone else remembered a shop on Montmartre where they were sold. Someone else had the temerity to knock the shop-owner out of bed, hustle him downstairs in a flapping nightshirt, and make him sell us his stock. We hung the Mercedes with lanterns and offered ourselves to the gendarme.

This time he gave up.

'English! Bohemians! Get on with you!'

We drove round and round the Bois until dawn, and ended up with breakfast at a little *brasserie* near the Rond-Point.

It doesn't sound very extraordinary, now, any of it. Rather as though it were something everyone had done at some time or other. But the last time I was in Paris, I was at the Rond-Point and there was the very same *brasserie*, or so I thought. For fun I stopped and ordered a coffee. The old waiter set the cup down on the table before me, slopping a little coffee into the saucer according to custom, or tradition, or the rules of the Waiters' Guild.

'Ah, Mademoiselle Alda,' he said. 'Do you remember the morning you watered the flowers here at six o'clock?'

There were other escapades, too. Not all of them so innocent. Fruit of one of them was the young Russian who pretended to adore me and who stole my jewellery. Then, hearing that I had been invited by Marchesi to dine at her house to meet Madame Ambroise Thomas — a great occasion on which it was to be expected that I would appear in gala attire — he sent me a wire to which he signed Marchesi's name, that the dinner was off.

I think what most infuriated me was his bland telling me, next day, when it all came out, that he had really needed the money he got by pawning the jewellery, to pay court to me as he felt I merited!

Well, at least I've never lost my head over another Russian. Not even over Chaliapin.

We sang together at La Scala. And when I went to Buenos Aires for a season, Chaliapin was singing there, though not in the same company. I remember Gatti's adjurations to me to have nothing to do with 'that Russian.'

What Gatti didn't know was that I had been cured of Russians, in Paris, years before.

When I had been studying with Marchesi for five or six months she obtained for me engagements to sing concerts at various private houses in Paris. These were my first appearances under my new name 'Alda,' which Marchesi had given me. She had given Nellie Mitchell Armstrong her name 'Melba' from the city Melbourne, where she was born.

My first concert was at the Duke de Pomar's. I remember that my fee was five hundred francs ($100), and that the Duke sent me later a bracelet set with pearls and sapphires and a very old painted fan. I have them both, to this day.

Through Marchesi I came to know many of the members of the old society of Paris, still living then in the Faubourg St. Germain. Some of them remembered my grandmother. For many years, whenever I was in Paris — and I kept an apartment there until 1915 — I used to sing at some of those houses.

It was at a concert at the Princess de Murat's, I think in 1912, that Marie, then Crown Princess of Roumania, was the guest of honor. How beautiful she was, seated in her gilt armchair! And how gracious to me afterward! Fourteen years later I was to meet her again, in New York, at a dinner given for her by the directors of United States Steel. The Queen and I were the only women present at that dinner, at which she spoke on the financial situation of Roumania and I sang several songs.

After dinner the Queen, with that marvellous memory for times and places and people that is a mark of royalty, recalled to me that other occasion in Paris, long before.

She smiled. 'I have never forgotten how beautifully you sang, and what a lovely dress you wore. It was pale green and silver. I remember I asked you who made it and you said Doucet. I will tell you now. I went round to Doucet next day and ordered one just like it.'

A queen, yes. But also a woman. Being a woman myself, I remember that little incident as the highest tribute anyone ever paid me.

IT WAS Marchesi who chose *Manon* as the opera in which I was to make my début at the Opéra Comique. That was on April 15, 1904. Massenet himself, the composer of the opera, had taught me the rôle, word by word. It is one I was to sing hundreds of times, though I prefer Puccini's *Manon Lescaut* to the French composer's. Massenet left Paris for the Midi before the date of my début, and wrote me the following letter:

En route, *January* 20th.

All our thoughts are with you, and we send you our faithful remembrances.

If I could have news of you how that would interest me! Some day, in some hotel, I shall know through my wife (who reads the papers) that you have played. I know you can have only a great success.

From both of us, our admiration —

J. MASSENET

Curiously enough, my impressions of that first night at the Opéra Comique have blurred into memories of so many other *Manons* that nothing remains very clear. I remember that I was surprised at myself because I was not more excited, now that my MOMENT had come. I remember looking up at the boxes and catching a glimpse of Marchesi and with her as her guest in my honor — Melba. And wickedly I remember the day when I was singing and someone flung open the door of Marchesi's music room, exclaiming:

'Who is it, screaming like that?'

And Melba had walked into the room!

I remember knowing how imperfect my French pronunciation was, and hearing myself make an absurd mistake in grammar that brought a ripple of amusement from the audience. That made me laugh too; with them, at myself. Afterward, Albert Carré scolded me.

'You mustn't do a thing like that; this isn't musical comedy.'

But I didn't take it seriously. I couldn't. I know now the swiftness of my rise was a liability. The best singers are seasoned slowly, as the best wine is ripened with time. Perhaps too much of the hoyden schoolgirl remained in my nature. It seemed to me vastly amusing that I should be singing the leading rôle in a performance at the Opéra Comique, and before that vast audience. It didn't seem real. Presently, I remember thinking, I shall find myself back in the theatre under the eucalyptus trees in the garden at St. Kilda.

It was this casualness of mine that brought the comment from Melba that I have already quoted. I never completely abandoned that attitude, or began to take my career as a singer really seriously until, after that first night at the Metropolitan, the critics' comments awoke in me a grim determination to conquer New York and the critics with it.

PART
III

LIVING ADVENTUROUSLY

Je marche sur tous les chemins
Aussi bien qu'une souveraine,
On s'incline, on baise ma main,
Car par la beauté je suis reine.

Mes chevaux courent aux grands pas
Devant ma vie aventureuse.
Les grands s'avancent, chapeau bas,
Je suis belle, je suis heureuse.

Autour de moi tout doit fleurir
Je vois à tout ce qui m'attire
Et si Manon devait jamais mourir
Ce serait, mes amis, dans un éclat de rire.

MANON

III

I SANG *Manon* four or five times that season, and always
with success. I had the youth, the piquancy, and that
quality the French call 'the Devil's beauty,' that the rôle requires.

I wanted to add *Traviata* to my repertory, but Mary Garden
was singing it, and the company had no need of another Violetta.

I quickly saw that I might wait several seasons before I would
have my chance. And I was impatient. One day I went out to
an agent's to see if any of the opera companies in any of the
other European cities had need of a lyric soprano to sing leading
rôles.

Sitting in the agent's waiting-room I could hear, from behind
a closed door, a woman singing the Jewel Song from *Faust*. Then
the music stopped and a few moments later the door opened and
a woman came out and passed me on her way to the street. On
her face was the look I had worn when the manager of the
Gaiety didn't find me good enough.

'What is going on in there?' I asked the clerk.

'It is the Directors of the Théâtre de la Monnaie in Brussels.
They are hearing soprano singers.'

I opened the door and walked in on the three surprised
Belgians.

'Gentlemen,' I said, 'I am Mlle. Frances Alda of the Opéra
Comique. Will you hear me?'

Once again, it worked. They engaged me on the spot. I had a
contract for a season in my pocket when I went back to the
Comique and resigned. Marchesi did not approve at all of this
high-handed way of creating a career. Still, she reminded me,
the Monnaie had a magnificent reputation. Melba had sung

there for a season or two. So had Frances Saville. With many admonitions Marchesi taught me the rôles the Directors had said I should be required to sing that season.

Brussels is a little city, and then it was a gay one. The stream of gold from the Congo was pouring into it. Old King Leopold and the bankers who had upheld him in his African ventures rubbed their hands, even though the world beyond Belgium told dark and terrible tales of Belgian domination in Africa. They bought jewels and yachts and built themselves ornate ugly palaces in Brussels and villas at Ostend. They were immensely proud of their opera, where Melba and Eames and Frances Saville had scored great triumphs. They supported it loyally and royally.

On the night I made my début as Marguerite in *Faust*, one of the Directors, M. Guido, came to my dressing-room before the performance to tell me that the King was in the royal box to hear La Monnaie's new prima donna. He was so impressive and solemn about it that I couldn't resist teasing him a little.

'All right,' I said. 'When I move down stage to the spinning wheel to sing "There was a King in Thule," I'm going to look up at the royal box and give the King a wink.'

Guido was horrified. 'Mademoiselle, I beg you not to do such a thing.'

'Nonsense!' I told him. 'Of course I shall. Do you know, I think the King would like it.'

As a matter of fact, I believe he would have. Though I spared M. Guido's feelings and never lifted my eyes from my spinning wheel as I sang the song.

Leopold was then a bad, old man. Traces of his dissoluteness were marked on his face, as the results of many of his cruelties were evident in the life of his city. It was just at that time that the courts were handing down the decision in the suit brought by the creditors of his daughter Princess Henriette, and by Princess Stephanie, widow of the Archduke Rudolf, against the Queen's estate. Scandal concerning the royal house was rife everywhere.

Jaroslavna in *Prince Igor*

Manon

Martha

Violetta in *La Traviata*

I have always spent much time, thought, and effort on having gowns
beautiful and becoming

Princess Clementine was the only one of the King's three daughters who had remained on anything like friendly terms with her father. She continued to live in Brussels — she had not yet married. The rumor was that she was engaged to the Duc D'Orleans, who had been greatly enamored of Melba. Princess Clementine was extremely kind to me. I think the fact that I was English and young rather won her. She used to come frequently to the opera on the nights I was singing, and always came round to my dressing-room between acts to tell me how she was enjoying the performance, and several times I had tea with her.

There were two great artists in Brussels whilst I was singing at La Monnaie whom I came to know well. One was Jacques Thibaut, who today is recognized as the greatest French violinist.

Then Jacques was young, about twenty-five. And full of rapturous dreams about music and the arts and the artistic life.

I couldn't help teasing him sometimes. He, in return, would reproach me with taking my art too casually, of playing with my career.

'But why shouldn't I have fun?' I would argue. 'I work hard. I want to play too. I love the parties and the flowers and the admiration you get when you're a singer, and a woman that men like the looks of. I'm jolly frank about saying so, that's all.'

'Some of it, perhaps,' was Jacques' reply. 'But not too much. *La belle vie des grandes artistes*, that is what I wish for you, my little friend. You have everything for that.'

The other member of the company at La Monnaie whose friendship touched me deeply was the tenor Ernest Van Dyck.

He was then no longer young, but still a very great artist none the less. He had sung at the Metropolitan in New York for a number of years under Grau's directorship, and whilst my aunt Frances Saville was also a member of the company, as I have already told.

He had the gift of expressing sentiment charmingly, as when

he wrote in my album after my first performance of *Manon* at La Monnaie:

'Manon, Manon, Sphinx étonnant,'
   dit des Grieux. (le fils)
'Elle est charmante et je comprends
   qu'on l'aime,' dit des Grieux. (le père).
Et je dis comme ces deux des Grieux
   à la toute belle Mademoiselle Alda.
Bruxelles, le 22 Novembre 1904.

VAN DYCK

There has been one point, at least, in which my life as an opera singer has been radically different from the lives of other singers I have known. Always, in whatever city I was singing, I have made my friends not among the other artists, but in the society of that city. In Paris, of course, Marchesi had given me introductions to members of the old nobility whose genuine interest in music made them immediately cordial to a young singer, and whose kind hearts drew me to them with real affection. It was the same, later, when I was singing at La Scala. It was said that I was the first opera singer who had been received by Milan society, not as a singer alone, but as one of them. In Brussels, I found my life full of friends and gaiety and good times. Baron Empain was at that time, one of the most powerful bankers in Europe, and one of the most influential men in Belgium. He had financed many of the King's ventures in the Congo. His younger brother François Empain became a friend of mine. He was always at the opera on nights when I sang, and he kept my dressing-room and my suite at the Metropole filled with flowers. It was he who gave me the first *griffon* I ever had. Since then I have never been without one of those clever, ugly little dogs. That first one, I remember, came from one of the cages in the Dog Market in the square before the Hotel de Ville. There have been three or four others between that Pitchu and the Pitchu who runs about after me all day at Casa Mia. They all have had the same name, which is Flemish for 'little man.'

Immediately after my début at La Monnaie I received the following letter:

88, Rue Jouffroy
7 *November*, 1904.

MY DEAR FRANCES,
Thank you for the telegram. All my congratulations for the very big success.

Mrs. Gardiner has said it was very great.

Now, my dear Frances, take the advice of Maman Marchesi:

1 — Sign up for next year. That marks your success. Melba did that.

2 — Do not sing four times a week. That tires the voice and makes it tremble, and the public ends by treating you with indifference.

With tenderness,
MATHILDE MARCHESI

In great haste.

Excellent, shrewd advice.

I followed the first half of her counsel and signed a contract for the season to come. It was harder, well-nigh impossible, to follow her second warning. The people of Brussels seemed to have an insatiable appetite for *Manon, Traviata, Faust,* and *Les Huguenots.* In ten months (two seasons) I sang fifty-two Manons and seventy-four Marguerites.

But I had youth and tremendous vitality, and I loved to sing. Each morning I had a good breakfast, which meant porridge and kippers and tea and toast and marmalade — we believed singers needed to eat in those days. If one put on weight — and this one did — well, the more pounds the more power. (Think of Alboni, who though she was seventy, and so fat she could not walk alone, still sang the aria from *Roméo et Juliette* at the Paris Opera and took all the laurels from the other singers.) After breakfast, and a walk in the park, I practised for an hour with an accompanist from the opera.

Refreshment after this — and practising operatic rôles is real work that provokes real hunger — consisted of a dozen raw oysters and a bottle of stout. Then I went for a drive, at the fashionable hour of the midday, and lunched about half-past one, as only the Belgians do lunch, on *waterzooi Gantoise*, which is a stew of chicken and vegetables in a very rich sauce; or, on the days when I was singing, on *boeuf tartare*. What is *boeuf tartare*? According to legend, it is the dish which the Tartars partook of and which gave them strength to ravage Asia and Eastern Europe. To make it, you chop a raw onion very fine! On a nest of this you mound half a pound of raw chopped beef!! In a little hollow of the beef you drop a raw egg!!! The whole is garnished with capers, and is eaten with three or four generous tablespoonfuls of olive oil poured over all!!!!

After that, if you can't make your voice heard to the topmost seat in the gallery and out into the square before the Opera House, you'd better stick to radio that furnishes mechanical amplifiers.

Lots of hard work, and plenty of fun in between. I know no prescription so potent as this to work happiness. And I was happy.

Also, I was in love.

He was a singer, and the only singer I ever did fall in love with. Not a tenor — I've been spared that. But a big, magnificent man, six and a half feet tall, with a glorious bass voice. His name doesn't matter here and now. Besides, when I was in Paris, in 1933, in a theatre one night I saw him. His wife was with him. He brought her over and introduced her to me and we chatted pleasantly about nothing at all. Then they went away.

'Where did you know her?' she probably asked him before they got home.

And probably he told her some vague story about our singing together at Covent Garden, years ago. Which, of course, we did.

But I'm certain he didn't tell her that when I was in Brusseis and he was singing at The Hague, he used to make the journey to see me, and that once we enjoyed ourselves so whole-heartedly that he forgot all about trains, and missed the last one. Motors weren't so fast in those days, so though he promised the chauffeur an exorbitant tip, he still arrived in the Dutch city too late for the curtain on the night he was supposed to sing.

A crime for which no director knows forgiveness.

W HAT is there about me, I wonder, that seems to exert a fatal fascination over opera directors?

Not that the two gentlemen who directed La Monnaie were slaves to my charms. They were only pleasantly cordial and appreciative of my ability as a singer and my cooperation with them in their work. I had to be married ten years or so to Gatti-Casazza and to have sat on the side lines at some of his bouts with prima donnas and even more temperamental tenors to appreciate to the full the compliment implied in the lines M. Guido of La Monnaie wrote in my autograph album:

> To the charming Manon, to the ravishing Marguerite, to the excellent pupil, to the devoted artist — to Frances Alda.

Or Messager's attestation:

> If all the artists were as charming as you, dear Alda, the career of a Director would be simply a foretaste of Paradise.
> With all best wishes —
>
> A. MESSAGER

There they stand, in black and white. They're a great consolation to me sometimes; particularly when I've been coming in for a round of abuse for being egotistic and demanding, and generally prima donna-ish.

'I'm always having to explain you to people, Alda,' Mary

Garden told me not long ago. 'Half of them think you're a grand person, and the rest think you're a bitch.'

'Both are right,' I said.

At that, am I so different from most women?

ALBERT CARRÉ, tall, handsome, and dignified, never gave me a glance when the seductive Mary Garden was about. But Harry Higgins, Director of Covent Garden, where I went to sing in the season of 1906, was gratifyingly admiring of me as a singer and as a woman.

He had engaged me to sing Gilda in *Rigoletto*, with Caruso, who was to be at Covent Garden after the close of the Metropolitan's season in New York in April.

When Marchesi heard this, she wrote me:

> Several of my friends in Brussels, on their way through Paris, have come to see me. They all speak of you and admire you enthusiastically. But they report that your singing is not so careful as it used to be and that your voice shows signs of trembling. They fear for your artistic future. You have truly a great future as an artist before you, and your début at Covent Garden will decide that future.
>
> London is a difficult city, and where there are numerous jealousies to be encountered. Why have you not had recourse to my advice? (That is what Melba did for two years.) You have every opportunity of doing so, since you have a pied-à-terre in Paris. That would be of much greater value to you than trusting yourself exclusively to a singing master from the Brussels opera, as I learn from the photographs in the papers you sent me.
>
> I am frank, and entirely and above all an artist.
>
> Do not hesitate to come to me.
>
> All the operas that you are going to sing over there, and above all the one in which you will make your début, you should work over very carefully with me.

The rôle of Gilda that you will have to sing in Italian
is very difficult. It is the rôle in which Melba made her
début in Brussels, and it is the one which established her
future.

It is impossible for me to send you the partition in
Italian. I have constant need of it. But I can have one sent
to you from Ricordi, and we will make the necessary
changes in singing it when you come.

Probably you do not know that I have been gravely ill.
For the past two days I have been on a chaise longue after
an attack of bronchitis which nearly removed me from my
friends.

I embrace you with all my heart —

MATHILDE MARCHESI

A Covent Garden audience is different from any in any other
opera house in Europe. In some ways it resembles the audience
at the Metropolitan. On the Continent, in nearly every city,
society may go to the opera or stay away; but opera goes on,
supported, well or ill, by the vast music-loving populace.

Not in New York, nor in London. In both those cities no
opera house without society as a factor will ever be a success.

Oscar Hammerstein, grand old man as he was, and with a
wonderful personality, tried it in London with excellent artists,
chorus, and orchestra. But society was not interested. And his
opera venture there was a failure.

In New York, the Metropolitan's Diamond Horseshoe was as
important to the success of the company as any of the artists.
Gatti knew this, and he made money for the shareholders by
that knowledge.

'People come to the theatre to be entertained,' he told one
of the stage directors. 'Don't forget that. To you Germans
[that stage director was an Austrian] the theatre is a church. To
the Italians, it is a ballroom.'

And what is a ballroom without society?

Covent Garden always had society's seal on it. An opera
night there was the nearest thing to a Buckingham Palace
Garden Party. Landed gentry, up from the country to have

their débutante daughters presented at the spring courts, felt that they must appear at the opera several times during the season. The Bank of England must have been called on to disgorge half a ton of family jewels — tiaras, stomachers, necklaces, and brooches like the Albert Memorial. The house glittered; feather fans fluttered. Matchmaking went on in the boxes regardless of what went on upon the stage. The applause for Caruso or for Melba or for Emmy Destinn would die away, and immediately the chit-chat about Simla, Capetown, Devonshire, and the Derby entries was resumed.

A marvellous people, the British!

Only a nation trained in the hunting field could take the fences with such sublime nonchalance.

My contract was to make my début in *Rigoletto* with Caruso. As a matter of fact, my first appearance at Covent Garden was in *Faust*, as I have already recounted. But I still looked forward to singing with the world's greatest tenor, whom I had gone to hear in Paris the year before.

What thrilled me most about that performance of *Rigoletto* was finding that Caruso's voice and mine blended so perfectly. He often spoke of it afterward, when it was the accepted thing at the Metropolitan that we should sing together.

But I had my own moment of triumph at Covent Garden on the night of my official début.

The King and Queen attended. During the entr'acte they sent for me to come to the royal box to be congratulated. Alexandra was gracious and charming, as she always was. Edward was imposing and magnificently severe.

But I thought I discerned a twinkle in one eye.

'Have you played golf lately, Frrrancesss?' he asked.

THE baritone who sang Rigoletto at that performance was Battestini. I consider him the finest singer I have ever heard. Not only for his magnificent baritone voice, but for the perfection of his art of singing. He had had countless offers to go to America, but he would never accept any of them.

'I will never cross the sea,' he told me. 'The Channel is enough. The very thought of six or seven days and nights tossing about on the waters fills me with terror.'

'Pooh!' Caruso would retort to this. 'It isn't the sea at all that you are afraid of, Battestini. It's those American Indian savages in war paint and feathers sitting in the boxes in the Metropolitan, ready to jump down on the stage and kill you with their hatchets if you should break on a top note.'

Battestini would laugh at this. But not too heartily. And not entirely sure that Caruso was joking.

Meanwhile, Cleofonte Campanini, who was conducting at Covent Garden that season, was telling me a different story.

The two brothers, Italo and Cleofonte Campanini, had been engaged by the Metropolitan Opera Company in its very first season, back in the eighties. Italo was a tenor; Cleofonte played in the orchestra. Occasionally, when Italo was singing, the younger brother was allowed to try his hand at conducting. Later, Italo Campanini retired to become manager of his own opera company. He took the company to New York to give Verdi's operas, principally *Othello*, at a time when the craze for German opera ruled the Metropolitan. Campanini's venture was a financial failure. It was saved artistically by the ability of Cleofonte as a conductor, and by the fine singing of Eva Tetrazzini, who later became Madame Cleofonte Campanini. When Oscar Hammerstein opened his Manhattan Opera House in New York in 1906 as a rival of the Metropolitan, he engaged Cleofonte Campanini as conductor. To a great extent, he gave the artistic direction of the performances into his hands.

'The Metropolitan is losing its prestige,' Campanini told me in London. 'Hammerstein has secured the American production rights to the new operas of Debussy, Richard Strauss, and of Charpentier's *Louise*. The list of singers is magnificent — Melba, Mary Garden, my sister-in-law Luisa Tetrazzini. . . .'

And he offered me a season's contract.

'Well,' I said pointedly. 'How much will Mr. Hammerstein pay me?'

Campanini mentioned a sum which seemed to me very good.

I agreed to go, if Messager would release me from an engagement to sing at the Grand Opera in Paris, of which he had become Director. Actually, I signed a contract.

Then Campanini went on to speak of something else. He was to conduct a week of Verdi operas at Parma, the composer's birthplace, during the next October. He asked me to sing Gilda in *Rigoletto* at the festival.

Well, things in the career of Frances Alda, late Miss Frances Davies, were looking pretty good. Carré wanted me back at the Opéra Comique, which Mary Garden had left for Hammerstein's in New York. I had engagements for several concerts at big private houses in London during the season. And here was Campanini with two offers up his sleeve.

Also, I had just met someone who interested me enormously. This was Franko Alfano, the author of *Resurrection*. Actually, he was one of the ablest composers of our time. Years later, when Puccini died, Alfano was chosen to complete *Turandot*, the opera Puccini had been working on and left unfinished at his death.

That Franko was also a very attractive man, and obviously attracted to me, didn't detract from his fame in my eyes.

Meanwhile, François Empain, over in Brussels, was writing me to know when I should be coming back. He had his yacht at Ostend and would run across the channel to fetch me.

Wasn't I coming? Soon?

I sang jubilantly in my bath, and when I went to Tosti for my daily singing lesson.

That dear, gentle old man was adored by everyone who knew him. He was a great friend of Caruso's, who, whenever he was in London, would descend on Tosti's house in Mandeville Place, embrace his 'Ciccio' fervently, pour out all his troubles, joys, business arrangements, and confidences about Giachetta. Then, before Tosti could answer a question or give a word of advice, Caruso, still talking volubly, would sweep him off to Pagani's restaurant to eat ravioli, or for a day in the country.

Tosti had been a great favorite of Queen Victoria's and was still of Alexandra's. He was invited everywhere in London. People adored having him sit down at the piano and sing one of his own songs in his little fluty voice, that was still very true and sweet.

That is one grand thing about the British: they remain loyal to the end. There's something rather glorious when you find some elderly singer like Albani still drawing the crowds and still enjoying royal favor, long after her voice has lost its beauty and richness. Or is that loyalty just a subconscious desire to show the world how tenacious the British bulldog can be?

Anyway, there's a lot of goodness and kindness in it.

If you're an artist, and if you've worked hard for years, first to perfect your art and then to give the public what you had to give of beauty or art or entertainment or just sheer fun, it's warming to your heart to know that even after your gift has faded, as all those gifts do fade, people really have grown to care enough about you as a person to be sweet, and to be still grateful for the past.

What artist wants to be treated like a spigot? Turn it, and for as long as the tank is full, fill up your glasses, boys. But when the tank gets low, or empty — then to the junk heap with it!

The singer receives the least compensation of any artist. If you write a book, there it is. Something tangible. You can take it up from time to time and read it over. You can admire it, or disagree with it. You can throw it at your husband when he irritates you beyond what words will take care of. Paint a picture, carve a statue, and what have you? Something your friends may think awful but be too kind to say so. Still, there the thing is. And there's always the off chance that long after you're dead somebody will come along and christen it ART and sell it for an enormous sum to some museum where the public will go on paying money just to look at it.

But sing a song — perfectly — and where is it?

Vanished completely before the last quiver has ceased ʲin your throat.

It's that sense of being intangible and evanescent that singers suffer from. Those who don't understand call it egotism and conceit.

But psychologists, please take notice.

It was part of that feeling that I was riding on the crest of the wave that I should find myself one night, while in London, seated at dinner opposite a man whose face was vaguely familiar to me.

Where had I met him before?

I asked who he was, and was told:

'The Manager of the Gaiety.'

I felt my toes inside my gold slippers begin to curl up iɾ amusement.

When someone at the table spoke admiringly of my singing I looked across at my vis-à-vis. I said:

'Well, would you give me an engagement at the Gaiety?'

'It's yours tonight if you'll take it,' was the prompt reply.

'Oh, no, you wouldn't,' I retorted. 'You turned me down.'

And I told the story of my first visit to London, and how that same theatre manager's refusing to engage me was really the foundation of my career as an opera singer.

WHEN I started for Parma in the first week of October, all down the Midi and across Lombardy the vintage was in full swing. The air was heavy with the scent of wine. Great carts heaped with grapes creaked along the sun-baked roads. In the vineyards, laughing, bare-legged youths and girls were dancing out the year's Chablis, Médoc, Borolo, and Chianti.

It was evening when my train got in. Madame Campanini was at the station to meet me.

She told me they were singing *Loreley* that evening. We had just time to drive to the opera house to hear the performance.

Never shall I forget what I heard that night. There were years when, if I had a bad dream, some of that night's experience would be woven into it. Only, in the dream, it would be I on the stage, singing Anna in Verdi's *Loreley*.

Alice Zepelli was singing the second rôle, of Anna, at that performance. She was a fine singer, but when she came to the aria (and I knew just how hard that was to sing, because Tosti had taught it to me in London), she broke on a high note.

Immediately the audience broke into hisses and jeers. And then, as the poor woman stood there, defenseless, *the audience began to sing that aria through, as with one voice, and perfectly!*

Horror filled me. I turned round to Madame Campanini. She told me later my face was white.

'I can't sing here tomorrow night,' I said. 'I simply can't face an audience like that.'

But I did face them. I had to.

I sang with Bonci and with Battestini and I was inspired to my best.

There were no jeers, no hisses, thank God. Instead, thunderous applause and generous 'bravos' (some of these I suspect, for my extremely feminine thighs and legs, well shown off by smooth, skin-tight trunks in my Third Act costume). When it was all over, and I went out the stage door with my arms full of flowers, there was a crowd waiting to cheer me again, to unharness the horses from the victoria and pull me through the banner-hung streets, singing, to my hotel.

Among the flowers, the telegrams, and the general hubbub of excitement that inevitably attends a début performance and that eddies and swirls about a singer's dressing-room, there was a very formal note, in Italian, brought to me between the acts by one of the ushers.

Signor Gatti-Casazza presented his compliments to Signorina Alda, and asked the favor of an interview.

I tossed the note to Cleofonte Campanini to read.

'Who is Gatti-Casazza?' I asked.

Campanini made a face of distaste.

'Oh, you don't want to have anything to do with him,' he replied. 'He's no one of any importance.'

I dropped the note on the floor and thought no more about it.

Next morning while I was still in bed, the valet brought the morning post. Among the letters was another one from that same persistent Signor Gatti-Casazza. My Italian was pretty limited but I was able to translate its message. The writer regretted that Signorina Alda had not replied to his note sent the evening of her début in *Rigoletto*. He still wished very earnestly for an interview. Unfortunately his duties at La Scala necessitated his immediate return to Milan, but would not Signorina Alda, in passing through Milan on her return journey to Paris, stop over there and allow him to see her on a matter of importance?

Milan ... La Scala. ... La Scala was the greatest opera house in all Europe. ... Gatti-Casazza ... I *had* heard that name before. ... WHAT had I heard about Gatti-Casazza?

'A person of no importance,' Campanini had said. And I recalled the look on his face as he said it.

I began to have my suspicions. After all, I had not been singing with various opera companies for three seasons without learning that the world of opera is a hotbed of intrigue, petty jealousy, spite, and politics.

I said nothing to either Cleofonte or to Madame Campanini

about receiving the second note. Instead I went to Battestini.

'Who,' I demanded, 'is Gatti-Casazza?'

'The ablest director of grand opera in the world,' he said promptly. 'Why do you want to know?'

'Tell me more about him first,' I hedged.

'For eight years he has been directing La Scala,' Battestini told me. 'The house was closed for nearly a year and a half when Duke Visconti, who was President of the Board, and the other directors, heard about Gatti. Then he was managing the communal theatre in his own city, Ferrara, and doing this so well, though just as an amateur and for love of it, that everybody in Italy was amazed. The directors of La Scala offered him the position of Director of La Scala. The shareholders and the city of Milan advanced the money for the first season. And Gatti has made money for them. He has brought *il bel canto* back to Italy — he and Maestro Toscanini, his conductor.'

'And what about Toscanini?' I said.

Battestini exploded in a volley of ecstatic praises:

'Marvellous... incredible... an extraordinary genius...,'

Wickedly, I interposed: 'I don't suppose Campanini is any too fond of him?'

Battestini began to laugh. 'I'll tell you something. There was a row of some sort between Gatti and Toscanini. The maestro is temperamental and Gatti is obstinate. Toscanini left La Scala and went to conduct for a season at Buenos Aires. Gatti engaged Campanini for La Scala. But things didn't go very well. There was the première of *Madame Butterfly* when the audience hissed poor Puccini, and Rosina Storchio who sang it. The musicians began to get rebellious. At one rehearsal the orchestra formed a cabal. They played the whole overture to *Tannhäuser* half a tone lower than it is written. And Campanini went on conducting, apparently none the wiser. Well, after that, was there a scene? Campanini was out. Gatti got a new director. The minute Toscanini came back from South America Gatti and he made up their old differences, and they have been together at La Scala ever since. No,' he concluded, 'I don't think Campanini cares very much about Toscanini or Gatti-Casazza.'

So that was how the wind was blowing.

I began to understand a lot of things now.

I wrote Signor Gatti-Casazza that I should be passing through Milan in two days' time and would be at the Hotel Milan, where he could communicate with me.

It seemed a part of the drama that was shaping my life that that very afternoon in Parma, Campanini should come to see me. He wore an anxious and shamefaced look.

'What's the matter?' I asked him.

'Apparently Mme. Melba has heard that I have engaged you to sing in New York next season.'

'Well, has she anything to say to that?' I demanded.

For answer he pulled a crumpled telegraph blank out of his pocket and showed it to me.

The message was brevity itself:

'Either Alda or myself.'

Of course, as far as box-office receipts went there was no choice open to Campanini. Melba was the best-known soprano in the world. To American audiences Frances Alda would be just a new singer to be appraised. It relieved Campanini no end that I should offer no objection to cancelling the contract he had drawn up with me in London.

So Melba went to New York that winter.

Meanwhile, Frances Alda turned her thoughts on Milan, and so went on to another adventure.

MY FIRST meeting with Gatti-Casazza took place in the Hotel Milan. This, he told me in almost his first words, was the hotel in which Verdi had died in 1901.

Later, he insisted on escorting me to see the very room.

I refused to go in.

Standing on the threshold I could see the square, gloomy chamber with the floor of black-and-white marble, the heavy draperies, the oppressive carved furniture, the high, dark bed like a catafalque, where Verdi had lain for two days in a coma, while his relatives and friends and admirers thronged the ante-chamber, weeping and sobbing and praying. Gatti-Casazza had been a witness to that scene. He pictured it to me.

Ugh!

I shivered.

And I wondered at the temperament of this grave, middle-aged man with the heavily bearded face in which the dark melancholy eyes seemed to brood on unfathomable things. Yet he had lodged in him somewhere the extraordinary genius of an impresario who could direct a great opera company for the entertainment and delight of the crowds and for the solid enrichment of its shareholders.

In a mirror beside the deathbed I caught a glimpse of our two figures — Gatti as I have described him, myself in a yellow Vionnet frock, a wide black hat trimmed in ospreys — a prima donna's hat — long gloves, high-heeled, shining slippers, and a frivolous ruffled parasol.

There was something macabre in the reflection of us given back by the mirror that had recorded the death scene Gatti was describing in its fullest details.

I said very hastily, in French (Gatti did not speak English and I did not speak Italian; I did not know until later that he hated having to converse in any language except his own, even in French):

'I should like to go down and have a drink.'

Seated at one of the tables in the outdoor café, I breathed a sigh of relief. The dust and confusion of the *piazza*, the jangle of the trams, the rattle of carts over the cobblestones, the clatter of donkey hooves, the whining of the bootblacks, sweetmeat and lottery ticket sellers, even the smell of unwashed Italian humanity, seemed good after that experience upstairs.

Meanwhile, over my frappé, I studied the man who sat opposite to me.

At that time Gatti-Casazza was thirty-eight years of age. And a bachelor. Though he had been engaged for a time to the Spanish singer Maria Barrientos, she had broken the engagement in 1906. (In 1916, he engaged her to sing a season with the Metropolitan Opera Company. She sang the title rôle in *Lakmé*, I remember, in the first performance of that opera that had been given at the Metropolitan in ten years. She was not at all pretty and she made tremendous grimaces as she sang; but she was a very *chic* little person. Her voice, when I heard her, was a light coloratura soprano. She was not a success in America and, as I remember, she remained with the Metropolitan only two seasons.)

Can one ever hope to understand the grown man unless one has had glimpses into the childhood and youth that were the crucible in which the man was fused?

I think not.

Certainly a great deal of the secret of Frances Alda was to be found in the impulsive, fiery-tempered, ardent little girl playing prima donna in the lath and burlap theatre in the garden at St. Kilda; rebelling against her plain white linen frocks and cotton stockings, against Grandfather's mandates and having to scratch his bald spot as he sank into his afternoon nap; trembling with the ardor of her devotion to her first actress idol, Cora Brown-Potter; violently taking things into her own hands and by the very force of her self-confidence forcing Mr. Williamson to engage her as a singer in his road company.

How much of the secret of Giulio Gatti-Casazza could be read in his hands, extremely small and delicately formed for a man of his proportions!

'Too small for the piano,' his early teachers had told him when he first went to Milan to school.

His father had served under Garibaldi among the famous Thousand who made the march on Rome, which re-echoed, in our time, in the tramp-tramp of Mussolini's Black Shirts. Later, he married a lady of a noble family of Ferrara. When he retired from military service he took his wife and their two sons back to that city to live. Later he went into Parliament. Senator Gatti-Casazza was charming, witty, debonair. He sang in a delightful baritone voice, and he loved the theatre as he loved nothing since he gave up fighting for *Italia irridenta*. In Ferrara he became head of the Board of Directors of the Teátro Communale. There, under his direction, Toscanini, at twenty-five, had his first engagement in a theatre of any importance.

After that early judgment on his hands which kept him from studying the piano, Giulio Gatti-Casazza turned his attention to mathematics. He determined to enter the navy. He did spend several years at the Naval Academy in Leghorn, but failed in an examination and went home to Ferrara to enter the university there. Later he was graduated, in Genoa, as a marine engineer.

But whilst he was in Ferrara he discovered the theatre. Not from the boxes, as a place of entertainment — he had known it in that way all his life — but from the Director's office.

That experience discovered in him his true genius.

Later, after he had graduated and was serving his military duty in Ferrara, his father was elected to Parliament. He resigned his post as President of the Board of Directors of the theatre and the municipality begged his son, Giulio, to take his place.

What Giulio Gatti-Casazza was doing at the Ferrara theatre was soon talked of all over Italy. He introduced Wagner, when nothing could have been more unpopular in Italy than German music. He produced Verdi's *Othello* and *Falstaff*.

Puccini then lived in Ferrara. Gatti was often with him at a time when the composer was working on the score of *Manon Lescaut*. He went with the composer to Turin to see the première of that opera in 1893.

Ferrara was, of course, just a small and relatively unimportant city. Gatti's contribution to its theatre was so spectacular and so successful, financially as well as artistically, that he became the most talked-of man in theatrical and musical circles in Italy. The Directors of La Scala in Milan could not fail to hear of him and be impressed.

Milan's famous opera house had been closed for sixteen months. In the century of its existence it was the first time such a thing had happened. The municipality refused to invest any more money in a losing venture. Then the Directors sent for Gatti-Casazza. He had been recommended to them by Mascagni, Franchetti, and Puccini. They offered him the post of Director.

It was the most coveted post in the European operatic world.

Under Gatti's management La Scala shook off its dust, awoke from its bad days of debt and shame, and began to give opera that attracted the attention of all the musicians and musical critics in Europe. Equally important was the fact that it began to pay dividends.

One of Gatti's first acts as Director had been to go to Turin with Boito, the author of *Mefistofele*, and engage the services of Toscanini as conductor. 'The first performance he conducted there was *Die Meistersinger*, with Scotti in the rôle of Hans Sachs.

Even at that time Toscanini was famous. In fact, he is one of those artists about whose gifts no one had ever had any doubts. I have among my treasured possessions a letter written by Catalani, the composer of *La Wally*, to a friend, who ultimately gave it to Toscanini, who in turn gave it to me.

The letter tells enthusiastically of having heard a '*Giovane maestro*' eighteen years old, named Toscanini, who, Catalani prophesied, would some day take the whole world of music by storm.

During my first season at the Metropolitan, Toscanini gave *La Wally*, with Caruso and Destinn. He has great partiality for the music of that opera; he must have, since he named his two eldest children Walter and Wally for the hero and heroine of the piece.

La Wally was not a great success in America, chiefly because it was never given often enough for the opera-goers — who invariably like best what they already know well — to become familiar with it.

How much of La Scala's success could be attributed to its conductor is not for me to say. To put it mildly, it was decidedly a fifty-fifty proposition. Toscanini's supreme artistry and Gatti's shrewd business sense made a perfect and unfailingly successful partnership for any opera house.

Those two men, working together, could accomplish great things. They did it then, in Milan, and they continued to do it during many years there and in New York.

Haven't I seen them do it?

Of course, even in those youthful days there were times when the two temperaments were too much for each other. There were ruptures. There was the time that Battestini had told me about, when Toscanini had shaken the dust of La Scala from his feet and sailed to Buenos Aires to conduct for a season there. Gatti had engaged Cleofonte Campanini as conductor, until the musicians mutinied and he had to let *him* go, and engage a substitute until Toscanini was back in Italy and could be approached with dignified offers to return to La Scala.

Guilefully, Gatti would mention some opera not already on the program that he would like to introduce at La Scala.

Toscanini would rise like a trout to the bait.

'To give — whatever it happened to be — we must have so many violins; so many brasses; so many choristers. Who shall we get to sing this rôle or that?'

Immediately Toscanini would be in it, heart and soul.

And Gatti, sitting to one side, leaning his cheek on his hand as he so often sat when considering some new project, would be thinking shrewdly: 'If I get as many violins as he says he wants and as many choristers and all the other singers, not to mention new scenery and costumes for the ballet, what will it cost? If we sell ninety per cent of the seats how much profit can we make?'

CONTRASTED with Gatti-Casazza, Toscanini appeared alive, vibrant, electric.

They made an extraordinary pair.

They had come together to see me at the Hotel Milan. (I didn't know I was establishing a precedent in Gatti's life as a director when I refused to go to see him in his office at La Scala, as a note from him, which I found waiting when I reached Milan, asked me to do. I replied that if he wished to see me, he must come to my hotel. And he came.) He brought Toscanini with him.

Now they sat in the salon of my suite and asked me questions.

Could I sing this rôle? Could I sing that? Could I sing the other?

'Yes, yes, yes,' I said to all their questions.

To judge from my replies, I was the most accomplished opera singer at large anywhere. I know Toscanini's eyes twinkled and the corners of his mouth quirked into a smile.

But nothing shook the evenness of Gatti's solemnity.

He was planning, so he told me, to present Charpentier's *Louise* at La Scala for the first time. The opera was to be sung in Italian. Having heard and seen me as Gilda at the Verdi Festival in Parma, he wished to engage me to create the rôle of the French sewing girl who is Charpentier's heroine.

Toscanini — alive, vibrant, electric

I had Melba's telegram in my dressing-case. I had made Campanini give it to me. That, plus the honor of creating a new rôle at La Scala, with the wide publicity attendant on such an achievement made the proposal very attractive to me.

I was hesitating before I replied, and Gatti went on to tell me that the première of *Louise* was set for a date in February. It was then October. I should have three months in which to prepare myself for the rôle before I should be required to return to Milan for rehearsals.

Also, in the coming April, Chaliapin, the famous Russian bass, was returning to La Scala to sing Boito's *Mefistofele*, which he had sung there several seasons before. Gatti offered me an engagement to sing Marguerite in that opera with Chaliapin.

I agreed to both proposals, signed the contracts, and next day after that visit to Verdi's death chamber that I have described, I went back to Paris.

Gatti-Casazza saw me off at the station — the old, grimy, barn-like station of pre-Mussolini days. Franko Alfano, whom I'd been seeing a lot of in Milan, was there too. He and Gatti exchanged glances that didn't altogether reflect the punctilious courtesy of their greeting. My last glimpse of Milan included the two men — Franko gay and smiling, Gatti very grave, very formal, and yet (as well to admit it, I said to myself, as I arranged my cushions, travelling-rug, books, flowers, and my griffon Pitchu for the journey) very interesting.

WHEN I went round to the rue Jouffroy and told Madame Marchesi all that had happened to me in Italy, she was triumphant.

At the thought of a new rôle to be created her eyes snapped.

Here was a challenge to all my powers, and to all hers.

She got out the score of *Louise* (in Italian), and we set to work on it together. I had seen Mary Garden in the rôle at the Opéra Comique a number of times. Louise was the rôle in which Mary made her sensational début in Paris. She had been engaged by Albert Carré, Director of the Opéra Comique, as an understudy. On a night when *Louise* was being given, Mary was sitting in a box.

A few moments after the curtain fell on the First Act, one of the employees came to her.

'Mademoiselle, the Director wishes to see you. At once.'

She followed the man down to Carré's office. There she found that the thing that every understudy dreams of happening some day, had actually occurred. The singer who had been singing Louise had been taken ill during the First Act; she could not continue. It was too late to find another prima donna who knew the part, or to change the opera for another. An understudy would have to go on in the next act, as Louise.

It was Mary's chance.

And it made her.

Her performance that night was magnificent. The house went mad, entirely forgetting the singer whose illness had opened the way for a newcomer. Next morning all Paris rang with it. Here was the city's own opera, and the heroine most dear to them played, as no one had ever played the rôle, by an American girl whom nobody had ever heard of before. Sybil Sanderson was then at the height of her career, and people remembered Emma Eames and Emma Nevada. But this American Mary Garden had something those other, finer singers had lacked. Something the French understood and adored — that quality they call '*chien.*'

Well, sometimes life behaves like a story.

Could any fiction writer invent a neater turn of events to follow after the Americans who had financed Mary's musical studies in Paris had been told by some busy-body that their protégée was having too good a time, and in too Parisian a manner, to suit their starched ideas of moral behavior, and had withdrawn their support? Mary had found herself stranded and penniless. It was Sybil Sanderson who made it possible for her to go on with her studies. She took Mary into her own home, and later sent her to Carré. He engaged her as an understudy. That, as I have told, led to Louise and fame.

My own type was so different from Garden's that I knew I must forget her Louise completely, and create my own from my own interpretation of the character.

For two months I worked on the rôle, though I was singing occasionally at concerts during that period. I went about Paris and saw the sewing girls going home from the workshops in the evenings, tired but bravely gay; defiant in their youth and their poverty and their eagerness for life. I saw how meagre their lives were, and how desperately they reached out for any scrap of pleasure or excitement, and how, because of this hunger of youth in them, many of them became caught in the toils of a city like Paris; became its victims and its captives.

I began to understand Louise as I felt Charpentier wanted her understood, and as I must understand her in order to present her to an audience in a foreign city so that they would feel with her, through my interpretation of the rôle, that all that she did and all that happened to her was logical and inevitable, and had in it the beauty that all things that must be have in them.

I had to make Louise real, as well as sing the music her creator had written for her to sing, perfectly.

There were, too, the costumes to be designed and ordered.

The dresses for my rôles have always been tremendously important to me. (Is this another phase in which I have never outgrown Grandmother's strict censorship over my wardrobe in my childhood days?)

I have always spent much time and thought and plenty of effort on having the gowns in which I sang not only appropriate but beautiful, and becoming to me. Many of them I designed myself. I have had an extra thrill, sometimes, when, after a performance, the reporters commented admiringly on 'Madame Alda's beautiful costumes.' Celia, the maid I had at the theatre for thirteen years, was trained to take perfect care of them. After I wore one it was sent immediately to be cleaned, to be ready for the next time of wearing.

No torn lace, draggled chiffon, or satin skirts with traces of the Metropolitan's dirty stage for Frances Alda.

I still keep carefully a dozen and more of those I loved best: the rich rose and silver brocades I wore as Lady Harriet in *Martha*; the pale grey crinoline and little jade-green shoulder shawl in which I loved to sing Mimi; the lace underskirt and rosebud-sprinkled panniers in which I danced the gavotte in *Manon Lescaut*; Francesca da Rimini's scarlet and purple mediaeval draperies; the barbaric gold and jewelled robe and head-dress of Jaroslavna in *Prince Igor*.

The costumes for Louise, of course, were extremely simple. All the more reason, therefore, that they should be made of fabrics and colors that were most becoming to me. They had to convey, too, that indefinable air of *chic* that even the poorest of the Paris *midinettes* has the gift for achieving with a scrap of lace, a twist of ribbon, or the exactly right angle at which she wears her hat.

JANUARY first, 1908.
I saw the New Year in at Ciro's with a gay party. I remember we toasted each other and the new year in champagne, and wished each other luck and good fortune.

What would my luck be in 1908?

I had a premonition that the year would be an important

one for me; the end of one cycle, leading into something new. I sensed, ahead of me, changes and opportunities. But I did not guess — I could not — how many these would be. Nor that before I drank a toast to another new year I should have sung in Milan, in Warsaw, in Buenos Aires, in Paris, and in New York.

Franko Alfano lifted his glass and smiled at me:

'To the most beautiful lips in Paris,
To the most beautiful eyes in France,
To the most beautiful face in Europe,
To the most beautiful hair in the world.'

Next day I made him write it in my autograph album. It was one of those lovely, extravagant, heart-warming compliments that a woman cherishes. And needs sometimes to buck her up.

VERY early in the new year, I went to Milan for my first rehearsal with Toscanini.

In the rehearsal room at La Scala, Gatti sat off in one corner. He leaned his elbow on the arm of his chair and rested his cheek against his hand, eyeing me gravely. He had the most beautiful eyes I have ever seen in a human being. Like deep pools.

Toscanini sat beside the pianist. He kept his eyes closed as he listened, only lifting a finger now and then to mark the time.

I began to sing.

Act One, Scene One, enter Louise.

I sang the rôle straight through; through the big aria in the Third Act that is so difficult to sing, through the final scene in which Louise spurns her dying father's plea to return to the security of her home, pushes off his detaining hand, and goes back to her lover and to the wild life of the city that has marked her one of its victims.

The pianist struck the final chord.

Its echoes died away in the still room.

No one spoke. Then Toscanini leaned across the pianist's shoulder and closed the music book on the rack. Only then did he open his eyes and look at me.

Blandly, in Italian, he asked:

'In what language were you singing?'

Furious?

Of course I was. Who wouldn't have been?

I glared at Toscanini, at the cowed and silent pianist, at Gatti-Casazza brooding in his corner. Without deigning to reply I marched out of the rehearsal room, out of the theatre and back to the Hotel Milan.

For three or four days I remained there in a state of injured dignity.

Now, recalling my mood then, I know what a fool I was. A spoiled girl of twenty-three who just couldn't take it. But, remember, life hadn't given me many knocks up to that time. It had all been smooth sailing. Successes had come as thick as blackberries in summer. My Italian pronunciation had drawn no adverse comments in Parma or at Covent Garden. Who, I demanded fiercely, was this *maestro* Toscanini to criticize me now?

Meanwhile, Gatti-Casazza came to the hotel to apologize and to ask me to come back to La Scala.

Indignantly, I refused.

He sent me notes.

I tore them up.

More notes followed.

In the meantime, and secretly, I was studying Louise harder than I'd ever studied any rôle before.

Finally, I relented to the point of considering Gatti's proposals.

He pleaded with me to return to La Scala. There, he said, Toscanini would go through the score of *Louise* with me word by word, as Massenet had taught me Manon before my début at the Opéra Comique. In that way, my pronunciation of the Italian words would be perfect, so that at the première every syllable would be understandable to every person in the audience.

I went back. Of course I did. I had never had any intention of giving up singing Louise, which would be a great step forward in my career. But I did have every intention of humbling that *maestro* Toscanini who had injured my pride.

No queen was ever more careful of her dignity than was I at the next rehearsal. No one was ever more punctilious than Toscanini in teaching me the correct pronunciation of the phrases as we went through the score.

Only once his puckish humor bubbled up again.

He mimicked my pronunciation of a word.

Immediately I stopped singing. I lifted my finger at him.

'I must tell you, *maestro*,' I said in French, 'if you do that once again, just once, I shall walk out of here quicker than you can say Jack Robinson.'

He took it from me.

Why, heaven only knows.

Now, recalling that childish fit of temper and hurt pride on my part, I think too of the innumerable times later on that Toscanini taught me the rôles I was to sing; his infinite patience and inspiring enthusiasm, and all that I owe him. And I feel like humbling myself before the forbearance of a very great artist.

I have seen him respond quite differently when other prima donnas turned haughty and asserted their temperaments and their pride. I shall never forget his scene with Farrar. At a rehearsal he stopped her, correcting her singing of a phrase. Repeating the passage she sang it exactly as she had sung it before.

Again Toscanini stopped her.

'You forget, *maestro*,' she said magnificently, 'that *I* am the star.'

Without opening his eyes, Toscanini shook his head wearily.

'I thank God I know no stars except those in heaven which are perfect,' he replied.

The passage, needless to say, was sung as Toscanini wished it to be sung.

B UT to come back to *Louise*.
  Does any singer ever make her début at La Scala without feeling that she is singing not just to the living audience, but also to the shades of the great singers who have made the fame and the traditions of the opera house?

As always in those days I was following in the footsteps of Melba. As a New Zealander — which to most persons, except New Zealanders — is accepted as the same thing as an Australian, despite the little matter of a four days' and five nights' sea journey between the two islands — it was inevitable that my voice should be compared and contrasted with Melba's. I was following, too, after my Aunt Frances Saville, as these two great singers had followed Patti and Jenny Lind and the great Italian singers of my grandmother's day.

It was a great tradition, that of the foreign singers who have won Milan's critical acclaim.

I must not fail it.

On that night of the première of *Louise* the house was filled. Every seat in it. From the wings, waiting for my entrance cue, I could see the vast sea of faces in the orchestra, the tiers of boxes filled with the aristocracy of Milan— men and women with names that had been sounded as mediaeval battle cries. and with the city's rich and powerful bankers and manufacturers

and merchants. My eyes went above these to the packed galleries. There, leaning forward, intent and highly critical, were
the music-loving people. Many had gone without their dinners
to pay the price of a gallery seat at that night's opera. Many
carried memories of great singers heard at La Scala through a
generation. All were jealous of their city's reputation for the
best opera in the world.

All, nobleman and bourgeois, rich and poor, the fashionable
and the unknown, had come to judge of a Frenchman's ability
to compose music — an art most of them quite frankly believed
belonged exclusively to the Italians. And to judge of an Englishwoman's voice and her art of singing.

Il bel canto.

Could a Frenchman create it? Could an English voice pour it
forth to satisfy their ears and hearts?

Next morning all the reviews spoke of the impatience during
the first two acts, 'which was curbed only by interest in and
appreciation of the new singer.'

My experience of that appreciation began the minute I came
on the stage. The Scala is so built that there are two rows of
boxes on either side of the stage and looking down directly on it.
One of these belonged to the officers of the garrison in Milan.
That night it was full of uniforms.

When I made my entrance I saw the officers lean forward in
unabashed curiosity.

'Che bell' occhi!' a voice exclaimed.

There was something so impudent and young and debonair
in this admiration so frankly expressed that I returned the
compliment by singing directly to that box through a good part
of the opera. Which obviously delighted the occupants.

At the close of the aria in the Third Act there was tremendous
applause from the whole house, and calls for me. I had to bow
again and again, holding up the progress of the act, a thing, as I
was to learn later, that infuriated Toscanini. He always wanted
each act to be played and sung straight through from beginning

to end without interruptions, like a perfect composition. And without the intrusion of the singers' personalities on the work of the composer.

Audiences at La Scala were not always so hospitable to new works. When *Butterfly* was given there for the first time, the house had hissed and booed. And this, even though Rosina Storchio, Milan's adored prima donna, was singing the title rôle. In the scene where Butterfly comes on with her baby in her arms, there was a howl of derision:

'*Il piccolo* T——,' naming the man who was known to have been Storchio's lover and the father of her crippled child.

I was present at the première of *Pelléas et Mélisande*, which was given a few nights after that first performance of *Louise*.

I sat in a box with Gatti.

The house was packed, and one felt the antagonism of the audience immediately after the overture. That antagonism was grimly silent, however, until the scene in which Golaud and Pelléas wander in the vaults underneath the castle, Golaud brooding on his jealousy and his desire to murder his brother.

Then the distaste for Maeterlinck's mysticism and Debussy's musical rendering of it burst all bounds.

Such hoots and shouts and stamping of feet!

At the conductor's desk I could see Toscanini, magnificently imperturbable, going right on conducting, as though perfect, sympathetic silence reigned. I could see the violinists and cellists draw their bows, and the pianist's fingers move over the keyboard. But not one note could I hear above that raucous din.

Perhaps to placate the public after that failure, Gatti staged a marvellous ballet.

That, I well remember, was the first time I ever saw Rosina Galli dance.

She was then a child of fourteen or fifteen. Her mother, who was a caretaker in a Milan apartment house, had brought her at the age of eight to the Scala's ballet school to be taught. Even then Rosina was a marvellous little artist.

I told Gatti so as we sat together that night and watched her.

'Perhaps,' he said.

His eyes were not on the stage. They were on me.

How strange, when one thinks that this girl whom we watched together should have been the one to come between us after we were husband and wife.

TWO other singers I met at La Scala that season whom I was later to sing with many times in New York, and know well.

Amato, whose Metropolitan début was made a few weeks before my own. And the tempestuous Russian artist, Feodor Chaliapin.

Chaliapin had sung at La Scala before. Soon after Gatti became Director he arranged to produce Boito's *Mefistofele*. Boito was one of the Board of Directors of La Scala and one of the ablest, most gifted musicians of our time. He had been Verdi's friend and the librettist of many of his operas. But *Mefistofele* was his own creation, words and music.

Gatti considered several basses for the title rôle. But not one seemed to him good enough.

One day a Russian nobleman, passing through Milan, presented letters to Gatti-Casazza and asked to be shown about La Scala. Finding that the Russian knew much about opera and music, Gatti confided to him his difficulty in finding a bass singer for *Mefistofele*. The Russian recommended his own countryman Feodor Chaliapin. He assured Gatti that if the performances at La Scala could be set some time during Lent, a season when the theatres in Russia used to be closed, Chaliapin would be allowed to come to Italy.

It was so arranged. Chaliapin came, to find himself, before he had sung a note, the centre of a terrific storm.

Were there not basses in Italy? the press and the public were shouting? What need had Gatti-Casazza to send to Russia for one?

Only Chaliapin's superb singing and acting of the part saved the day. Not even the most rabid chauvinist could fail to give praise to so great an artist, whatever his nationality was.

When Chaliapin returned to La Scala in April, 1908, to sing *Mefistofele* again, this time with me as Marguerite, he received a tremendous ovation. He played the part naked to the waist, with a leopard skin thrown over his hairy chest. A Satan far removed from the suave tempter in black and scarlet tights and cape and point cap such as Marcel Journet had worn when I sang *Faust* with him.

Chaliapin was morbidly sensitive to any criticism. He could not forget that when he had sung in New York — I think it was in 1905 or 1906 — he had not been well received. The American public had been affronted by his unconventional costumes and by his impassioned acting.

'Don't ever go to America, Alda,' he kept telling me in Milan. 'It's a terrible place. Nothing would induce me to go back there again.'

He did come back, of course. Later. And New York went quite mad about him that time.

But he was still the temperamental Russian, full of whims and notions, and a despair to the stage managers and stage hands because of his always wanting some bit of scenery changed or some property arranged differently to allow him a chance for some new stage business. Everyone connected with the Metropolitan could understand the desire for revenge that prompted one of the stage hands, after hoisting Chaliapin in armor onto the mule for his entrance as Don Quixote, to stick the mule's haunches with a pin.

Up went the mule's heels. Down went its head.

Up, down; up, down.

Chaliapin went on the stage in a series of bucks that made him appear like a clown at a rodeo.

Chaliapin's warning to me against America came too late.

Immediately after the première of *Louise*, I had received a visitor. Mr. Rawlins Cottenet of New York. He was, he told me, the secretary of the Board of Directors of the Metropolitan Opera Company. He had heard me the night before at La Scala, and he had gone out and promptly wired Mr. Otto Kahn, then Chairman of the Board, and asked permission to offer me a contract with the Metropolitan for the 1908–1909 season.

Melba at Hammerstein's. Alda at the Metropolitan.

What a turn of the wheel!

I accepted the offer Mr. Cottenet made me. When Gatti-Casazza came one afternoon to take me for a motor drive I told him that I should be singing in New York the next winter.

H OW long does it take a woman to find out that a man — any man — is in love with her?

I think, even before I said good-bye to Gatti at the Milan station after he had engaged me to create Louise, that I knew he was going to fall in love with me, if he wasn't so already.

There were those unmistakable signs . . .

But why go into them? Every woman has seen them at one time or another.

Is there a woman alive who isn't secretly pleased when she finds a man has fallen in love with her? If there is, I never met her. That first, elemental pleasure has nothing to do with what she thinks of the man; or whether she feels that delicious falling-in-love sensation coming over her when she is with him or thinks of him. It is ever so much more primitive than that. It hasn't so much to do with the man himself as with the woman's sense of her power and power to charm. It's a symbol of her success as a woman. And everybody knows that women have a keener appetite for success than men ever have. It means more to them. They take it more seriously.

Which may be the reason why most successful women are so much less attractive than the majority of successful men.

I am not concealing the fact from anyone that I am not a feminist. You couldn't make a feminist out of a woman who knows, and doesn't care if the world knows it, too, that in some things she's as elemental as Eve, and as unashamed.

It was my woman's *amour propre* that was flattered by having the dignified director of La Scala waiting humbly to take me out to parties in Milan, and writing me notes full of extravagant Italian expressions of admiration of me as a woman, even more than as a singer.

When I went to Warsaw for a month's engagement at the opera there, before I was due to return to Milan to sing with Chaliapin in *Mefistofele*, the notes followed me into Poland. Telegrams and letters every day.

Warsaw was interesting in those days. One felt the barbaric mediaeval splendor of old Russia. Society was gay, vivid, extravagant. People came to the opera in great sleighs, curved like seashells, with the coachman sitting high at the back of the sleigh, and the ladies and gentlemen wrapped in magnificent furs.

I was welcomed and fêted and made much of.

And I loved it.

One amusing incident I have never forgotten. After the performance one night there were a lot of people in my dressing-room waiting to take me out to a supper party. Presently, one of the theatre employés appeared at the door. He was positively staggering under a huge basket of flowers. The thing was colossal, so enormous that at sight of it and the man's legs appearing below it while his body and face were concealed by roses and more and more roses, I laughed. To a man standing beside me about to put on my cloak, I said:

'Well, whoever it was who sent me that must be in love with me.'

The strangest expression came over his face.

'It was I who sent it to you,' he burst out. 'I am in love with you. Madly in love with you ...'

There seemed no stemming his Polish fervor.

'But,' I said hastily, 'do you know what I've heard about you? That you fall in love with every opera singer. I've heard you were in love with Frances Saville.'

'I was,' he admitted.

'She is my aunt,' I told him.

Somehow, that seemed to end *that*.

Meanwhile, as I learned later, Gatti had been in communication with the director of the Warsaw Opera. He asked that I be released from my engagement before the date set in the contract, giving as his reason for asking this, that he wished to start rehearsals for *Mefistofele* immediately. He brought all the prestige of La Scala to bear on the Warsaw director, who finally acceded to his demands and informed me that I might terminate my engagement there several days before I had expected.

'Well, at least that is better than nothing,' Gatti wrote me, admitting without apology that he had been pulling wires to get me back to Milan.

I WENT back to Italy in April ...

Snow on the St. Gothard. ... Mimosa in the villa gardens at Bellagio. ... Almond and peach trees wreathing Milan in a rosy garland ...

Mefistofele, with Chaliapin and Alda, Toscanini conducting. And Milan wild with delight and approval of the three of us. Boito taking both my hands and kissing them. Giving me his photograph with the inscription:

> *To the most charming and eminent artist*
> *Signorina Frances Alda*
> *with admiring homage.*
>
> ARRIGO BOITO

Franko Alfano there to play the gallant, and teasing me because that gallantry was obviously very displeasing to Signor Gatti-Casazza.

And Gatti telling me that the directors of the Metropolitan Opera Company were making offers to him and to Toscanini to come to New York next season and to re-establish the prestige of the opera there.

Telling me that the fact that I would be a member of the company the coming winter was an added inducement to him to consider the offer and to leave La Scala, where he had been for nine years.

ANOTHER brief engagement in Warsaw, then I was back in my apartment on the Avenue Bugeaud.

Gatti came to see me there.

He had come to Paris for a conference with Otto Kahn. He and Toscanini had signed three-year contracts with the Metropolitan, he told me.

There were howls of grief in Milan when the news was known. Lacking Gatti and Toscanini, La Scala's fame was burst like a pricked balloon.

But true to his nature, Gatti was already full of gloomy forebodings about America and the Metropolitan, and the magnitude of the task ahead of him. It was not as though the Metropolitan were New York's only opera house. Two years before Oscar Hammerstein had opened the Manhattan Opera House on Thirty-Fourth Street and advertised French opera with some of the best singers imported from Europe. At first, the Metropolitan directors had merely smiled at Hammerstein's venture. They recalled that thirteen years before he had done the same thing — had even opened his house in the same street. That experiment had lasted just two weeks. And this at a time when the Metropolitan was closed after a fire had destroyed the interior.

But Hammerstein's second attempt had not failed. It had had two increasingly successful seasons. Melba (didn't I know it?) had appeared there, and Emma Calvé. True, the Metropolitan had Caruso, but the Manhattan had Bonci, the great tenor with whom I had sung at the Verdi festival in Parma. And it had Mary Garden.

New York society, which for three decades had been linked with the Metropolitan, had decided to notice the new Manhattan Opera Company. Many of the younger members of the fashionable set were going there in preference to the Metropolitan, which, under the management of Conried, the director whom Gatti was to succeed, had been giving German opera almost exclusively, and none of the novelties which those same fashionables knew were being produced in Paris and Milan.

Perhaps I wasn't as sympathetic a listener to all this as I might have been if Gatti's visits had not found me in the midst of packing.

And a prima donna's packing can assume appalling proportions.

Trunks of operatic costumes and of my own wardrobe, hat boxes, shoe boxes, jewel cases, valises, portfolios of music were everywhere. Emilie, my maid, was darting in and out of closets, bringing dresses and yet more dresses. Thirty-two hats, each on a separate stand, stood waiting to be disposed of. And every day more and more exciting white cardboard boxes with the labels of Worth, Doucet, Vionnet, and Paquin were delivered at the door.

I was going to South America.

Gatti regarded me dolefully over the welter of silks and chiffons and laces.

'How long will this engagement in Buenos Aires last?'

I told him; until August.

'And then?'

'We sail from Genoa. The company will come back there.'

'I will go to Genoa to see you off. Then I must go to New York to confer with the other members of the Board of Directors and to see the opera house and its personnel. I shall be back in Italy when you return.'

'Chaliapin is going to Buenos Aires, too.' I told him. 'Not with us. But he will be singing there during our engagement.' Gatti frowned at this.

Later, after he had seen me off and was himself on board ship en route for New York, he wrote me, cautioning me against seeing too much of the Russian singer. He added that he had not liked the way Chaliapin had tried to be friendly with me in Milan.

He expressed himself as already regretful that he had signed the contract with the Metropolitan. With every mile that the *Kaiser Wilhelm* brought him nearer to America, his discontent and homesickness apparently increased.

The impression I had from the letters and the cablegrams he began sending me as soon as he arrived in New York was of a shivering victim being led across the sea to be offered, a live sacrifice, on the altar of the Metropolitan Opera Company.

THE company which Signor Camillo Bonetti had engaged to take to Buenos Aires that summer for the opera season there and in Montevideo was entirely Italian, with the exception of myself. Bonetti had made me the offer, and I had accepted it, immediately after the première of *Louise* in Milan.

At once, on shipboard, I found myself faced with the necessity of learning Italian. Not just to sing my rôles, but for the needs of everyday conversation and social enjoyment with the other members of the company.

(Gatti had warned me too against being friendly with my fellow artists. And against making a confidante of any of them. Oh, well, I have always talked too much. And sometimes too soon. Caution was never part of my nature. Things might have been better for me sometimes if it had been. Still, there were times when I felt the darkness of Gatti's temperament like a shadow over my natural high spirits and young enthusiasm.)

I plunged into the intricacies of Tuscan, Roman, Venetian, and Neapolitan dialects, floundered after a few rules of grammar, and began to assemble a vocabulary that extended beyond operatic arias.

Didur was a member of the company. And de Segurola.

We three began a friendship that has lasted ever since.

Didur had been singing at Hammerstein's Manhattan Opera House, but was joining the Metropolitan Company under Gatti's management that autumn. A fine bass singer, he later created the rôle of Boris Godounow at the Metropolitan in 1913. De Segurola, too, belonged to the Manhattan Company, but later joined the Metropolitan.

'Seggy' was one of the very few artists who ever came as guests to Gatti's and my home. During the War years, when it was impossible to follow our usual plan of going to Europe, I rented a house at De Soris Point, Long Island. It was a lovely house and quite famous. Charles Dana had built it. Later, it belonged to Harrison Williams. It was there he entertained the

Duke of Windsor, then Prince of Wales, when he visited the United States for the International Polo Match. The house is gone now. J. P. Morgan bought the site and tore it down, and has built there a house for his son.

Every week-end that summer we spent at De Soris Point we had many guests staying with us. Seggy often came. I always rang him up and asked him when I wanted to be sure of having someone with a grand sense of humor to add zest to the party. He used to love to tell how he had taught me Italian — in the vernacular.

But as a linguist I had the laugh on him after my birthday party, one thirty-first of May.

We were a big table full of guests: the Oliver Harrimans, the George Goulds, Mr. and Mrs. Otto Kahn, Beatrice Chandler, Elsie de Wolfe, big Ham Fish, Malvina Hoffman, and a lot of others, including Scotti and de Segurola.

Seggy pounded on the table to command attention. He pushed back his chair and stood up. He raised his glass of champagne, proposing a toast:

'Alda,' he began, 'you permit? I speak on your behind...'

Yes, I was better at the intricacies of Italian than he was with English.

I remember I had just bought a Twin-Six Packard. It was one of the first of those made, and I was tremendously proud of it. One day I drove up to the stage door of the Metropolitan in a rented car of another make.

Seggy was just coming along the sidewalk. He helped me out, staring at the car.

'But, Alda, where is your Six Twins?'

H OW I love going places!
If there is anything in heredity, I suppose you could say it's in my blood — the eagerness for wider horizons, new shores, fresh obstacles to meet and conquer.

My father's family, the Davieses, went out from England to New Zealand in the days of clipper ships and when the islands were still much as Captain Cook found them. Grandfather and Grandmother had not hesitated to set forth into the unknown with few more possessions than a violin and a baby or two. I, at sixteen, had taken to the road in a mixed company of a light opera troupe. A year later I had left Australia and everyone I knew, except Alby, with not one qualm.

Was there something symbolic in the fact that I made my operatic début as Manon?

Certainly I could sympathize with Massenet's heroine in her zest for *'une vie adventureuse.'*

I LIKED Buenos Aires at once.
It was big and vigorous and young and rich and vulgar and kind. There was a frank lavishness about everything, from the scenery and the women's figures to the way the men made love.

The audiences were eager for *Manon*, for *Traviata*, for *Faust*. They came to the opera not from any grim determination to prove themselves cultured and fashionable, but for enjoyment. They gave themselves over to the sensuous delights of music and movement and color and the dramatic values of life with a spontaneity that poured across the footlights to us on the stage.

How easy they were to sing to!

And how warmly appreciative of all that a singer had to give!

There were invitations to this party and that, to go to see this or that famous sight; to spend a week-end at one of the great ranches back in the country; to watch the *vaqueros* ride herd and hear them sing their roundup songs, part Spanish, part Indian, but all romantic. Invitations to *verbenas* held in the patio of one of the *haciendas* with yellow roses and jasmine twining the galleries, and the starry night sky for a roof.... Guitar music, and the click of castanets, and then, while we foreigners watched, the young girls of the family dancing the Spanish dances taught them by the dancing master imported from Spain.

And on the nights when I was singing at the opera, flowers and more flowers, until my dressing-room was heaped with roses and camellias.

When I began this book I announced that I was not going to do any pretending in it. It was going to be ME, as I am, sometimes with my makeup on, sometimes with it off.

Starting from that premise, why should I lead anyone to suppose that I haven't always enjoyed immensely being a prima donna?

On the stage and off it.

Bouquets, telegrams, twenty-seven wardrobe trunks, maids and secretaries darting hither and yon, sable capes, pearls, birds of paradise, diamond bracelets, silver foxes, people to see you off at stations and piers, and more to welcome you when you arrived at others, men kissing your hand, paying you extravagant, gorgeous compliments that later, alone in your room, you chuckled over, relishing the humor of all that happening to YOU ... of course I enjoyed all these.

I'm quite frank about that enjoyment.

The only difference between Frances Alda and every other prima donna is a few degrees of honesty.

No use my making believe to be a *pot-au-feu*. I haven't the gift for it. I'm not the kind of dear little woman who runs away from her career the minute the curtain is down, and hurries home to cook supper for her husband and darn his socks and listen to him read carloadings from the evening paper.

And I never made up in a gingham house-dress and a smudge of flour on my cheek and did some business with a long spoon and a mixing bowl against a kitchen cabinet setting while the news-reel cameras clicked.

I'd rather dance all night with three men who were crazy about me than sew on buttons for any one of them by daylight. I like my food cooked by chcfs and served by a perfect butler. I'd rather ride a surf-board on Long Island Sound behind the speedboat Walter Chrysler gave me than tend home fires for myself or anyone else.

And I've never felt the necessity for pretending not to enjoy all the fun life has to give me in order to appear arty or important or delicately blasé.

I remember one evening whilst I was singing at the Metropolitan, I knew that four of my beaus were in the audience. Each one had carefully let me know where he would be sitting. The impulse to play a little joke on them all was too much for me. As the opera went on, I proceeded to sing passionately to each one in turn, gazing at the part of the house where each had told me he would be. Each one thought the singing and the expression was addressed to him alone, and none of them ever knew. Only Boo, my secretary, who was in the secret, was standing in the wings, laughing.

So, accordingly, I enjoyed myself in Buenos Aires that summer.

When the company moved across the bay to Montevideo for an engagement, I experienced the joy of singing in the city where my mother had been born.

It seemed to bring me closer to her than I had ever been, except when I sat on a hassock in Grandmother's bedroom back in St. Kilda, and listened to her stories of my mother's girlhood.

I drove about Montevideo, through the old Spanish streets, telling myself it was in this frowning fronted old house, or there that Grandmother had had her lodgings and where her baby Leonora — my mother — had been born.

EVERY mail brought me some reminder of Gatti. Letters ... cablegrams ...

He must have spent a small fortune on the latter.

In all he protested in the most extravagant, poetic phrases, in which the Italian tongue abounds, his devotion, his admiration and his need of me. He seemed to glory in the confession of his love, and told me that I should be proud of having inspired such passion in a man who had always been known to be indifferent to women. He would repeat that though I might find many men who were more handsome, with more wealth, and of higher worldly position, never would I find one whose love for me was more sincere, or more worthy of my love in return.

Few women, I suppose, have ever received love letters as marvellous as these.

I read them over now, and it is easy to see how the man's extraordinary genius shines in them. All that he found it impossible to express in speech or in personal contacts, he was able to put into words on paper with a pen.

'A melancholy man,' he often called himself. And he would cable me that unless I replied to his letters and to his cablegrams he would fall ill of temper and despair. Life, he would insist via Western Union, held no joy for him, no brightness until he was with me again. He reminded me that he had followed my advice in going to New York and attending to his business there and trying to keep his spirit tranquil and his hopes high, but though he did this he was full of unrest, and all his thoughts turned away from the Metropolitan Opera Company toward South America and me.

How to reply to this torrent of affection?

I didn't know.

Did I love him?

I wasn't sure.

The difference of seventeen years between his age and mine was a barrier more insurmountable than the difference between

Gatti-Casazza so dark, brooding, introverted;
I so gay, adventure-loving, enthusiastic

our nationalities and our temperaments: his so dark, brooding, introverted; mine gay, adventure-loving, enthusiastic.

But he interested me enormously as a person, as well as the director of my career during the coming year. He was, I was even then aware, the most intelligent man I had ever met. And the best read. When he wanted to, he could talk marvellously on world affairs, history, art, politics. Often, at a dinner party, I have seen him hold the whole table of guests spellbound, while the food cooled on their plates and the bubbles died out of the champagne in their glasses. When he wanted to, that was. There were other occasions when he would not speak at all, to anyone, whether they were guests in his house, or he was a guest in theirs.

His mother told me later that once, during his boyhood, he did not speak to any of his family for six weeks. No one of them ever knew why.

A strange nature.

When the letters and cablegrams became very insistent on his having some message of affection from me, messages that my ignorance of Italian made all too difficult to write, I would run through the score of the Italian opera I was working on, choose a few love passages from one of the arias, copy these out on a telegraph blank, and despatch them to Gatti in New York.

OUR South American tour ended late in August. The company sailed for Italy. When the ship docked at Genoa, Gatti was on the pier to receive me.

I spoke to him in Italian, I remember, for the first time. He seemed so affected by this that I hadn't the heart to disabuse his mind of the idea that I had learned the language expressly for him. He had brought me a true lover's gift — a little volume bound in green leather in which, every day that I was at sea and beyond the reach of his cables (no radio then), he had written me a love letter.

I read them in the train on the way to Venice.

Gatti came to Venice for a fortnight whilst I was there. Every morning I could look out of my window at Danieli's on the Grand Canal, and see the director of the Metropolitan Opera Company seated in a gondola waiting for me to come down to carry me off to see some sight in that wonderland of cities.

What a mine of information the man was!

He made old Venice live for me, golden and glorious, as I always, forever after, used to think of it when I sang Desdemona.

But he had no interest at all and no patience with the gay social world there that promptly began to open its doors to me.

That world revolved then — it still does — around two of the most interesting women in Europe.

One of these is Princess San Faustino. She was born Jane Campbell, of a New Jersey family. Her marriage to Prince San Faustino was one of those international unions that gave birth to the novels of Henry James and Edith Wharton. She had an apartment in the Barberini Palace in Rome, where she was one of the great hostesses and social arbiters, very popular with the royal family and very powerful. Her summers she spent in Venice at the Hotel Excelsior at the Lido.

Annina, Countess Morosini, was the other. Annina was then the most strikingly beautiful woman I think I ever saw. And with the most perfect figure. She was an intimate friend of the German Kaiser. Whenever he came to Venice in the years before 1914, his yacht would be anchored before the Palazzo Morosini, opposite the famous Hotel Danieli. A portrait of him, really very magnificent, hung in Annina's boudoir. He had given it to her. She told me herself, the last time I visited her, about three years ago, that when the Germans began shelling

Venice the portrait was shaken from the wall to the floor. The only thing in the house that was injured.

These two women, more than any other persons, started the vogue for the Lido as a summer resort. They knew everyone in Europe who was interesting or important or entertaining. And, Jane San Faustino anyway, knew everything about everyone, and could tell it to you with wit and a keen relish for the foibles of human nature.

Jane, seated in her *cabana* on the sands, made or broke destinies. Jane, dressed in her inevitable all black or all white, sometimes with the coif she copied after that worn by Mary Queen of Scots, playing bridge all night when the game is good and the stakes high enough to exite all her gambling instincts, is a *person*.

Some day someone will write a book about her. No book could be written about international society today that left her out.

She was darling to me, and she gave me letters to several of her friends in New York.

'I don't see what you can see in all that sort of thing,' Gatti would remonstrate with me, when I would leave him to go to one of Jane's or Annina's parties.

He would remind me that he was sailing for New York in three days' time to take up his new duties. Remind me that I was to make my début in December in *Rigoletto*, with Caruso. He would groan because December was two months off and we should be separated all that time.

'Remember what you have promised me. Remember that you are going to marry me.'

Was I?

I wondered.

PART
IV

METROPOLITAN MERRY-GO-ROUND

'*Si, mi chiamano Mimi.*'
LA BOHÈME.

IV

A T FIRST sight of the Metropolitan Opera House, I gasped.
Then I laughed.

That an opera house?

It looked more like a storage warehouse. Dirty brown brick.
Shabby. Old, weather-stained posters hanging in tatters in the
sleety winter wind. The sordid everyday business of Broadway —
the hawkers, the actors and actresses out of jobs, the hotel touts,
out-of-town sightseers, sandwich men, dope peddlers, gangsters,
the thousands who make a living off the weakness and ignorance
of other human beings — swirling in a greasy tide around its
doors.

I remembered the stately Opéra in Paris; the dignity of La
Scala — a palace dedicated to music and as noble as the palazzo
of any Visconti in Milan. I thought of the magnificent opera
house in Buenos Aires where I had sung that summer . . .

And this was New York. The richest, most modern, most
progressive city in the world.

It seemed to me incredible that with all the great private
fortunes in America, and with the American reputation for
giving education a very high place, no one person had ever
come forward and built for New York an opera house worthy of
the city and of the art of singing.

It still seems to me extraordinary.

I have never got used to the complaisant stagnation of
America's *soi-disant* society. The sentiment among the Metropolitan's box-holders in 1908 seemed to be that what had been
good enough for their fathers and for themselves back in 1883
was still good enough.

And a bit too good for the new rich who were pressing in on
their sacred circle.

This childish conservatism seemed all the more incongruous considering the history of the Metropolitan. It had been built by and for the new rich of the late seventies and eighties, for whom the Academy of Music, at Fourteenth Street and Irving Place, which had succeeded the opera house in Astor Place and which was the resort of old Knickerbocker New York, was not adequate. The Astors, Vanderbilts, Goelets, Drexels, Mortons, Iselins, Warrens, and Havens who had figured prominently among the first directors and box-holders still swayed destinies and determined the policies of the company.

No Jew was permitted to own a box. Mr. Otto Kahn, the President of the Board, subscribed to seats in the orchestra.

That season of my début was the first season that Mrs. Astor's box, Number Seven, was not occupied by society's Queen-Dowager. She had died that year. I never witnessed what I was told was the usual procedure on Monday nights. It had been Mrs. Astor's custom to arrive at the opera at exactly nine o'clock. And this no matter at what hour the curtain rose. As what she did was copied slavishly by the rest of society, it developed that the opera's first act was sung to a house more than half empty.

As nine o'clock drew near, there would be the swish and rustle of silk trains, the tramp of feet coming down the orchestra aisles, the scrape of chairs being moved to better positions in the boxes.

Interest in happenings on the stage dwindled. Opera glasses were raised and focussed on the curtains of Box Seven.

Nine o'clock.

A hand parted the curtains.

Mrs. Astor came in and took her seat.

An audible sigh of satisfaction passed through the house. The prestige of Monday Night was secure. Only, then, was the attention of all but the ardent music-lovers in the audience turned to the singers and orchestra.

I laughed when all this was described to me. This, in democratic America? All this kowtowing to an old lady, the widow of a descendant of a line of pork-butchers?

I thought of the wicked, autocratic, but gallant Leopold of the Belgians; of the genuine, sincere friendliness of English royalty toward the great artists who have sung and played for them; of Duke Visconti, coming round to my dressing-room after the première of *Louise* to pay his respects to the singer, and to take me to the ducal box to meet his wife.

Well, if this was America, I must accept it.

But I couldn't take it seriously.

The interior of the Metropolitan, when it was lighted and the boxes were filled, was impressive. But backstage was a disgrace.

The dressing-rooms were ill ventilated and unbelievably dirty. They had no toilet facilities and not even running water. There were several with no windows at all. None of the singers had her own dressing-room except Farrar, who had pre-empted a small windowless room that no one else wanted, so her possession of it remained undisputed.

I stood those conditions for years. Though not uncomplainingly.

Gatti would shake his head and motion me to be quiet whenever I protested that the whole place needed a vigorous housecleaning. But nothing was done.

Then, one year, while Gatti was in Europe, I descended on the Metropolitan with scrubbing brush, mop, and scouring soap.

At least, figuratively speaking.

I did inspire the plumbers to pipe water into the dressing-rooms and to install toilets. I marshalled the painters and got them to paint the floors and walls and furniture. Next I ordered cretonne hung on the walls so that it could be taken down frequently and cleaned and rehung. Then I moved on to the room used by Gatti as an office. I had it cleaned, painted, and the walls panelled in grey lampas.

Gatti shivered with horror at my temerity when he returned

and discovered the extent of these innovations. But the job was done. The Director's Office remains today as I decorated it — a charming, dignified room.

As I have already told, Gatti came to America to start preparations for his first season there whilst I was still holidaying in Venice. He wrote me frequently. The letters were full of the difficulties he encountered:

'The Metropolitan is a sack of troubles which I have inherited from Mr. Conried,' he complained. 'I would pay three hundred and fifty lire to put the tip of my nose into Italy.'

I am afraid that I did not pay much attention to his grumblings. I was too occupied with my own affairs. I had been engaged to sing several concerts in Paris during that autumn before I had to leave for New York for the opening of the Metropolitan.

One of those concerts was at the home of the Marquise de Brou at Versailles. I was to sing with Pol Plançon, the famous bass who had sung several seasons in New York and with Nordica, Sembrich, Calvé, the two de Reszkés and my aunt, Frances Saville.

The audience, I remember, was very smart and all of them very good friends. There was a persistent buzz-buzz of greetings, conversations, compliments of how well this one or that looked after taking the cure at Vichy or Marienbad, whose daughter had recently been engaged to whose son, and so on.

Nor did any of this die down when I stood up to sing.

The accompanist played the opening bars of the first of my group of songs, then paused on a note, expecting me to open my mouth and begin.

But I did not.

He threw me an anxious glance, started off again, and again paused for me.

Nothing happened.

The Marquise, a darling old lady, rose from her chair and came toward me:

'Mais, ma chère, qu'est-ce-qu'il y a?'

In good full voice I replied:

'I know I am supposed to have a very strong voice, but even so it would be impossible for me to make myself heard above all this *tohu-bohu.*'

Magnificent silence.

A pin dropping in it would have sounded like a cannonshot.

The accompanist didn't trust himself to look at me. But he played for the third time the opening of the song, and this time I sang it with him. And so through the three songs of the group.

There was gratifying applause; I bowed and stepped through the curtains into the hall.

And bang into Pol Plançon!

He threw up his arms, then threw them around me.

'Mon Dieu!' he exploded. 'To have the courage to do a thing like that!'

Well, I've always had that courage, and I pray God I always shall have it. The courage to insist that a singer — good, bad, or indifferent, even if it's some hoarse 'blues' singer in a fifth-rate night club — shall have the courtesy of attention.

After all, it isn't as though it were the easiest thing in the world for even a very experienced singer to stand up before an audience and sing. And the supposition is that he — or she — is at least trying to please and entertain you.

Isn't that attempt in itself worthy of your consideration? If you don't like it, you don't have to applaud afterward and you can then go out. But during the singing, it's only good sportmanship to give the singer a chance by keeping silent.

At least that's how I feel about it.

There are hostesses in New York who know very well what is apt to happen when they invite me as a guest to one of their musicales.

I've stood up and said: 'SSSH!' to a room full of cackling New Yorkers as boldly as I said my say that day at the Marquise de Brou's. And, likewise, I have led the applause for some young singer who was simply scared to death, as I could see and feel and sympathize with.

And what's more, I expect I'll go on doing that as long as I live and go about to concerts — which will be as long as I can get about to anything...

Unless people begin to get the same point of view on this matter as I have.

The audience at the Marquise de Brou's was delightfully forgiving of my reprimand, and terribly appreciative and sweet to me after the concert was over. Pol Plançon drove back to Paris with me in my *électrique*, still exclaiming over the degree of my courage.

Perhaps our admiration of ourselves and of each other tempted the gods.

Suddenly, round a bend in the road, came a man riding a bicycle. As he approached he began to wobble horribly from side to side, his feet slipped off the pedals, the bicycle careened to one side, and it and the rider tumbled in a heap nearly under our front wheels.

The chauffeur jammed on the brakes.

It was raining that day. And is there anything more slippery than French asphalt? The *électrique* skidded across the road and shot over a low stone wall.

The two eminent artists landed on their faces in a freshly ploughed kitchen garden, with an automobile on top of them.

Plançon, miraculously, wasn't hurt at all. When they dragged me out of the wreckage I was unconscious. My left arm was broken in two places and my shoulder was badly out of joint.

They laid me out on the roadside, a pitiable object.

But my luck held. For along that same road came no less a person than Doctor Doyen, the great surgeon. It was undoubtedly to his skill that I owe the full use of my arm today.

So it happened that when I sailed for New York I was still strapped in bandages and my arm was in splints. These were taken off just in time for that performance of *Rigoletto* that was my début at the Metropolitan. But the memory of the accident and the pain I had suffered was fresh in my mind. Whenever Caruso, singing the Duke, came close to me in loverlike advances, I winced and drew back — a more timid, reluctant Gilda than I ever played before or after that night.

I had arrived in New York in time for the opening night of the opera season. This was, by tradition, the first event of New York society each autumn. That year's opening was no exception to the rule. Every seat in the vast house was taken. In the boxes of the famous Diamond Horseshoe sat the dowagers and débutantes. Their rich dresses and the glitter of their jewels made the audience as thrilling to look at as any stage could have been.

The opera was *Aïda*.

And what an Aïda!

With Emmy Destinn making her American début as the captive princess of Ethiopia; with Caruso, Amato, and Louise Homer!

And with Toscanini conducting!

No one in my time ever sang an Aïda to compare with that of Emmy Destinn. Especially in the Third Act she was magnificent. Hers was one of the greatest voices, and she was one of the greatest singers I ever heard.

That night I had my first view of a Metropolitan audience. Gatti had invited me to sit in his box with him. But what actually happened was that Dippel had calmly appropriated the Director's Box for that evening, and Gatti had to find himself and me another box.

Needless to say, this put him in a very bad humor.

Having Andreas Dippel as co-director was galling to Gatti's pride. Also it gave rise to all sorts of difficulties with the personnel of the opera house, and it was very disastrous to Gatti's authority over the company.

The German singers were up in arms against what they considered the 'Italianization' of the Metropolitan. Some of them openly resented having a director who did not intend to take them into consultation on every little point that had to be decided. Formerly, it seemed, the year's program was made out by the leading artists, sitting about the director's desk, and each one claiming as many performances during the season as possible. The contracts of the women singers carried a clause that if the singer cancelled a performance on grounds of being indisposed, the management was to pay her just the same as if she had sung that night.

One of Gatti's first acts as director was to cancel this clause in all the contracts.

It was remarkable after that how few singers ever felt compelled to cancel a scheduled performance.

Gatti was determined to institute a régime of law and order where little of either had existed for some time. The theory seemed to be that singers were temperamental fools, and would continue to be so, whatever rules you laid down for them. You might just as well throw up your hands and let them go their own way.

But that was not the way Gatti intended to run his opera company.

His phenomenal success with the Metropolitan originated in his regarding the opera company and all its affairs as a business to be managed exactly as he would have managed any other business venture. At his coming, twenty-five per cent of the seats in the house were sold by subscription. He increased the list of subscribers to the point that by 1926, nearly ninety per cent of the house was sold out in this way before the season opened, thus assuring the company a fixed revenue. Also, he increased the number of performances. During the season 1920–1921 we gave one hundred and fifty-five performances. Conried had plunged the Metropolitan in debt. Gatti took it out of the red and laid up for it a bank balance of over one million dollars. The first loss during Gatti's régime came when Otto Kahn insisted, and against Gatti's judgment, on their bringing over the Russian Ballet. The Metropolitan was out money on that venture, and a lot of money. But it still had a comfortable balance in the bank until the Great Depression hit it, along with every other business in America.

Contrary to so many stories one hears on all sides, Otto Kahn never had to put his hand in his pocket to help the Metropolitan. Kahn was the largest stockholder in the company, and he had more to say about what was done than anyone else had. But he never gave five cents to the opera house. When money had to be supplied it was raised by appeals to the public.

I HAVE already told the story of my début at the Metropolitan.

Driving up Fifth Avenue on the morning after my début, I had challenged the critics who had refused to be pleased with me or with my singing. I had challenged New York:

'I'm going to conquer you. See if I don't.'

Though I didn't understand the full significance of this at the time, in those words I challenged myself.

Up to this time I had regarded my career as an adventure — something to give me excitement, thrills, the pleasure of success, money to buy lovely clothes and beautiful furniture for my apartment in Paris and to keep prudently invested (there spoke the spirit of my French grandmother). But an adventure. If I tired of it, if it ceased to give me good things and began to bring difficulties and unpleasantness instead, why, I could drop it.

But now, subtly, with that challenge to myself, I began to view this career of mine in a different light. It was no longer a plaything in my hands, but something that possessed me. Something to which I was pledged irrevocably. It presented me, as now, with a battle ground on which I was forced to fight, whether the fight amused me or not.

By that challenge I ceased to be Frances Davies, having a perfectly grand time as Mademoiselle Frances Alda, opera singer. I became, in the very essence of my being, Frances Alda.

I know now, having seen the rise and making as well as the disintegration of many singers, how Marchesi would have rejoiced in that moment, the change it affected in me. Her wise old eyes would have seen it for what it was — the most important decision in my whole life. A rebirth.

YES, my hat was in the ring.

Characteristically, having accepted the fact that the fight was on and it was just a question of whether the critics or I got the worst of it, I began to plan my attack.

I was scheduled to sing seventeen performances that season. This included four Sunday concerts. The operas were to be *Rigoletto*, *Le Villi*, *Faust*, Massenet's *Manon*, and *Falstaff*.

Sixteen more rounds between the critics and me.

I should sing *Rigoletto* once again, in January. In the meantime there would be a performance of *Faust*, with Caruso. And the première of Puccini's *Le Villi*, with Bonci and Amato. This was scheduled for the seventeenth of December, and would be my next appearance.

I didn't care for the opera, which was Puccini's first, and written for a competition whilst he was still a student. The story is of a simple peasant girl in the Black Forest, whose betrothed leaves her to go to the city to claim an inheritance. While he is there, he is untrue to Anna, who dies of a broken heart. The false lover returns to the forest — naturally, not until after he has spent the inheritance on wine, women, and song in the big town — and there he is confronted by Anna's ghost, and a band of witch dancers (the Villi) who dance round him madly until he too dies.

The rôle of Anna had little opportunity in it for me. No gaiety, no *diablerie*, no wistful tenderness. The love scene in the first act was as unimpassioned as a glass of milk. And in act two, I knew perfectly well that I made a much too substantial ghost. Diet as I might, I couldn't lose my curves. I preferred rôles that allowed me to make a feature of them since, apparently, I couldn't avoid having them.

Too, I had a deep-seated contempt for any girl who let her lover walk off and leave her, and then died of it.

Frankly, Anna seemed to me the queen of the dumb belles.

But I was down to sing Anna, and Anna it must be.

Toscanini went over the score with me, teaching me the part word by word as he had taught me Louise.

I think he had been troubled by the reception the New York critics had given me. He felt the cabal at the opera house against Gatti and himself and me, 'the Italians,' who, according to the gossip that went round, threatened all sorts of changes and innovations at the Metropolitan.

Changes — as though the place didn't cry out for them! As though Gatti and he had not been engaged by the directors to introduce a few, so that the stodgy Metropolitan could hold its own against the vigorous competition Hammerstein was giving it!

He didn't pretend to think *Le Villi* great music, but it was sufficiently interesting to warrant its being produced. And produced well.

Certainly, no one who ever sang Anna ever worked harder at the rôle than did I, with Toscanini to inspire and correct and encourage me. Gradually, under his coaching, Anna became not a dull, flaxen-haired *mädel*, but the symbol of maidenhood and innocence. Her story was no longer a bit of sentimental folklore, but an allegory universal in its significance. I went through the rehearsals with Bonci, with whom I had sung at Parma, and Amato, who sang the rôle of Anna's father, with a sense of security and real optimism about the première.

Then it was the afternoon of December seventeenth.

The telephone rang. . . . Emilie answered it.

'Mr. Gatti-Casazza is calling, madame.'

'Tell him he may come up.'

He came. His anxiety about that night's performance enveloped him like a sombre cloak. He kissed me. But perfunctorily.

How did I feel? Was I in good voice? Did I realize how immensely important it was that I make a good impression that evening to counteract the criticisms on my début?

Instantaneously all my sanguine expectations went out the window, leaving me feeling flatter than a pancake.

A rather soggy pancake, at that.

'Is that any way to encourage me?' I demanded. 'Important? Of course, I know it's important. And it's terribly important, if I am going to sing well, that I keep my spirits up. How am I going to do that when you come in here and spread gloom all around me?'

'Now, now,' he pleaded. 'Don't get mad.'

'Mad? Of course I'll get mad. Here I've been working all day . . .'

He interrupted me to tell me how much harder than that he had been working. Listening to a rehearsal of another opera, 'that deserved to be eaten by dogs.' Dippel had been exceptionally annoying. The man had the head of a tenor. Could one say more than that? Nothing at the opera house was right. Nothing. He didn't know how he was to keep his own brain in its place. He was sick. Terribly sick.

'Excuse me for this nervous outbreak.'

He looked as though he actually were going to cry.

What can you do with a man like that?

I was to ask myself that question a thousand times in the

years ahead. How many times I was to go on the stage to sing a performance with every nerve in my body quivering after some such scene in my dressing-room with Gatti. The man's intensely nervous temperament, which he kept imprisoned within a severe and formal exterior to the world, sought in me an outlet, I suppose. Just as his dark melancholy was drawn irresistibly to my gaiety.

On that afternoon before the first performance of *Le Villi*, I did my best to soothe the distracted Director as though he, not I, were the prima donna of that evening's performance, and entitled to go through a bad case of the jitters.

Well, I was beginning to understand something that I know now to be true of men; of bank directors no less than tenors.

They are the real prima donnas.

Why talk about nerves, temperament, egotism, and so on, as though these were found only in women?

Having observed a number of directors with a new opera to be presented, I can truly say that I never saw a singer, any singer, as excited as they over a First Night.

Stage fright — but that's different.

That can happen to an artist who has sung a particular rôle half a dozen times. When the time for the seventh performance comes, for no reason that anyone can understand, she is sick with fear.

And I mean sick. Really sick.

The worst case of stage fright I ever saw was Eddy Johnson's. If the very able and charming Director of the Metropolitan Opera Company reads this book, he will remember, as I do, the time the company was singing in Atlanta. Eddy had been ill for several weeks; still he and everyone believed he would be able to sing the performance of *Faust* with me that was scheduled. He and I had sung it together at the Metropolitan a number of times, and without a hitch. But that morning in Atlanta, before I was out of bed, the telephone rang.

Eddy was at the other end of the wire. He was stuttering.

'Listen, Alda, I can't sing today. I can't.'

'What's the matter?'

'Everything's the matter. I can't sing *Faust*. I can't sing, I tell you. They've got to change the opera. Give something else. Get another tenor.'

'Hold everything,' I interrupted. 'I'm coming right over.'

I got into enough clothes to satisfy the proprieties of the South and went down the hall to Eddy's suite.

The man was in a panic, shivering under the bed covers.

Stage fright. Sheer, stark terror of he didn't know what.

'Listen to me, Eddy,' I said. 'Maybe you think you can't sing this afternoon. Maybe you'll sing like a pig. But you've got to sing. That's the point. You've got to do it, no matter how scared you feel, because if you don't — if you give in to it — you'll never sing again.'

Well, the way he was feeling he didn't care if he never sang again. In fact, he'd rather he didn't.

I stayed right on the trail all morning. I camped there in Eddy's room and talked to him, laughed at him, teased him. Everything except sympathize with him. When it came time to go to the theatre to dress for the performance his teeth were still chattering. But he went.

When the curtain went up on Act One with Eddy on the stage and me in the wings watching him, I don't know which of us was the more scared.

But he was game. His voice was shaky and he looked like the wrath of God. But he sang. He kept looking across at me in the wings and I kept applauding and smiling and repeating — though, of course, he couldn't hear the words, only guess them from the motions I was making — 'You're fine, Eddy. You're fine.'

Once, in the love duet with me, his voice began to tremble . . .

'Go on, you're all right. You're all right,' I whispered.

And he *was* all right. The fear that came so suddenly, so inexplicably, vanished as swiftly. He finished the opera in full command of his voice.

And probably, because that is the way stage fright affects most people, he was entirely cured of stage fright forever, by having refused to yield to it.

In telling this story of myself, I find myself always having to come back.

This time it is to the première of *Le Villi*, my second appearance at the Metropolitan. The performance was not on the regular subscription list, and Gatti had raised the box-office prices for the première. But the house was filled.

It's funny how quickly you sense the mood of the audience.

This audience was warm and ready to be pleased, and quick to express its appreciation. The applause was spontaneous and generous. Did that reflect the attitude of the critics, too?

(Wait for the morning, Alda. And the verdict.)

They came, both together. Again I found myself pulling the papers apart to find what was for me the kernel of the day's news; the reviews of the performance at the Metropolitan the night before. My grimness broke into a smile as I read:

How deliciously Bonci's and Alda's voices blended in the duet. Toscanini conducted with love.

Another critic who had found in me nothing worth listening to at my début, now reported that my voice was '*true and fresh and charming....*'

I cut out the reviews and pasted them in my scrapbook. Later, I showed them to Toscanini.

'Was I so much better? Did ten days develop a voice in me where I had had none before?'

'Perhaps the ten days developed a few grains of sense in the heads of those *signori* who write for the newspapers.'

'Aha, *maestro*, they're coming round. They'll have to eat their own words yet.'

'Wait for *Faust*,' he cautioned me.

We sang *Le Villi* again on the day after Christmas to a typical holiday audience: schoolgirls on vacation, sightseers, and out-of-town visitors. And again during the holiday week.

We also sang a performance of the opera in Philadelphia. I have occasion to remember that night because during the performance I had my first experience with Toscanini's bad temper.

The train bringing the orchestra and their instruments was delayed, or something else happened. At any rate, the curtain did not rise until 8:45. Toscanini was so angry he could hardly speak. He proceeded to conduct, but in double tempo, and never looking up at the stage.

I became breathless, trying to keep pace with him.

When it came time for my prayer, 'Hey, wait a minute,' I said to the prompter.

The audience heard me, and there was a ripple of laughter.

THE opera for New Year's Day was *Faust*.

Another new year beginning!

Twelve months ago, and I had been in Paris, with Franko Alfano coming up from Milan to spend the holidays near me. Making love to me ... teasing me about that melancholy director of La Scala who was so jealous of me ...

Twelve months ago, and I had been looking forward to singing Louise, with no thought of New York and the Metropolitan Opera Company except as possibilities for me sometime in the far future.

Twelve months ago, and I had taken my career lightly, with amused satisfaction and a kind of roguish delight in its triumphs.

Like a big, good-natured joke that Life was playing on me. And an attitude of *je m'en fiche* for anybody and anything that threatened to interfere with my fun.

Twelve months ago, and I had spent a New Year's Day filled with gaiety and pleasure ...

On this New Year's Day in 1909 I was up at eight in the

morning, and at nine was out in Central Park for an hour's stiff walk around the reservoir. Then, while last night's revellers were just stirring in their beds, back to the Ansonia for an hour's practice at the piano. Then lunch, and a rest and a drive. At four o'clock two cups of strong clear tea, and at six o'clock I was going in the stage door of the Metropolitan.

I always allowed two hours to dress and make up for a performance. And I always made myself up. Bodin, the wig-maker in Paris, who had made all Garden's wigs and mine too, taught me how to do it.

For more than twenty-five years *Faust* had been New York's favorite opera. Christine Nilsson, singing at the old Academy of Music, had created a Marguerite whose traditions still lingered. When the Metropolitan was opened, the opera chosen for the momentous First Night was *Faust*, with Nilsson and Campanini. Marcella Sembrich made her American début two nights later. She, singing Marguerite in her turn and through all the years of the Metropolitan's history until I came to the company, had kept alive the traditions of Nilsson in the rôle.

New York opera-goers had also heard Nordica as Marguerite. And Melba. And for several seasons at the Metropolitan, Emma Eames and the two de Reszkés had sung *Faust* to packed, enthusiastic houses.

I was following in an illustrious company.

But any slight nervousness I might have felt was dispelled by the broad wink Caruso gave me when we met in the crowd of villagers in the second scene of the First Act.

The audience was in a happy holiday mood. One felt their friendliness. And how that friendliness loosens a singer's vocal cords and lets him sing!

Too, I was feeling a great joy that in the rôle of Marguerite I had at last something real to sing.

'I want to sing' — that had been my desire even as a child. That desire — it is really a need — has never left me. *Bel canto* — that is what I love. Give me something to sing, something that is beautiful and calls for artistry in singing it, and then let me stand still and sing it — I ask no more happiness than that.

I was looking forward to the Second Act in *Faust*, in which I would have the Spinning Wheel Song, and then the great Jewel Song:

> 'Comment n'être pas coquette?
> Ah, je ris de me voir
> Si belle en ce miroir —
> Est-ce toi, Marguerite, est-ce toi?'

And then those phrases of ineffable love and tenderness, of all the musical passages that I have ever sung the one that I love best:

> 'Je veux t'aimer et te chérir.
> Parles encore.
> Je t'appartiens, je t'adore,
> Pour toi je veux mourir.
> Parles, parles encore!
> Ah, je t'adore.'

As everyone knows who has ever heard *Faust*, when the curtain rises on Act Two it discloses Marguerite's garden with her spinning wheel beside a bench among the flowers. And to one side, the porch and door and window of her cottage.

Marguerite comes on, singing of the handsome youth she has seen at the village festival. She finds the flowers her lover has left for her, and exclaims over them. Then she goes to her wheel, takes the thread in her hand, and begins to spin, singing as she spins her ballad of 'The King of Thule.'

All went according to the best opera traditions up to the moment that I was to begin the Spinning Wheel Song. I took the thread in one hand, and with the other gave the wheel a gentle push to make it revolve.

Nothing happened.

I pushed harder, and stepped on the treadle.

The wheel would not turn. Someone had nailed it fast.

All this was terribly disconcerting, of course. I felt so silly standing there, holding the thread, beside a motionless wheel.

Caruso caricature of Gatti-Casazza

But the worst was to come.

At the close of the scene, Marguerite is supposed to go into her cottage. Darkness falls on the stage. A light glows in Marguerite's window. She throws wide the casement and sits there, dreaming of Faust. Presently, he comes stealing into the garden. He approaches the window. They have a love duet, and then he goes into the cottage, and the curtain falls.

I had sung the 'Jewel Song, and, as I knew, sung it beautifully. The audience had applauded warmly. The rest of the scene moved perfectly. I had forgotten the awful contretemps of the spinning wheel when I went up the steps of the cottage and tried to open the door to enter my little house.

The door would not open.

Suddenly I began to feel as though I were in a bad dream. I pulled at the door. It would not budge. It, too, had been nailed fast.

There was nothing for it but to make my exit through the wings, and once backstage, to find a stage hand who could open that door from the inside so that when Faust came on the farce would not be repeated.

Nothing more disturbing happened that night; though my nerves were on edge, expecting I knew not what. Caruso and I took our curtain calls, smiling and bowing. I knew — and the papers next morning bore me out — that the critics would approve of that performance of *Faust*, and of the Metropolitan's new Marguerite. And this, even though I was entering on the domain of the retiring Sembrich.

But I knew now that it was not the critics that I had to contend with. Whoever it was who was determined to wreck my career in America was not someone on the outside, but some person, or persons, right in the opera house. Perhaps even another artist, a member of the company.

I KNOW now, at least I believe I know, who it was.
But I shall not tell.

We opera folk can be very childish sometimes in our jealousie and resentments. People say it goes with the artistic temperament. Maybe.

'The head of a tenor,' Gatti used to say, meaning thereby that the person under discussion couldn't make an unprejudiced decision, or be trusted not to fly off at a tangent. That had been his experience of tenors. He wasn't any more complimentary to women singers, for that matter.

Well, we are like that.

But at least we know it. And in most of us there's a degree of forgiveness for other artists, even for those who have been jealous of our moments of triumph, or have tried to prevent our success.

Perhaps it comes out of our self-knowledge. Who could possibly know better than one of us who has been fed for years on applause and flattery and bouquets and extravagant compliments and attentions what it feels like to see the tide of these ebbing from your shores and flowing toward someone else? It's no good putting it down to egotism or adult infantilism or any of the other names the psychologists have invented for hurt feelings. That doesn't explain it unless in the same breath you admit that the temperament and the egotism have been inspired in us and fostered and developed by *you*. *You*, the *public*.

It is you, fully as much as our own temperament, that has decreed the row of footlights between us. It's for you that we have made up and costumed ourselves and played our parts. For you we have poured our individualities into the moulds of Mimi, and Tristan and Canio and Thaïs and Parsifal and Butterfly. And done this until sometimes it would seem as though we left in those rôles something of our own real natures, and took away from them instead a portion of their melodrama and unreality.

Don't judge us too severely.

As we forbear to judge each other on these counts; knowing at heart our own vulnerability.

But don't believe either, for a minute, that the stage, and especially the grand opera stage, doesn't breed hatreds as bitter as any in politics.

There was the feud between Emmy Destinn and Geraldine Farrar. Nobody knew exactly where or why it began. Possibly in Berlin, where both had been members of the opera company. But for all the years that she was with the Metropolitan, Destinn steadfastly refused to appear on the stage with Farrar.

I remember when Gatti wanted to produce *La Donna Curiosa*. He and Toscanini spent half a day at Destinn's apartment trying to persuade her to forget her vow and to sing in the opera with Farrar. But she would not. She had the fanatic tenacity of her people, the Czechs. During the War, she was interned for a time in Austria, where she suffered great privations, and ever afterward she vowed she would never speak the German language. From this all sorts of difficulties arose at the opera house, where practically no one spoke Czech, and Destinn's Italian was not very fluent.

I had heard her first, and met her, when I sang at Covent Garden. Destinn was singing there too, that season. I remember the first time I heard her voice was at a rehearsal of *Madame Butterfly*.

She was magnificent. Nobody ever sang Butterfly as Destinn did. Of course she was stout, and far from looking the part of the little Japanese lady. But her manner of singing was so perfect, her voice so divine — like drops of water — and the pathos she put into the rôle. . . . All these made her unforgettable.

The other Butterfly who stands out in my memory is Storchio, who created the part at La Scala. I heard her in 1929, in Chicago. She was singing with the Chicago Opera Company. It was nothing short of a tragedy that she should have come to America at a time when her vocal resources were not at their best. But her artistry and her reading of the rôle were absolutely supreme. That was twenty years after the first time I had met her in Milan. But in Italy, even today, when one speaks of Storchio, the eyes roll and nothing but enthusiastic compliments are heard.

Destinn, Amato, and I were all newcomers to the Metropolitan in the season of 1908–1909. Sembrich, who had made her début when the Metropolitan Opera House was opened in 1883, sang her farewell that winter. Eames, too, left the company that February. Fremstad and Gadski remained to sing the big Wagner rôles, and Louise Homer for the contralto parts.

And, of course, Farrar.

She and I were never friends. It was a very distant 'Good-morning, Miss Farrar,' and 'Good-morning, Miss Alda,' when we met. This happened not very often. During the first years I was with the company we never sang together, except on the night of Sembrich's 'Farewell,' when all the stars of the company appeared as supper guests in a scene from *Tosca*. It was not until the season of 1914 that Farrar, Caruso, and I sang *Carmen*. The story of two of those performances must be told later.

She sang *Bohème*, but to my mind she was too brittle for Mimi, who is a creature all heart and frailty. But her Butterfly was exquisite. I admired her, too, enormously as the goose girl in *Koenigskinder*. When she came through the massive town gates driving her flock of white geese before her, she was poetry itself.

Nor was I her only admirer. One was always hearing stories of this man, or the other, who was madly in love with her.

MEN and women in love. What a never-failing topic of interest and conversation this is! Not only in the dressing-rooms of the opera, but everywhere. Well, why shouldn't it be? If people ever reveal themselves in their true colors, it is when they are in love.

That first winter I was in New York, the love affair that engaged the attention of everyone I met was Bob Chandler's infatuation for Lina Cavalieri.

Cavalieri had come to America two years before. Hammerstein had brought her, and she had sung one season at the Metropolitan, where 'young' Willie Vanderbilt saw her, and fell head over heels in love with her. To the intense annoyance of his father. The elder Vanderbilt was one of the Metropolitan's directors. No one who knew how things were going was surprised when the management did not renew Cavalieri's contract.

That winter, 1908–1909, Cavalieri was singing at Hammerstein's on Thirty-Fourth Street. (Presumably young Mr. Vanderbilt found it just as easy to drive down there as to stop off at Fortieth Street!) Also, she had opened a beauty shop — one of the first in New York to be owned and managed by an actress or a society woman.

Cavalieri's extraordinary beauty evoked all manner of legends.

It was generally accepted as truth that she had begun her career as a flower-seller in Rome. There an elderly marquis had seen her and discerned under her peasant dress a beauty that the whole world was to acclaim. Like Shaw's Galatea, Lina repaid washing and feeding. The Marquis's generosity ran, I believe, to an apartment and lessons in singing and dancing.

The last took Lina to Ronacher's in Vienna, and out of the reach of the Marquis. Success in Vienna sent her to Paris and the Folies Bergères, where she was billed as 'The Most Beautiful Woman in Paris.'

When I went to Paris to study with Madame Marchesi, Cavalieri was all the rage. She was famous for her beauty, her jewels, and her lovers. She had already started her career in Grand Opera by singing Nedda, in *Pagliacci*, in Lisbon. She was not a success in it, however; though later, in Paris, she sang *Fedora* with Caruso. I remember going to the first performances thinking she would be laughable, instead of which I was impressed by her singing and acting. And she was unbelievably beautiful.

I remember, too, seeing Cavalieri once in St. Petersburg. I was dining at that famous restaurant on the island in the Neva. Suddenly a hush fell over the place, the chatter of voices died away. Even the *tziganes* muted their strings. Every head was turned to watch the progress of a woman in a gown of pale-yellow satin that was moulded over the most beautiful figure I had ever seen. Above the low décolletage rose a small, proud, dark head with classic features. The woman's neck, bosom, arms, and the crown of her head blazed with emeralds.

Beside her walked a magnificent-looking Russian officer in a pale blue uniform. It was Lina Cavalieri and Prince Alexander Bariatinski.

I was to see and meet Lina many times that first winter I spent in New York, at Bridget Guinness's house in Washington Square.

It was at Bridget's too, that I first met Bob Chandler. Bridget and Bob's sister-in-law, Mrs. William Astor Chandler (she had been Beatrice Ashley, and the original 'San Toy'), put their heads together and decided it would be a good thing for Bob to fall in love with, and marry, Cavalieri. After all, didn't America's greatest artist deserve the most beautiful woman in the world?

Chandler was distinctly a world person. A Bohemian, by natural selection, and with the background and training of a conservative aristocracy. As I believe, all the greatest Bohemians in the world have had. He understood completely the

world at which he thumbed his nose. There was in him, therefore, none of the latent envy or resentment that frequently
colors the 'bohemianism' of men and women who have come
into this world less richly endowed than he.

Bob, when I met him, was recently returned from a long stay
in Europe, during which he had been divorced from his staid and
shocked wife, and had launched himself seriously on his career as
an artist.

And what an artist!

There was no denying the flame and the fury of his genius.

He had a big, untidy studio in a building on Fifth Avenue
where he was working on some murals designed for the Pennsylvania Station. But he came often to Bridget's, where he
roamed about, shaking his great head at you, like an enormous,
friendly Saint Bernard. And talking — when the mood was on
him, shouting — like a character out of the pages of Rabelais.

Bob fulfilled Bridget's and Beatrice's expectations by falling
passionately and absurdly in love with Cavalieri, to the interest
and enjoyment of all New York. There was nothing silent or
unobtrusive about Bob's love-making.

When, that spring, Cavalieri, who had gone abroad, cabled
him that she would marry him, he exulted openly and loudly.
Then he caught the next boat to Europe.

They were married in June, in Paris. I was in my apartment
in the Avenue Bugeaud at the time, and I was among those
asked to the wedding breakfast, which was held at the old
Elysée Palace Hotel. It was tremendously gay; but the gaiety
did not conceal the calculating shrewdness of Lina's beautiful
long eyes.

One of the messages to the bridegroom was a cablegram from
his brother in Virginia, who had been adjudged insane in the
State of New York. It consisted of one line: '*Who's loony now?*'

Almost on the heels of that ironic question, Lina delivered her
ultimatum to her husband.

Let him examine the terms of the marriage settlement he had

made and signed. (It had been shrewdly drawn up by Lina's lawyers.) He would see that he had made over his entire fortune to his wife. Very well, she proposed to make him an allowance, but only on condition that he go to work and paint some pictures to sell.

Bob's bellowings of rage resounded across Europe and the Atlantic. Meanwhile, Lina and her Russian prince — Bariatinski's successor — enjoyed the Chandler fortune.

How far away all that seems now. There have been so many divorce scandals since; that one was newspaper headlines and club gossip. But this particular scandal had a slight effect on my own fortunes. So indignant against Cavalieri were a good many of the women of America, that at least one of the concert engagements that had been booked for her that winter was cancelled.

I remember that I went hurriedly to St. Paul to sing with the St. Paul Symphony Orchestra for an audience that had refused to receive the notorious Mrs. Chandler.

I still have the manager's wire:

> Send contract, photographs, obituary, and copy of marriage contract. We may need it. We take Alda in place of Cavalieri.

MEANWHILE, my first Metropolitan season was drawing to a close. I had sung seventeen performances in five operas, and four concerts. In March, there was the famous performance of *Falstaff* with Toscanini conducting. And sung by Destinn, Homer, Scotti, and me as *Nannetta*.

If I put Toscanini first, it is because any performance of *Falstaff* without him is, for me, as flavorless as a salad without garlic.

When I took stock of that first season in New York, it seemed
to me that, on the whole, things had not gone too badly.

At least, it finished with me one lap ahead of the critics.

They had spoken warmly of my Manon and were enthusiastic
about me as Nannetta. Three months after my début, they
proclaimed my voice was sweet and true, and that I 'sang with
feeling.'

And these were the same gentlemen who, in December, had
thought me unworthy of the Metropolitan.

My contract was for three seasons. I was glad to think of the
two seasons that were ahead of me. When I sailed for France,
late in April, I had the feeling that I was leaving friends behind,
and that I wanted very much to come back.

THE Avenue Bugeaud again.
Oh, how good it was to be there!

To be home!

I walked about, through all the rooms of the apartment, and
touched this piece of furniture and that. I rearranged the photographs and the little silver boxes and the vases that had been
filled with lilacs for my welcome.

Emilie took her good nature out of storage, and actually
smiled for the first time since we had landed in New York.

I ordered my car to drive in the Bois, and began telephoning
and sending *petite bleus* to all my friends.

The months in New York fell from me with the dust of travel.

I seem to have the faculty of finding myself quickly and completely at home in whatever environment I happen to be living.
And, for the moment at least, to separate myself completely
from all previous environments.

Maytime in Paris . . . what does that mean to you, if you're a woman? A love affair, if you're sentimental. But certainly, it means clothes.

I have been biding my time all this long way through this story until I could begin to talk about clothes. Isn't there some terrible fate held out for 'the man who has no music in his soul'? I'm sure the same, or a worse, nemesis hangs over the head of the woman who at any season of the year, but especially in the spring, has no clothes on her mind.

I don't think I am more frivolous than most other women. In fact, no matter what my enemies may say of me, events prove that I have a strong sense of responsibility, deeply ingrained habits of promptness, and a capacity for continued hard work. But I know this: no matter what bitter disappointment Life brought me, I should meet it more gallantly in a dress and a hat that I knew were becoming and smart. And if ever I have any repenting to do, it won't be in sackcloth and ashes, or in last summer's sun-faded print. It will be in trailing grey chiffon cut by somebody who has an inspiration about gores, and folds, and trailing drapery.

All this by way of introduction to the fact that, no sooner did all my senses tell me I was in Paris again, than I set about getting some new clothes. There was the summer to plan for — I was going to Marienbad for a few weeks to take off some pounds; and later to the Lido. There was also next winter in New York to be thought of.

When I first went to Paris to study, someone advised me to go to Doucet for my clothes. I went, and there I was fitted by a quiet, skilful little woman whose fingers did marvellous things.

Her name was Vionnet.

She made me two dresses; one was of blue serge, the other was of very small black and white check. They were made alike, the blouse cut like a Norfolk jacket with pleats down the front. They had turn-back collars and cuffs of white, with some color in the embroidery.

When I appeared at Madame Marchesi's for my lesson,

wearing the blue serge dress, I remember she made me stand up before the class, while she complimented me on it, and announced that that was the sort of frock a young lady should wear.

That was my first experience with Vionnet. Always after that, and when she had her own establishment, I went to her. And always the clothes she made me, I loved more than any others. All her clothes were always very simple and beautifully cut.

The first dress ever made on the bias Vionnet made on me.

Literally.

I know I stood for hours while she cut and draped and pinned until the dress was created. It had long hanging side pieces, and a little cape, also cut on the bias.

Vionnet was famous as the originator of the *bateau* neck line. Her first one of those dresses she made for me. I had that particular dress copied nine times.

In 1919, Vionnet made me a concert dress that had tremendous *réclame*. It was of black velvet, ornamented with a peacock embroidered in gold. The head of the bird was at the corsage, the long neck and body curved around the waist to form a girdle, and the enormous, wide spread glittering tail went down the back of the skirt.

How I loved the moment when, my song finished, I bowed and then turned, allowing the audience the full glory of that golden bird, before I went off the stage!

Peacock, indeed!

ALL the while I was in Paris, and later when I went for my 'cure' and then to the Lido, the letters and the telegrams from Gatti continued to keep me aware of him. He was in Europe, visiting his parents in Ferrara, going with Toscanini to consult with Puccini, who was then working on *The Girl of the*

Golden West, and hearing new singers who might be possibilities for the Metropolitan.

I remember it was that summer he went to Buseto to hear Lucrezia Bori. He wrote me that he had heard her sing Nannetta; he found her *'vivace,'* but inferior to me in the rôle. However, he engaged her, and she joined the company that coming season.

W HEN I went back to New York in November of that year for the opening of my second season, my interest was centred about *Othello,* which Gatti planned to give six times that year, and in which I was to sing Desdemona.

Already Gatti's and Toscanini's hard work during the previous season was showing results. There was genuine and widespread interest in the Metropolitan, and much curiosity about 'the novelties' that would be introduced into the program that winter. Among these was Tschaikowsky's *Pique Dame* and Gluck's *Orfeo ed Eurydice,* which New York had not heard in many years.

That winter, too, saw the opening of the New Theatre on Central Park West.

Had New York gone opera mad?

It seemed so.

They had already the Metropolitan, and Hammerstein's Manhattan Opera House. Now, the very men who were directors of the Metropolitan built the New Theatre where they planned to give light opera. The New Theatre, however, was never a success. Its location was against it. New York opera- and theatre-goers couldn't apparently get used to the idea of going away from the theatrical district. And the acoustics were so bad that those sitting in the second row could not hear the words spoken or sung on the stage.

I opened the New Theatre with the French tenor, Edmond Clément, singing *La Fille de Madame Angot*. The night of the première was one of those times when everything seemed determined to go wrong.

When we were called for the First Act, my costume for Act Three had not been delivered. I went on, played and sang my rôle, storming inside all the while at the perfidy of dressmakers and the carelessness that had allowed me to accept promises rather than performance.

'Has it come?' I demanded of Celia, my theatre maid, when I got back to my dressing-room after the curtain.

She shook her head.

Had she telephoned the costumer? Had she sent a messenger with orders to bring the costume, finished or not?

She dressed me for the Second Act. Still no box had been delivered. The call boy sounded his warning.

I shook Celia by the elbow.

'Listen, in the next act I have to appear in a wedding dress. I've got to have a wedding dress. Instantaneously! If that costume isn't delivered, you've got to make me one.'

I went on the stage.

'What'll I do? What'll I do?' went through my head all the time I was singing. Then, suddenly, I caught sight of Celia standing in the wings. She held up a big white pasteboard box. Her face was one huge smile.

Saved!

My relief from the worry as to what I could possibly wear to pass muster as a wedding gown was so overwhelming that I felt a great friendliness for the audience. I remembered it was Christmas Eve.

'Merry Christmas!' I said suddenly in English in the middle of the last act.

There was a little ripple of surprise, then laughter. Back to me, from the audience, came:

'Merry Christmas!'

But the Christmas spirit didn't hold backstage. I got hell.

AFTER that opening week at the New Theatre, I looked forward to the rôles I was scheduled to sing at the Metropolitan. That season they were to be Desdemona, Nannetta, and Manon.

Then, one day, while I was at lunch, Gatti came to see me. He looked at me a moment as though wondering what my mood was, then, without any warning he asked:

'Can you sing Mimi, in *Bohème*?'

It seemed to me there was a challenge in it somewhere.

But there was more than a challenge. There was my chance.

Gatti had no way of knowing, for I had never said a word of this to anyone, that of all the operatic rôles, the one I wanted most of all to sing was Mimi. I had practised it by myself. And Toscanini, hearing me one day, had sat down at the piano and taught me the rôle, as long ago he had taught me Louise.

'Some day you will sing Mimi, and sing it beautifully,' he said.

And here was Gatti asking me if I could.

'Yes,' I told him.

'Good! You shall sing it tonight, then. With Bonci.'

Farrar had been scheduled to sing that night, but she was ill, and it was too late to arrange for a different opera.

Well, that performance of *Bohème* duplicated in some measure Mary Garden's *Louise* at the Opéra Comique. For the rest of the season, and for many seasons to come, no one in the company sang Mimi as often as I did. No other rôle that I have sung belongs to me in quite the same way. And there is no other that, in the singing of it, gives me so full an expression of myself.

'*Si, mi chiamano Mimi.*'

I have sung it with all the great tenors America has heard in the past twenty-five years. With Caruso, Bonci, Riccardo Martin, Luca Botta, McCormack, Crimi, Orville Harrold, Gigli, Hackett, Lauri-Volpi, Johnson, and Martinelli.

And always, when we sang it, and no matter who the tenor was, the house was sold out and the standees crowded about the aisles, and Gatti, sitting in his office, but so intensely aware of everything that was happening in the whole opera house, would be gravely pleased.

When funny things, accidents, absurd mistakes, happened to me on the stage, it seemed as though they always happened during a performance of *Bohème*.

There was the time I was singing it with Caruso. As Mimi, I wore a crinoline, with ruffled white pantalettes showing beneath the hem. The pantalettes were fastened about my waist with a button and buttonhole. At the point where I bent over to pick up the key, I felt (and with what consternation!) the button give way. Beneath my crinoline I could feel the muslin pantalettes slipping down. I clutched the sides of my skirts, even as I was singing, and began stepping backward and to one side, manoeuvring to get behind the sofa which was at one side of the stage. I thought, if only I can get behind that piece of furniture, I can let the pantalettes slip down to the floor. No one in the audience will be able to see them. I can step out of them, leave them there, and finish the act, with no one the wiser. I should have mistrusted Caruso, but I was too concerned with my own predicament to do so. I got behind the sofa, I let the pantalettes slip to the floor, I stepped out of them, and then came forward again, congratulating myself on my cleverness and presence of mind. Then, to my horror, I saw that dangerous gleam in Caruso's eye. He moved over to the sofa. Still singing, he stooped, picked up the pantalettes, lifted them so that no one in the audience could fail to recognize them for what they were, and bowing to me, laid them on the sofa, while the house roared with laughter.

And there was the time we went over to Philadelphia to give a performance of *Bohème*.

I had invited Freddy Bull and Susan Dresser — whom later he married — to go with me as my guests. They wanted to see what life backstage was like.

They saw it that day.

Caruso was in one of his mischief-making moods. We had a lot of fun going over on the train, but I thought all the practical jokes were over until I made my first stage entrance.

To my surprise and mirth, the three men on the stage, Caruso, Scotti, and de Segurola, turned round toward me. In the left eye of each of them was a trick monocle.

That was only the beginning. Later, as I bent to the fire to warm myself, some one backstage (Scotti, I think) squirted soda water from a siphon into my face. In the café scene, Freddy Bull suddenly appeared made up as a waiter. The snow scene came, and from aloft came the stage snowflakes, but along with them bits of string, paper, buttons, nails.

Zingo! they hit the top of my bonnet.

The whole performance had gone completely haywire.

De Segurola lifted his top hat from the table to put it on, and found it filled with flour that powdered his wig and shoulders. A glass supposed to hold water turned out to be filled with ink. We were all of us hysterical by the time we came to the final scene — Mimi's deathbed.

To my horror, I found that the practical jokers had removed two of the bed's casters so that it shook and wobbled at every movement I made, and threatened to fall apart. And I am a fairly substantial person. I managed to 'die,' but immediately the craziness of the whole performance was too much for me. I began to shake with hysterical laughter. And to shake the bed. Mimi simply couldn't stay dead till the curtain fell. I had to roll over, turn my back to the audience, and stifle my laughter in the bedclothes.

The management fined each of us one hundred dollars for that evening's roughhouse.

'But wasn't it worth it?' Caruso exulted.

There was one performance of *Bohème* I sang with John McCormack, which will always stay in my memory.

John was very anxious to sing at the Metropolitan. I persuaded Gatti to engage him for a couple of performances. John

had his own following in New York. Whenever he came there to
give a concert of Irish ballads, the enormous Hippodrome would
be packed to its limits, and there would be lines of McCormack
fans waiting outside, in the vain hope of catching a few strains of
'Mother Machree' or 'I Hear You Calling Me.'

But whether he would be a success at the Metropolitan remained in doubt.

We went on to sing *Bohème* that night without any stage rehearsal. I had played the part too many times to need one, and
John sang it with the Chicago Company. It didn't seem to us or
to anyone else that we should need more than a musical rehearsal.

But when I rapped on the door for my entrance in the first
act and opened it and came in — poor, hungry, fainting Mimi
with her unlighted candle — there to my horror was McCormack standing between me and the chair in which, by all the
rules of the stage director, I was to sink down and faint.

'You're in the way, John,' I whispered.

He did not move.

'Get out of the way!' I was urgent now.

I saw a look of consternation come over his face.

'What'll I do?' he whispered back.

'Move, you fool.'

Heaven knows what he thought was going to happen to him.
But his hand went up, instinctively, and made the sign of the
Cross. Then, and only then, he got back his presence of mind,
moved a few paces, and let me stagger to the chair.

I BELIEVE I gave more care and thought to the costumes
for Mimi than I gave to my costumes for any other opera. I
had a great number of them; but all of them I loved. Especially

the grey crinoline and the little jade-green shawl, and the bonnet, in which I loved to sing the Second Act. I was always very particular about the snowflakes on my costume when I came on. Philip Crispano, the head stage hand at the Metropolitan, and still my devoted friend, always used to take care of my snowflakes. He would sprinkle my bonnet and shoulders with salt — the only thing that, across the footlights, looks like real snow.

I have seen Mimis come on, out of the storm, as fresh and dry as though they had arrived in cellophane!

And in high-heeled satin slippers!

Perhaps there was something in that entrance out of the storm that stirred in me memories of the day in San Francisco when Alby and I pressed our childish noses to the pane watching the snow. Memories of my mother coming in with the snowflakes on her shoulders and in the folds of her little sealskin hat; and the last time we saw her.

THE costumes for Desdemona were gorgeous Venetian gowns sewn with pearls. All but that in which I sang the last act, in which the jealous Othello murders Desdemona. For that I had made a nightdress of white chiffon to be worn over pale pink tights.

My hair (a wig of a richer shade of red than my own and long) hung in loose curls to my waist.

At the dress rehearsal, when I came on the stage, Toscanini took one long look at me. Then he raised his baton for silence.

'*Senti, Aldina*,' he said commandingly. 'You will kneel and sing the "Ave Maria." Then you will get up, without turning your face to the audience. There will be not one smile. Not one bow. There will be no encores. You will not lift your eyes. You will just get into bed like a good pure virgin.'

The most touching of Desdemonas

We played and sang it that way, though after the 'Ave Maria,' which ends on a tender high note, the audience burst into tremendous applause. But I felt Toscanini's eye upon me. I dared not look up. The scene went on with its poetry uninterrupted.

Slezak sang Othello. He was like a big Newfoundland dog. But he had a voice and he could sing. He had tremendous physical force which he threw into his acting. When he came to murder me for my supposed infidelity, he would shake and strangle me with a realism that probably appealed to the audience more than it did to me.

We were singing *Othello* on a night in March. It was the final performance of the opera for that season. For several weeks I had not been feeling my usual vigorous self. There was a nasty pain that hovered about my right side. That night I felt it again as I dressed for the First Act.

'Tomorrow I go to see a doctor,' I promised myself.

I was getting along all right until, in the quarrel, Slezak got his foot on my train, so that when he threw me down I fell not on my knee, as my custom was, but on my right side.

Suddenly all the world was one terrible, excruciating pain.

I managed to lift my head, to finish the act, and then I fainted.

In my dressing-room, when I came to, we held a council of war. Could I go on and sing the last act? That would mean singing the 'Salce' and the 'Ave Maria.' Could I?

I was terribly sick. But I swallowed down a glass of brandy, neat, and said, Yes, I could sing the last act.

And I did — the 'Ave Maria' and the 'Salce.' Perhaps there was in my voice that night a realism there never was before, for I was in agony. When Othello choked me to death I was already unconscious.

They carried me off the stage, and I revived sufficiently to refuse having a physician summoned there.

'Take me home. I want to go home.'

Scotti took me, in a taxi. Still in my chiffon nightgown with my opera cloak wrapped about me. At my apartment Emilie, my maid, undressed me and put me in a hot bath. I looked at my side. It was jet black.

When the doctor came he took one look at me, said, 'Appendix; ruptured,' and began telephoning right and left for a surgeon, nurses, hospital equipment. That night, in the sitting-room of my suite, I was operated upon.

I came out of the ether to find myself front-page news in all the morning papers.

Gatti, who had been out of town during that evening's performance, came and stood by my bedside, and shook his head mournfully over what might have happened.

'If you had died!'

He looked so stricken that I almost felt as though I had.

I F I hadn't had that ruptured appendix and the operation, and been ill for weeks, would I have married Gatti-Casazza? I've wondered, sometimes.

For more than two years he had been asking me to marry him; pleading, begging, protesting the depth and the sincerity of his love for me. Every letter he wrote me breathed an ardor that was extraordinary in that melancholy man. He was, decidedly, the most interesting man I had ever met; a man of world interests and world knowledge. He had position and power in the world that was *my* world . . .

For two years I had been more or less evading the issue, putting off the decision.

Then came long illness and the realization that I was without any relatives nearer than Australia; when I felt, for the first time in my life, alone.

'Yes,' I said to Gatti, when he asked me again, that April. 'I will marry you.'

We were married in my apartment. It was a soft, sunny day. I remember that the windows were open and the pigeons that always flew about the tower and that I used to feed every morning came and perched on the window ledge. They preened their iridescent feathers and turned their curious faces and cooed.

One lifted delicate, coral-colored feet and stepped inside the room close to the vase of tall white Easter lilies . . .

Only a few friends were there to see us married. Among them Mr. Rawlins Cottenet, who had offered me my first contract with the Metropolitan.

Gatti had asked Toscanini to be one of the witnesses.

He refused.

I think he did not approve of the step for either of us.

We left the hotel to face a barrage of reporters and cameras. Gatti stopped, pulled a spray of lilies from my bouquet, and slipped them into his buttonhole. It was his concession to the gaiety the occasion demanded.

After luncheon we drove to the Grand Central Station to join the rest of the company on the train for Chicago, where we were to sing several weeks.

There was no honeymoon.

But at the train a little crowd, determinedly festive, pelted us with rice and confetti to the delight of the reporters.

The train began to move.

I turned and looked at my husband.

Disgustedly, he was picking grains of rice out of his beard.

PART

V

TRIALS OF A DIRECTOR—AND A DIRECTOR'S WIFE

'*Je veux t'aimer et te chérir,*
Parles encore!
Je t'appartiens, je t'adore
Pour toi je veux mourir
Parles — parles encore.
Ah, je t'adore.'

FAUST

V

Remember you married as a woman. Don't give up the position you have attained.

THAT was Fremstad's message to me on my wedding day. And here was Gatti suggesting that from henceforth I should be known on the opera stage as Madame Gatti-Casazza.

I was a long way from being a feminist or taking a keen interest in suffrage. Mrs. Pankhurst and Rosalie Jones and the other vigorous exponents of women's rights who were then making the front page for picketing government offices in Washington, or getting arrested for haranguing crowds from soap boxes or leading parades down Fifth Avenue, seemed to me rather pitiful and ridiculous.

But I was a worker, and I loved my work. I was honestly proud of the career I had made for myself and which belonged to the name ALDA which Madame Marchesi had given me.

As for suddenly letting Frances Alda fade out of existence and becoming Madame Alda Gatti-Casazza ...

'In the first place, nobody can pronounce a name like that,' I retorted to Gatti. 'No. I am Frances Alda. I have made that name known to the public, and I am going to continue to be known by it.'

So, still as Frances Alda, I went with my husband and the other members of the Metropolitan Company to Paris, in that spring of 1910. That was the first and only time that the Metropolitan ever had a Paris season. Gatti had leased the Théâtre du Châtelet.

(How many bons vivants have dined in its famous restaurant! Few Americans know it, except those who have friends in Paris who are real gourmets and may have led them up the stairs and into that big room, still decorated with the faded gilt and crimson plush left over from the days of the Second Empire.)

Our season there was a great success; artistically, as well as financially. The Metropolitan had the reputation of having the finest artists of any opera company in the world. Hundreds of Americans who were in Europe came, proud of their own company. The French music-lovers stormed the box office for the privilege of hearing Caruso, Destinn, Amato and me, in performances with Toscanini conducting.

Our orchestra was French. And as bad as only a French orchestra can be.

I was sitting in the stalls during one of the rehearsals when suddenly Toscanini, without a word, thrust his hand into his pocket, pulled out his watch, and flung it across the seats at the wall.

The abandonment of despair conveyed by that gesture was sublime.

For a moment it touched even the violins.

They actually stopped sawing wood and began to play.

I got up, went round, and groped in the dust till my fingers closed on the watch. Any injuries it had sustained were internal. I went quietly up behind the *maestro*, handed him the watch, which he accepted without a look or a word to me. He put it back in his pocket.

Perhaps that had a fatal effect on the orchestra musicians.

Anyway, it wasn't long before they were out of tune and out of time. I saw Toscanini's hand steal toward his pocket. Out came the watch. Again it skimmed the tops of the orchestra seats and landed BIFF-BANG in a distant corner.

Again the startled orchestra recalled that they were supposed to be musicians. They paid sudden concentrated attention to their scores. I went quietly and retrieved the watch, now much the worse for wear, and with its sufferings registered on its face. I went up to Toscanini, handed it to him, and gravely he replaced it in his pocket.

This time it stayed there.

During that season at the Châtelet I sang performances of *Falstaff* and of *Othello* with Slezak. (How careful he was of me, his

> *'Gentilessima Desdemona, a quella io ho rompato*
> *il appendicte di suo.'*

as he wrote in extemporized Italian in my autograph album.)

The critics wrote enthusiastically of those performances, and, being French, they did not omit to mention their pleasure in my costumes, and my acting. 'The most touching of Desdemonas ... in whose expression, as she sang, there was an ineffable seduction. ...'

For me it was like coming home to be singing again on a French stage and for a French audience.

I sang several concerts at the houses of old friends, and one that I took for Bori. She fell ill and could not keep her engagement. She called me up, told me of her dilemma, and I sang for her that evening, though the fee was less than I was receiving for concerts at that time. Next morning I sent her the cheque in a little gold mesh purse set with turquoises, with a chain to hang around the neck.

Our season at the Châtelet was over.

I wanted to stay on in Paris, where I always had a good time. But I was counting without Gatti.

'Now we can go to Italy,' he informed me. 'We must go at once to Ferrara so you can meet my father and mother.'

And we went.

South of the Simplon the heat of Italy's summer burst upon us like a blast from a furnace. The fields were already burnt brown; the leaves of the olive trees hung listless and covered with fine white dust. When the train stopped one heard the sibilant, long-drawn note of the cicadas. Even at the railway stations the usual flurry and bustle of Italy *en voyage* — the excited greetings and farewells, the cries, the snarls of rival porters, the vociferous salesmanship of the wine and salami and sweetmeat vendors — were hushed by the intense heat.

Ferrara, when we came to it, was like a dead city. The clop-clop of the horses' hoofs as the carriage rumbled over the cobblestones from the station reverberated against the blank, closely shuttered walls of the houses along the way. Grass grew between the paving stones. And over all there hung a sickly sweet smell — the smell of malarial marshes and old tombs and the cerements of the past.

The coachman — he was an old family retainer; he had looked at me appraisingly, as he might look at any purchase his master's son brought home from the Fair — clucked to the horses; we rounded a corner and drew up before the expressionless, dusty white façade of the Palazzo Gatti-Casazza.

'Here we are,' said Gatti.

Within, waiting solemnly in the long salon with the Pompeian frescoes and painted ceiling, were my husband's parents, to welcome their new daughter-in-law.

Gatti's father I loved at first sight — his alert, ruddy face with the bristling white mustaches ... his air of a military man who was also very much a man of the world, with an eye for a beautiful woman.

And he loved me. We remained friends up to his death. In any arguments or altercations, he always took sides with me, even against Giulio. Naturally, this didn't please his son. But then, it was I, and not Giulio, who used to ask Senator Gatti-Casazza to visit us at the Lido, or in Paris or London. He would come, revelling in the gaiety and the people and the parties his son frowned at. Most of all, on those visits, I think, he enjoyed taking me about to museums and art galleries, to the antiquaries' shops and auction rooms, where we 'shopped' enthusiastically for beautiful, rare old furniture and brocades. Senator Gatti-Casazza was a connoisseur of such things.

Signora Gatti-Casazza, 'la contessa,' as she was in her own right, was a dark-browed, grim woman, entirely lacking the wit and the social grace that made her husband so charming as a companion. There was something strangely morose in her nature. I was told that there were years when she never went beyond her own garden, and for no reason that any member of the family understood. And if ever I saw a chin that had obstinacy carved in its every line, it was hers.

It was the feature of her face she had handed down to her son Giulio.

Gatti's mother and I looked at each other as I suppose mother-in-law and daughter-in-law must often look at each other. I wondered what part of her I had to encounter in the man I had married.

She, no doubt, wondered what *her* son could see in *me*.

The other members of my husband's family there to welcome me were his brother 'Beppino' and his wife. Giuseppe (Beppino) Gatti-Casazza is today one of Italy's leading architects; a famous collector of antiques, whose *palazzo* in Venice is filled with treasures. He and his wife, Antonia, are still among my dearest friends. Their daughter, Andrea, then a baby, has inherited her father's cleverness. She studied medicine, took her degree, and today practises at the children's hospital in Milan.

On the day after our arrival, Gatti said: 'This afternoon we will go for a drive.'

Both historically and artistically Ferrara is, of course, one of the most interesting of all the Italian cities. The d'Este family, who were its hereditary dukes, left the stamp of their individuality on mediaeval and Renaissance history throughout Italy.

What they could not win by warfare apparently, they attained by marriage. Their daughters who went to Mantua and Milan and Florence, their sons who went to Rome as cardinals, were patrons of the arts and letters. They built superb palaces and enchanting gardens. And all this glory had come out of the little ages-old city near the Adriatic.

I was eager to see the city that was most closely associated with them and for which they had created the most. Especially, I looked forward to being shown all these things by my husband, whose knowledge of history and its significance surpassed that of anyone I had ever known. I remembered how he had 'shown' me Venice in all its golden splendor — making it live for me forever. I was eager for what Ferrara might hold for me.

At five, the fierce, blazing heat began to abate, so that you could bear the thought of leaving the house. We went down to the street door. There stood the family victoria, drawn by a pair of gaunt, elderly horses. The old coachman — in faded livery — sat stiffly on the box.

We got into the carriage. Gatti gave a direction. We drove off.

The carriage upholstery was faded and gave forth the smell of musty straw. But I leaned back — in my loveliest, most fashionable Paris frock — and wide, flower-wreathed hat. I opened my parasol and tilted it against the sun.

'Where are we going?' I asked Gatti.

'To the cemetery.'

And to the cemetery we went — in our bridal state. Not to see the gorgeous d'Estes, but for me to pay dutiful respect to the graves of my husband's grandparents and collateral relatives — and the vault where —

'You will lie, some day.'

'Not if I have anything to say about it.'

No matter what life brought to me, I resolved then and there, I simply wouldn't die in Italy. Or anywhere near Italy. Frances Alda wasn't going to be gathered up and stored away in that dreadful place, along with those strange, dead Casazzas.

And then —

I laughed.

Out loud, and right in the face of those bead wreaths and marble angels and death's heads and sanctimonious inscriptions.

I couldn't help it, thinking what a terrible shock I'd probably give the ashes of Great-Grandmother Pia and Step-Uncle Eduardo in those shades. I was thinking they wouldn't find me a restful companion.

We stayed in Ferrara only a few days, but even in that short

My mother-in-law, sitting silent and slumped in her chair
with an air of brooding unfathomable things

space of time I saw enough of the life lived within the walls of the Palazzo to make me realize how wide was the gulf between my husband's early years and my own. I contrasted those close-shuttered, formal rooms, filled with relics of the past, the almost mediaeval attitude that prevailed in the relations of parent and child, husband and wife, master and servant; the austerity, the formality, the terrifying power of the family tie, with the sunny, breeze-swept house at St. Kilda, filled with children and pets, with music and the noise of games. And I wondered what unfathomable purpose had brought together a man and a woman from such separate worlds.

IF SINGING in Paris had been fun, even more thrilling was the engagement I had to sing with Caruso and Amato a special performance of *Bohème* at La Monnaie in Brussels.

The performance was set for a date in September, just before Gatti and I were to sail for New York.

Brussels was having its season. All the seats at La Monnaie were sold out days before our performance. A long queue of disappointed people trailed from the box office into the street.

Would we, the directors begged, give a second, repeat performance on the next evening?

We would.

To go back to the opera house where I had sung for two seasons was like turning back the page of a familiar book. Here I had first sung Marguerite in *Faust*. Here, I had sung the part of the Queen in *Les Huguenots*. And created for myself, not incidentally, a case of stage fright that hung over me for years.

Singing the big aria, one night, I had cracked on a top note. Just once.

But that one time never faded from my memory. It gave

me the jitters every time I had to sing the rôle from then on.

I remember once confiding this to Caruso. He returned the confidence by telling me that the same thing had happened to him once while singing *Bohème*, and he never started that particular aria without a live terror plucking at his heart.

But, apparently, no one at La Monnaie remembered that one moment that remained in my memory as so awful. When I arrived on the night of the first performance, there was a little crowd of old friends to welcome me. Not alone the two directors, but the wardrobe mistress and the plump little Flemish woman (who always reminded me of a tightly stuffed sawdust doll) who had been my maid, and three or four of the old stage hands, between whom and me there was a spirit of comradeship that might be hard for anyone not of the theatre to understand completely.

The caste system that prevails behind the scenes of any big opera house is as strict as that of India. But there is also a spirit of 'The play's the thing,' that makes each and every member of the company, from the topmost prima donna to the least of the stage hands and the call boy, feel a measure of personal responsibility for the success of each performance, and a corresponding measure of personal pride in every success.

In a way, it's that, as much as the footlights and the applause and the thrill of emotional acting, that gives a stage career its fascination.

But there were some changes at La Monnaie.

Old King Leopold was dead, and beautiful Cléo de Mérode was vanished, no one quite knew where.

King Albert and Queen Elizabeth sat in the royal box. They were charming in their appreciation of the performance and congratulated us most cordially after the Second Act.

After the Third Act François Empain stood in my dressing room. There was something like consternation in his eyes as he looked at me, and I spoke of Gatti.

'Alda! Alda! Why did you marry him?'

I SUPPOSE the first months of any marriage are full of bumps and sharp corners and steep grades, with innumerable chances for skidding and landing in a heap at the side of the road.

My marriage to Gatti-Casazza was no exception to this rule.

Neither of us had been married before. Gatti was over forty years of age and accustomed to his own ways of doing everything. I was seventeen years his junior, but most of my life I had seen to it that I had my own way.

Perhaps I was spoiled.

Certainly I was impulsive and high-strung.

As for patience — I hadn't a scrap of it in my make-up. Naturally, with two such temperaments, there were numbers of times when the domestic barometer registered all the danger signals at once.

The first time was in Chicago in the first week after our marriage. Remember, I had been ill and confined to my own apartment for six weeks. And during that period that subtle, mystic change we call 'spring' had come over the world. Spring affects some people one way, some people another. It infects me with a passionate longing for new clothes.

When my spring urge is on me, not only must I do away with my winter wardrobe, I must immediately go out and buy new, springlike frocks and shoes and accessories and hats.

Especially hats.

Accordingly, one morning while we were in Chicago, I set forth and followed that impulse up and down Michigan Boulevard. Then I went to the opera house and sang a matinée performance. Afterward, I drove back to the Blackstone Hotel.

There in my room stood six big intriguing white cardboard boxes. Within — fondled in sheets of tissue paper — waited the Hats.

I pulled off the box covers, scattered the tissue paper, and immediately began trying on first one hat, then the other.

Is there a woman alive who wouldn't do the same?

I was so happily engaged when Gatti came in.

He stared at me.

'But what are those?' he demanded.

It seemed ridiculous to explain that they were hats — something to be worn on the head. That was self-evident. But, of course, no male — except a man milliner — could be expected to know that these were the newest models fresh from Paris. I told him this.

'And you bought those hats? All the *six* hats!'

'Of course I did.'

He threw out his hands furiously.

'But what a fool! Haven't you hats enough, now, as it is? And why do you buy Paris hats — in Chicago — when in less than three weeks you will be in Paris . . . ?'

Well, any man who couldn't understand that a woman always wants new hats — especially Paris hats — no matter where she is or where she may be going next, was beyond sufferance.

I told Gatti so.

Not omitting to mention the fact that I had paid for the hats myself, out of my own money. And if I wanted to buy not six, but six dozen Paris hats in Timbuctoo, since I could well afford to pay for them out of the money I earned myself, I considered myself privileged to do so. My marriage to him had not altered my right to do as I liked with my own.

And then, was there a row?

I can see Gatti storming and finally kicking his foot through one of the hat-boxes, while the sheets of tissue paper flew about the room. And in the midst of it all I committed the one unforgivable sin a wife can commit against a husband.

I laughed at him.

Gatti — with his habitual solemn dignity, his black beard, his large mournful eyes — was the sort of man who should have remembered *not* to put his foot through cardboard boxes.

Cause of marital discord No. 1 — too many hats.

Cause of marital discord No. 2 — Verdi's piano.

It stood in one of the rooms of the Palazzo Gatti-Casazza, a darling little old rosewood piano. Its yellowed keys gave forth a tinkle like the voice of some old lady who had been a belle in her youth and still kept the lilt in her voice.

It had belonged to Verdi — his first piano.

Beppino had discovered it somewhere and bought it for his brother.

To me, it was the greatest treasure in the whole house.

'You shall have it,' Gatti told me. 'I give it to you.'

Immediately I suggested having it carefully packed and shipped to Paris for my apartment there.

Gatti made evasive replies. I very soon saw that though he had given me the piano, he had no intention of having it removed from where it stood in his parents' home.

I expostulated.

We were all in the garden at the time — a family gathering. My mother-in-law, who had been sitting silent and slumped in her chair, with an air of brooding unfathomable things, lifted her head and gave me a long look. Autocratically: 'Francesca, you should do as your husband wishes,' she said.

Behind the look and the command I felt the monstrous power of Family Authority! Not to be rebelled against, not even to be questioned. But to be obeyed absolutely, submissively, and, as far as one could judge, forever.

Until I, as the wife of the eldest son, inherited the position of Family Autocrat.

Or took my humble place in that horrible cemetery vault!

It wasn't tactful. It wasn't good manners. But then and there, in the presence of the Family, I made it unmistakably clear that in marrying Gatti, I had not married the Gatti-Casazzas and all their tribal traditions, customs, and household gods.

But I never did get the piano.

For the rest of that summer I gave a good deal of thought to marriage and what was required of a man and a woman to make their marriage a success.

I wasn't romantic about it. I knew I was not, and never had been, in love with my husband. But in many ways I respected him. I admired his genius. And I had had innumerable protestations from him that he adored me and desired no other woman.

And I, myself, meant to play fair. No love affairs on the side. No sentimental memories kept alive by letters and cablegrams on anniversaries and occasional meetings. No ghosts of past loves stalking the corridors of my marriage.

It seemed to me that September, lying stretched in my deck chair, America-bound, with Gatti in the chair next to mine, and engrossed in a book, that our marriage stood as good a chance as any other of being a success.

WE WENT to live at the Hotel Knickerbocker. Caruso lived there. So did Farrar. So did Scotti. The hotel was proud of us and coddled us. People used to come to lunch there not only for the food, which was exceedingly good — the best in New York — but for a glimpse of Caruso threading his way through the crowded restaurant to his own corner table; of Farrar, elegant and beautifully dressed and haughty, lunching alone at her table near the tenor's; of Gatti and me, and the Toscaninis, who were often among our guests.

It was one of New York's 'sights,' much as the luncheon crowd at the Algonquin became a 'sight' later on, with the newspaper columnists' rise to power.

I had forgotten about all that until last October when I was motoring across the Mohawk Trail and up into Vermont. The

Berkshires were in full autumnal glory, the sky turquoise-blue. I was with Ray Vir Den, an old friend. Ray has put on all the shows for the Dutch Treat Club for years. He loves nature as much as I do, and is a perfectly delightful companion. We stopped in Bennington and I went into the hotel to inquire about rooms and was met by an indifferent reply to my question, that the house was full.

Some word, some gesture of irritation and disappointment must have been peculiarly mine and familiar to the proprietor.

He looked at me sharply.

Then, suddenly, he had grasped me by both hands and was kissing them ...

'Signora, Signora, don't you remember me? Jorge. Jorge from the Knickerbocker?'

I did remember him then as one of the waiters who used to serve us there. A real Italian, who could whistle or hum the arias from a dozen operas; and reckoned Verdi and Puccini among the saints. And those who played or sang their music if not among the blessed, at least among those to be treated with awe, consideration, and tolerance for any sparks of temperament.

Gatti's first concern that autumn was for the première of *The Girl of the Golden West*, which Caruso and Destinn were to create. Puccini was coming over for the final rehearsals and for the first performance.

'*The Girl ... The Girl ... The Girl. ...*'

It seemed, that November and during the first ten days of December, that that was all I heard.

Caruso, always reliable and conscientious, had turned up in New York in October of that year, ready for the preliminary rehearsals.

But there was no Destinn.

Cables — frantic, imperious ones from Gatti, evasive messages from the diva — began to fly back and forth across the Atlantic.

'What's the matter with the woman?' Gatti wailed. 'First she is coming by this boat. Then she wires she will take some other boat. Then, when she finally sails, she leaves the ship at Cherbourg because she doesn't like it, and waits over for some other vessel. What will Puccini say if he arrives, and still we have no Girl? Women opera singers! Bah! they are more maddening than tenors.'

The fact was that Destinn was a phenomenally quick study, and she knew it. She knew perfectly well that she could stretch her holiday to the uttermost, and arrive in New York at the last possible moment, and still be perfect in her part in much shorter time than Gatti would ever believe possible.

The première was set for December 10.

It was the first time that New York had seen the world première of a new opera. It was, too, the first time in years that a great composer had a new work to present.

Was the creator of *La Tosca* and *Manon Lescaut* and *La Bohème* too old now to give birth to a creation worthy to stand beside these? True, Verdi had written *Othello* and *Falstaff* after he had passed his seventy-fifth year; and musically, they hold their place with, if not above *Aïda* and *Il Trovatore*, the works of his youth. But Verdi was — Verdi, and so completely himself that one could not draw parallels from his accomplishment to that of any other composer — even Puccini. So people argued it back and forth, while the eyes and ears and the critical attention of everyone in the international world of music were turned on the Metropolitan when that night came. The opera had been widely advertised, and there was a tremendous demand for tickets, especially by the ticket speculators who expected to reap a harvest.

Gatti, however, was determined to put an end to the racket in opera tickets that had always gone on, but was now on the increase as the performances at the Metropolitan became more and more popular.

That night he inaugurated a new system. No tickets were

sold in advance of the performance or sent out to the regular subscribers. Instead, the money was received at the box office and a receipt mailed or given to the purchaser. This receipt was to be presented at the box office just before the performance that evening to be exchanged for the ticket.

This method left the speculators gasping with rage and frustrated greed. Also, naturally it created no end of confusion and delay. And one, at least, amusing contretemps.

When Mr. Kahn arrived at the opera house, he was refused admittance.

'I can't help it if your name *is* Kahn,' the doorman told him. 'If you haven't got a ticket you can't go in!'

The audience was as fashionable and brilliant as at the season's opening night. As I looked along the parterre boxes it seemed to me that everyone in New York society was there.

There was the usual applause for Toscanini when he came into the conductor's box.

The curtain rose.

It seemed to me, watching stage and house, that the audience was following the action intently, even though the applause during the first act was slight.

But when the finale scene came and the curtain fell, there was no doubt of *The Girl's* reception by New York.

Spontaneous applause swept the house.

Destinn, Caruso, Amato, Gilly, and Toscanini were called repeatedly, and the applause continued until Puccini and Belasco were brought out. Both were cheered and forced to bow acknowledgment fourteen times. The same recognition was paid to them after the Second and Third Acts.

'My heart is going like a contrabass,' Puccini said. 'But I am unutterably happy. The performance has been perfect.'

The Board of Directors had arranged a reception for the composer immediately after the opera. Palms and flowering plants and ropes of smilax decorated the usually dusty, bare foyer.

I remember Blanche Bates was there, with tears in her eyes; and Elsie de Wolfe, chic and clever-looking and distinguishedly thin, at a period when most women tried to discipline their excess pounds with a corset, rather than dieting or rolling them off; and Madame Nordica, whose sweetness to me when I first came to New York I have never forgotten; Humperdinck, who had just come over for the première of his *Koenigskinder*; Mr. and Mrs. Stuyvesant Fish, the Vanderbilts, the Morgans, the Clarence Mackays, everyone of social and artistic importance who was in New York.

It was a Success.

At least the première was.

But the music of *The Girl* falls below that of Puccini's earlier works. There is some flowing melody, as in the waltz in the First Act. But Puccini's art did not suit the primitive Western scenes of the play. The opera ended by being neither American nor Italian. I believe this failure, which was inherent in it, more than any other cause, was responsible for its not being a long-continued success like the composer's *Bohème* and *Tosca* and *Manon Lescaut*.

This was not Puccini's first visit to America. He had come over for the presentation of *Madame Butterfly* several years before. It was during that visit to New York that he went one night down to the old Academy of Music to see Belasco's play, *The Girl of the Golden West*, in which Blanche Bates was starring. The house was sold out. Puccini bought standing room and stood up with a mixed company of melodrama enthusiasts. When the curtain went down on the Second Act Puccini extricated himself from the crowd and sought out Belasco in his office.

'I want the piece,' he said. 'I have already the minstrel's song in my head.'

It is an interesting coincidence that Puccini had also written *Madame Butterfly* from a play of that name in which Blanche Bates had played.

Puccini was intensely interested in all the craft of the theatre. Of course, he and Gatti were old friends — of nearly twenty years' standing, so he was often with us at the Knickerbocker. After dinner, he and Gatti would settle down with their cigarettes and liqueurs to talk four, five, six hours. Music, composers, operas, music publishers, directors, singers, opera house management, stage business — all these came up for discussion. Sometimes I sat with them, keenly interested in their comments and ideas. Sometimes I would go out to a party or to the theatre leaving them there, and when I let myself in, four hours later, they would still be at it; the room, with all the windows hermetically sealed, filled with a dense smoke fog through which the two men spoke to each other like veiled oracles.

Puccini had the creative artist's capacity for intense concentration on whatever he was at work upon. When the work was completed and the score published, he lost the sense of its being a personal possession. But while the creation was going forward — woe betide any of the servants he caught whistling or singing the airs they heard him composing at the piano.

Of course, they learned them — with that quick ear and gift for song that is part of the Italian heritage.

And, of course, they sang them too, for visitors and tourists, and in the cafés of Lucca, for a few centesimi and a glass of wine.

'Puccini's latest!'

We were talking one night about the brutal reception the audience at La Scala had given the première of *Madame Butterfly*. Puccini had walked out of the opera house with the score under his arm, thus preventing a second performance of the work.

'The very name *Butterfly* seemed horrible to me,' he said. 'I went back to Torre del Lago and tried to forget that I had ever written an opera of that name, or that it had ever been given. Then one day I heard about a simple bookkeeper in Lucca, who was so indignant at the reception given my opera that he named his baby daughter "Butterfly."

'"What!" the clerk at the registry cried. "Do you want to brand your child with the memory of a failure?"

'I was so touched by the father's tribute that I wrote to him. I asked him to come and see me. You know how you do those things.

'Well, one Sunday I was standing by the window looking out. There was a procession coming up the avenue to the villa. Forty, fifty, maybe sixty people, I don't know how many. At the head was a man carrying a baby and behind him came men and women, young and old, several priests, and dozens of children. The women were carrying flowers and one of the men had a flask of wine. It was Butterfly and her father — and all her father's relatives.'

During his stay in New York, Puccini wrote in my score of *Bohème*:

> Alle gentile diva
> Frances Alda
> Gatti-Casazza
> della voce pura, dolce, & chiara
> con amicizia sincere
> offre ammirando
> Giacomo Puccini
> N.Y. 1910

A little more than a fortnight after the première of *The Girl* New York heard, for the first time, Humperdinck's *Koenigskinder*, in which Farrar starred. Humperdinck came over for the rehearsals and the first night, and was fêted as Verdi had been.

Mrs. W. K. Vanderbilt gave a dinner for the two composers, to which, of course, Gatti and I were asked. I accepted the invitation, but on the afternoon before the dinner:

'I'm not going,' my husband told me.

'Of course you're going,' I said firmly. 'The director of the Metropolitan stay away from a dinner given for the two greatest composers living? Nonsense, you have to go. It doesn't matter how you feel.'

For a while he held out against me, but finally yielded.

A few minutes before eight o'clock we started, and drove up Fifth Avenue to the Vanderbilt house, which, in those days, still had its high, old-fashioned stoop with the flight of brownstone steps leading up to it.

Going up the steps, Gatti turned to me:

'I didn't want to come to this dinner, and you made me,' he said in Italian. 'Now I am here, but I tell you this: I shall not say one word to anyone all the time we are there.'

He was perfectly capable of doing just that, as I knew.

For the few minutes we were in the drawing-room before dinner, while the guests assembled, I watched my husband out of the tail of my eye. He stood, silent and remote, a most melancholy-looking guest.

Then we went in to dinner.

I found myself seated between Mr. Vanderbilt and Mr. Lydig at one end of the long table. From where I sat I could see Gatti, seated between Mrs. Vanderbilt and Mrs. Lydig, far away at the other end. I could see the two ladies trying to converse with him, and getting in reply only shakes of the head, or little, non-committal murmurs:

'*Si, si.*'

I spoke up; in French, so that everyone present would be sure to understand:

'Don't mind Gatti, Mrs. Vanderbilt,' I said. 'He told me when we were coming up the steps that he only came tonight because I made him come. And that he didn't intend to speak a word all the time he was here.'

There was a little gasp, then quick laughter. Everyone looked at Gatti with amusement. The black mood which had imprisoned him all day lifted as inexplicably as it had come.

Three minutes later he was talking away as delightfully as only he could talk when he wanted to, and the two ladies were listening to him eagerly.

Of all the houses I went to that winter, Bridget Guinness's old, red-brick, white-doorwayed house on Washington Square, with the two white cocks on the fence posts, was the one where I felt most at home.

The affairs of the Opera Company might be full of annoyances. My marriage might present me with problems of readjustment. Youth and good health, the abounding vitality and the love of fun that are my own blessed inheritance (to be wounded, perhaps, in the years that followed, but never to be lost entirely), carried me out of the doldrums, and into a circle where I could laugh and play pranks and enjoy myself.

I had grown to know and to love Bridget during my first winter in New York.

People used to say that she and I looked very much alike. It is true that we had the same curly auburn hair; our features were similar, and we dressed in the same style. She was one of the most vitally alive persons I ever knew. It is almost impossible for me to realize now that she is dead. I remember the last time I saw her, in New York three winters ago. We spent a whole day together 'shopping' for antiques and reminiscing over the good times we had had in the past, both in London in her house in Carleton House Terrace, and in Washington Square. I remember it was from the balcony of Bridget's London house that I watched the triumphal return of Great Britain's troops after the World War. (Just a few days before I had seen the French army's victorious entry into Paris from Nina de Polignac's house on the Champs Elysées. It seemed in those months that all my life long I should go on hearing bands and the march of feet!)

Bridget was a marvellous hostess. She did not share the belief that to enjoy yourself was slightly immoral. At her parties stodgy dowagers, temperamental prima donnas, Spanish dancers, statesmen, Hollywood celebrities, and bankers were mingled by some magic that was Bridget's own particular gift, into a harmonious and entertaining whole. At her house in

Washington Square, she had what amounted to a salon several years before Mabel Dodge arrived from Florence and set up her white satin bedroom on the corner of Ninth Street.

At those Tuesday Night parties you met, sooner or later, everyone of consequence who was amusing and original. Everyone who was famous, or about to be.

Mrs. John Jacob Astor was a friend of Bridget's whom I met there often. She was gracious and charming, one of the most beautiful women I ever saw. She was then divorcing her husband. (I had met him too, *not* at Bridget's but at a dinner given by Countess Leary. He sat next me, I remember, and all through dinner paid me extravagant florid compliments. But I was not impressed. I very distinctly did not like his style ...)

The parties at Bridget's consisted of a buffet supper, charmingly informal, but just the same very *comme il faut*. Afterwards, the artists among the guests willingly provided the impromptu entertainment.

I sang there many, many times. Sometimes Rachmaninoff accompanied me. Mischa Elman or Heifetz, if either happened to be there, would join in. I remember one night a wide space was cleared and Otero danced. His magnificent supple body in the smooth, tight, black Andalusian trousers, frilled white shirt, and crimson sash moved like a rapier in the hands of an expert swordsman.

At Bridget's there was none of the provincialism that I found so depressing in American society.

I confess, it astounded me when I first came to America, to find a wealthy leisure class, persons of prominence and power and who made at least a gesture toward the arts, but whose ideas and experience of their own country were drawn from summers in Newport, Bar Harbor, or Tuxedo, and winters in New York or Philadelphia. To them the Middle West might have been the Sahara. California was as far removed as Alaska. If you asked them about these places, they regarded you curiously.

The inference was that nothing outside that sacred circle they had drawn about themselves mattered at all.

Remember, I was an Englishwoman, a colonial. I had been brought up on the idea of an empire that meant a wide horizon of interests and associations. At my grandfather's home in St. Kilda, political events in France and Germany and Italy had been constantly under discussion. When I had been studying with Madame Marchesi at her house, I had lived in a world that was distinctly international. There had followed the years in Brussels, seasons in Milan and Warsaw, and three months in South America.

All my life I have kept my eyes and my ears wide open wherever I have been.

And I have never hesitated to ask questions.

So here was I, at twenty-five, with that background of education, not from books, but from travel and first-hand experience, plumped down in a society that took itself for the most part in dead seriousness, and that knew no more of Europe than a few hotels and shops, and the tourist sights in the various capitals.

The society, the thought, the vital essence of those cities and countries were entirely unknown to them.

As, indeed, was much of the pulse beat of their own country.

It took the Great War to pierce the armor of ignorance in which New York 'society' went encased. Through the years between 1914 and America's entry into the War I watched the gradual dissolution of many of those prejudices.

American provincialism went down on the *Lusitania*.

Do these social interests and gaieties seem incompatible with the busy life of an opera singer?

As a matter of fact, I did not sing at the Metropolitan at all during the season 1910–1911.

I knew, when I married Gatti, that inevitably there would be some carping among the artists about having the director's

Scotti, Paderewski, Alda, and Caruso
May, 1912

wife a member of the company. But I remembered Fremstad's counsel — not to let my marriage alter the career to which I had given so much work and study. After all, I argued, other prima donnas married and went on singing. Why should not I? It was only accident that made one singer's husband a naval officer and mine an impresario. But one night at a dress rehearsal before the opera season opened, I was sitting in my box. I heard voices in the next box, talking. I listened and recognized the two men as Otto Kahn and Henry Russell, director of the Boston Opera. I heard Kahn say:

'As the director's wife, it is much better that Alda should not sing here next season.'

I pushed back the velvet hangings that separated the two boxes. I believe the biggest shock in Otto Kahn's life was when he found me looking straight at him.

'I suppose it would be all right if I were his mistress instead of his wife,' I said. 'I resign right now.'

For a year I did not sing at the Metropolitan. I sang many times in Boston and in Chicago, and that winter began to make extended concert tours that took me back and forth across the United States.

I didn't realize it at the time, but those tours set a precedent that was to grow into a tradition. Every year thereafter, for fifteen years, I concertized. Now, looking back over those concert tours that took me like a weaver's shuttle from Brooklyn to San Francisco, from Toronto to Emporia, Kansas, back to Brooklyn and then by the Limited to Seattle before darting southward to Dallas, they seem like an entire separate life that I lived. Entire, in that in my memory the events of one season's concert tour merges now with those of the tour before and of the one after it. And separate, because those nights spent in train staterooms and in strange hotels, those days literally on the road, those arrivals in a welter of trunks, hat-boxes, telephone messages, telegrams, flowers, and press agents, and those quick dashes from the concert hall to the train in order to reach the next city in which I had an engagement, were so far removed from the busy but quite standardized routine of life in the opera house.

It was almost as though there were two Frances Aldas.

One who was by turns Mimi and Manon Lescaut and Desdemona and Nannetta.

And the other, who seemed to be perpetually on wheels.

Later on in this story I want to tell some of the adventures — funny, many of them — connected with those concert tours. But now I am writing of 1911, when the idea of turning myself and my accompanist, Frank La Forge, into a concert company was still startlingly new to me.

The first problem that presented itself for solution when I began to plan my first concerts was: what to sing.

Operatic arias, I felt, had no place on a concert program.

For one thing, the arias are written as part of a drama, to be sung in costume and usually to another character in the drama. To separate them from their rightful setting and present them without introduction or explanation, as 'songs,' is to rob them of their beauty and significance, no matter how well one sings them. Too, very few concert halls or hotel ballrooms are big enough for real operatic singing. The audience sits so close to the stage that they and the singer are uncomfortable unless she sings something *intime*, something written to be sung in a drawing-room. Therefore, no operatic airs.

What then?

Most of the singers America had heard in the years before I began to concertize had been German singers, or at least singers of German music. I, too, loved the songs of Schumann and Schubert, and Hugo Wolf. I intended to sing several of these; but I felt that I wanted to make my concert programs different and peculiarly my own. So I went back to some of the French music of the eighteenth century. I found a number of really exquisite little *chansons*, gay but often with a tear falling quickly on the gaiety at the close of the song.

This sort of song best suited my voice. It was what I loved to sing.

But the entire program should not be made up of old songs.

There must be some modern French and Russian music, for contrast. And, too, there must be a number of songs in English, not too high-brow songs either, for the people who couldn't understand a foreign language and were not so musical that the music alone satisfied them. Working with these ideals in mind I evolved this program. I sang it at a song recital in Carnegie Hall in December, 1911.

SONG RECITAL, AT CARNEGIE HALL
December 5, 1911
PROGRAM

Quand le bien aimé reviendra	Dalayrac 1786
Il était un oiseau gris	Monsigny 1764
C'est mon ami	Philidor 1762
Dites que faut-il faire (P. Viandot)	Air XVIII siècle
Ich liebe dich	Beethoven
Intermezzo	Beethoven
Ihre Thränen	Schumann
Auf dem grünen Balkon	Hugo Wolf
Botschaft	Brahms
Il pleut dans mon coeur	Debussy
Le Colibir ⎱ 1st time Apaisement ⎰	Chausson
Berceuse ⎱ 1st time O'Oiselot ⎰	Grechaninow
Thou art a child (1st time)	F. Weingartner
My Heart	Randegger
Jean	Spross
Expectancy (by request)	La Forge
The Voyager	L. V. Saar

Wherever I went on those far-flung concert tours I kept my eyes and ears open for any singers who might, I thought, be promising material for the Metropolitan.

It was so I found Luca Botta.

The tour had brought me to San Francisco, which I reached on the day before my concert engagement. I was just installed in my suite at the Palace — when the telephone rang. An old friend was at the other end of the wire.

Wouldn't I dine with her and go later to hear a travelling company then giving a repertory of Italian opera?

I hesitated before replying.

'You must come!' she insisted. 'They're singing *Bohème. Your* opera!'

I was tired and jittery from the transcontinental train journey. What I wanted more than anything else in the world was not three hours of hearing some worse than mediocre singers scream their way through my favorite opera, but to get into bed, release my hair from the extravaganza of pompadour, curls, and puffs in which the style of 1911 ordained I should wear it and shake it out over the pillow, have a simple dinner sent up on a tray, and read Arnold Bennett's *How to Live on Twenty-Four Hours a Day*, which someone had sent me with the challenging note —

> *Alda darling,*
> *Here's just the book for you!*

How to Live on Twenty-Four Hours a Day— as though ...

As though I didn't know more about that than any staid and conventional English novelist could possibly tell me.

But that book was electrifying America that season. Now in 1937 when all the New Yorkers I know are striving to *Wake Up and Live*, after Dorothea Brande's exciting recipes, or even to *Live Alone and Like It* (which, I for one, think can't be done), it flatters my British self-esteem — which hasn't been altogether eradicated by my becoming by marriage an Italian subject, then by divorce a woman without a country, and now by naturalization an American citizen — to remember that the first of the books on *How to Live* that jolted America out of complacent idleness was written by an Englishman.

'You will go, won't you?' my friend at the other end of the telephone urged.

'I'd love to,' I lied politely.

'Good! I'll come for you in an hour.'

Dressing, I regretted the unquenchable hospitality that is the hall-mark of all San Franciscans I have known. And the enthusiastic love of music, especially of grand opera, that is another of their characteristics.

Aside from the pleasure I should have in dining with my friends, I looked forward to the evening as wasted.

When we reached the opera house, the First Act was in progress. Mimi — such a buxom, well-fed Mimi who could not by any stretch of the imagination have come out of any city but Naples, or ever gone a single day of her life without plenty of spaghetti and ravioli or kept a single Christmas season without a feast of stewed eels(!) was singing to a solicitous Rudolfo the story of her life.

I looked at Rudolfo. He was young. In appearance, he resembled Caruso amazingly. As Caruso was the most widely publicized artist of the time I thought, naturally, that this young Italian tenor was exaggerating, for purposes of publicity, what was no more than a slight racial likeness:

Till he began to sing.

'*Che gellida mannina!*'

For me, the evening wasn't wasted after that.

The likeness to Caruso was not just of features and figure. His tenor voice had unusual purity of tone and power. Moreover, his singing was good. He gave Puccini's music its full value.

I looked at the program for his name.

Luca Botta.

That night I telegraphed Gatti recommending that he ask Luca Botta to come to New York for an audition for the Metropolitan.

Gatti and Toscanini liked his voice — and Gatti engaged him. He sang his first performances during the 1912–13 season.

'It is strange,' Gatti said to me after the first of these. 'His voice isn't as good as when we heard him last spring.'

'No, it isn't,' I agreed. 'But that may be nervousness. After all, it's a big jump from a travelling opera troupe to the Metropolitan's stage. He'll get better as he gets more accustomed to singing with the rest of the company.'

'*Va bene.*'

Gatti left it at that.

The rest of the story I must tell briefly.

Botta's voice did get better. The next season he sang several performances of *Bohème* — with me — and he sang them beautifully. We sang together frequently during 1915 and '16 in *Bohème* and *Prince Igor*. But there was no denying it, a warning huskiness had crept into Botta's voice. We all noticed it. Neither rest nor medical treatment seemed to relieve it.

And then the truth came out.

Cancer!

Luca Botta was one of the victims of that dread disease. He had to give up his stage career, and not long after that he was dead.

I still have and use frequently at Casa Mia a silver after-dinner coffee service, unusual in design and exquisite in workmanship, which Luca Botta sent me after our first performance together in *Bohème*.

I never lift the coffee pot to pour coffee for my guests that I do not remember — with sorrow — the too swift passing of Botta's rich and really beautiful voice — and the loss to the music world of a tenor who would certainly have become internationally famous.

Whenever I went away from New York to sing, Gatti's letters and telegrams followed me. Usually he wrote me about the concerts of the Metropolitan, which engrossed his mind and in which he knew I too was intensely interested, even though I was no longer singing with the company myself. So he would report his difficulties with this or that singer or director. He would give me businesslike accounts of the previous evening's performance, from the point of view of the box-office receipts, as well as artistically.

Sometimes the telegrams were more personal; like the one I found waiting for me, once, when I arrived in Minneapolis:

> *I don't know where to find my pearl buttons and studs what have they done with them?*

While Emilie unpacked trunks, answered the incessant telephone calls, held off reporters, arranged flowers, and kept warning me that the hour for the concert was drawing dangerously close, I tried to compose a reply wire to my husband telling him in which box, in which corner of which drawer of which bureau I felt sure he would find his shirt studs.

One day in January, 1912, while I was away on tour, among the telegrams was one from Otto Kahn. It read:

> *Come back — your place at the Metropolitan is waiting for you.*

Was I pleased?

Of course I was.

Not just because I really loved the opera house where I had met my first American audience, and in which lay my husband's career, but because I felt that this re-engagement was a tribute to me as a singer quite apart from (even in spite of) the fact that I was the wife of Gatti-Casazza.

I made my return to the Metropolitan as Desdemona. We sang *Othello* three times during the remaining two months of that season.

It seemed as though that opera, which Toscanini loved to conduct, and which had seldom been given in New York until I sang it in 1910, was becoming increasingly popular with the Metropolitan's audience.

On the morning after my return, among the letters on my breakfast tray was one in an unknown hand. I slit the envelope, and unfolded the single sheet of paper it contained.

And read as follows:

TO A CERTAIN MADAME FRANCES ALDA
AS DESDEMONA
AT THE METROPOLITAN OPERA HOUSE
February 22, 1912

If we had lived long years ago
And I had been born Othello,
I would not have strangled you in bed
At the hint of a lying fellow.

If we had lived long years ago
And your love had been given to me,
Iago and all the fiends in hell
Could never have slandered thee.

Poor Desdemona's fate was sad,
And I'm sorry too for Othello,
But a woman who's white should never wed
With a man who is black or yellow.

Well, anyway, the sentiment is all right.

A few days before my accident while singing Desdemona, I had made a record of the famous 'Ave Maria.' I remember the first time I heard it was while I was convalescing after my appendicitis operation.

They wheeled the phonograph into my bedroom, put on the trial record, and played it for me.

I burst into tears.

It was terrible!

If I sounded like that, it was no wonder Othello crept in to murder me. The only surprising thing about it was that the audience didn't rise *en masse* and help him do it.

When I was up and about again, I made another record. This time, to my satisfaction.

It was Caruso who first turned my thoughts toward phonograph records, and what a deep satisfaction these are to a singer, whose ever-present sadness is the knowledge that his art is so evanescent, so subject to the changes brought by age or ill health; so quick to be forgotten when the singer is gone.

Quite apart from being a source of revenue for many years,

the records a singer makes are his own treasury in later years, a real repository of his art.

The first records I ever made were with Caruso. He came to me one day and asked if I would sing with him the 'Miserere' from *Trovatore*. He had tried singing it with several sopranos, but the results did not satisfy him.

'You know what I have often told you,' he said. 'Your voice and mine blend perfectly. I have never found that with any other woman singer. The combination should make a record that is absolutely perfect.'

He told me he was going over to Camden, New Jersey, to make the trial record, and asked me to go with him.

I agreed.

I remember it was a cold, rainy, sleety day. One of those winter mornings that kill off all impulse to be anything more ambitious than a sit-by-the-fire. But we started in my motor from the Knickerbocker for the Pennsylvania Station.

On the way Caruso looked at my feet.

'*Sapristi!* Where are your rubbers?'

'I never wear them.'

'You don't wear rubbers and in a climate that can spit at you as it is doing now? And you aspire to be a singer!'

'I am a singer,' I retorted. 'Also I am a woman. Also, if you will notice, I have pretty feet.'

I stuck them out, in very high-heeled patent-leather pumps with cut-steel buckles.

'Why should I swaddle them in rubber overshoes when there are motors to take me where I want to go?'

He leaned to look out of the car window, searching (I could guess) for a shop that sold overshoes. Then he looked at his watch.

'There isn't time now, but when we get to Camden....' he threatened me.

During the journey he kept on lecturing me on the absolute necessity of guarding the voice from the effects of damp feet.

He did it humorously, in the rôle of the severe parent to a naughty child, but there was a sincere counsel in his words -- as I knew.

Even so, I was not prepared for what happened next.

At Philadelphia, we got into the car that had been sent to the station to meet us and take us to Camden.

'Drive to a shoe shop,' Caruso told the driver.

Arrived at one, he bundled me unceremoniously out of the car across the wet sidewalk, and into the shop.

'This lady wants a pair of rubbers,' he told the clerk. 'They must be the finest, most beautiful, stylish rubbers you have in stock because you will notice the lady has very beautiful feet and she is very proud of them. Now what have you?'

The amazed clerk had recognized Caruso at once, of course. Photographs of the great tenor appeared frequently in the newspapers, and Caruso in the flesh (unlike so many stage and motion-picture stars) looked unmistakably like his own photographs. The clerk began at once tumbling out boxes of rubbers of every sort and size.

I kept protesting I didn't want rubbers. I wouldn't wear them. But Caruso turned a deaf ear.

'Put out your foot!' he commanded me in Italian.

I put it out and he, dropped on one knee, took the rubbers from the clerk and began trying them on me, the while he repeated in Italian, from *La Bohème*, Rudolfo's love speeches. With extravagant emphasis on the most ardent phrases, and gestures, sometimes with a rubber, that made the clerk's eyes pop out of his head.

So on one day, I had my first pair of rubbers and made my first phonograph record.

I shall never forget how eager Caruso was to hear it, and how carefully he listened for any flaws or imperfections.

'It's perfect, *padrocina mia*,' he shouted, and caught me by both hands and hugged me. His confidence in it was proven by the sales of the record, which outran all others.

True enough, his voice and mine blended so completely that they became one voice. The voice of humanity — male and female — joined into one.

In those years while Gatti and I lived at the Knickerbocker, we saw a great deal of Caruso. When we went abroad after the close of the opera season, in May, 1912, and when the horror of the *Titanic* disaster was still upon everyone, he crossed on the same ship with us.

With every turn of the ship's engines he became more and more eager to see his sons and to immerse himself in Italy.

He would make two or three turns about the deck, the cynosure of all eyes, then he would drop down in the chair next to my own and talk to me for hours. About the boys; about his family, which was one of those closely entwined, truly Neapolitan families, almost patriarchal in its devotion to its own vine and fig tree; and, ultimately, about Giachetti.

The hours he talked to me about that woman!

Didn't somebody say somewhere: 'Never fall in love with a man or woman you could hate'?

Rubbish!

As though you could ever hate anyone with whom you could not, if the same degree of emotional intensity were directed in the opposite direction, fall in love.

The story of Caruso and Ada Giachetti, the mother of his sons, is one of those stories that shocks you because it reveals too much of what lies beneath and behind all violent love affairs.

They had met at Livorno, where he first sang Rudolfo in *La Bohème*. Giachetti was Mimi. She was older than Caruso, and already married. When they met, they fell in love. Of course, there is no divorce in Italy; which meant that the lovers had to choose between separation and living together without the sanction of law and church.

They chose the latter.

When Caruso came to America the first time, Giachetti came

with him as 'Mrs. Caruso.' Three children were born to them; two lived to grow up. Caruso proudly gave them his name.

Then Caruso learned that while he was in America Giachetti was unfaithful to him. She was living with a lover in the villa Caruso had given her. The lover was none other than their own chauffeur!

The emotional shock of that discovery almost unbalanced Caruso. (He told me the story himself, as simply as a child.) He went and stood before the gates of the villa and called Giachetti's name over and over till she came out. He prostrated himself in the dust and begged her to send the man away and not see him again.

She promised to do this, and they were reconciled.

That autumn Caruso returned to the Metropolitan while Giachetti remained in Italy with the children. Presently, it was reported to the tenor that the same handsome young chauffeur was being seen with Madame Giachetti. Instantly all the intensity of his love was turned to hate and to a frantic desire for revenge. It led him to make love to Ada's sister, Rina Giachetti, another singer. At the same time he took every means in his power to make Italy so uncomfortable for the woman he once had loved — that she was really forced to go to South America.

She died there, I have heard, in very tragic circumstances.

The memory of these recent bitter experiences, which at that time still had an emotional power over him, used to overwhelm Caruso at times and cast a darkness over his naturally gay and fun-loving disposition. Usually I could bring him out of the black moods with a joke, or by encouraging him to tease me, which he adored doing.

It was seldom he could resist an opportunity for a practical joke.

When Humperdinck arrived in New York, Caruso, in an overcoat with a turned-up collar and a muffler wrapped about his chin, and a large black slouch hat pulled down to conceal the upper part of his face, went to meet the composer of *Hänsel and Gretel*. Posing as a reporter, with a notebook and pencil in hand, he began shouting at Humperdinck all sorts of ridiculous questions about the new opera *Koenigskinder* whose première Humperdinck had come to America to attend.

When the composer's alarm and fear of this eccentric American newspaper man who was obviously quite crazy had reached the limit of endurance, Caruso pulled off the disfiguring muffler and hat, threw both arms about Humperdinck, and embraced him in true Neapolitan fashion.

His gift for mimicry was inimitable.

Once I remember, after a performance of *Bohème*, we were bowing before the curtain after the First Act, the ushers were handing many, many flowers across the footlights to me. (Then the custom was permitted.) There I stood, bowing, smiling, my arms full of roses, and ready to slip behind the curtains backstage when Caruso should take my hand to retire with me. One tall basket of roses remained on the edge of the stage. The chance for a bit of pantomime, which he dearly loved, was too much for Caruso. He refused to look at me, instead he went forward to the flowers. The exaggerated expression of discomfiture which he had assumed while the ushers handed me the bouquets, he changed now to one of equally exaggerated hopefulness. While the audience leaned forward, silent, watchful, not quite understanding what all this was about, any more than I did, he bent over the basket, found the card attached, read it, turned and looked at me, then at the audience, his face the picture of disappointment. By this time I was laughing. I dropped the flowers I was holding, ran forward, took up the basket, pulled out a rose, and gave it to Caruso. Whereupon his face broke into an ecstatic smile. He caught my hand, and together, while the audience laughed, we ran offstage.

I was so genuinely fond of him, and his emotional state after his final break with Giachetti was so distressing, that I was delighted when he brought Dorothy Benjamin and introduced her to me. She was a tall, beautiful blonde girl. Later Caruso told me they were to be married, though her father opposed the match bitterly.

THE *réclame* of *The Girl of the Golden West* may not have outlasted its second season on the Metropolitan's program, but like a busy hound, it started up the hare of American opera by American composers, and sung in English.

Why, some of the public argued, should a truly American theme such as was found in *The Girl* be handled by an Italian composer who could not be expected to give the libretto a truly American score? And why, if the opera were American in setting, sing it in Italian?

The idea of American grand opera, in English, was not new. When Gatti first came to the Metropolitan he proposed to the directors that they offer a prize for a new grand opera to be written by an American composer, and with a libretto in English. In May, 1911, the judges awarded the prize — one thousand dollars — to Horatio Parker for *Mona*.

The opera was given at the Metropolitan during the following season with Homer in the title rôle; but neither the critics nor the public approved it sufficiently for it to be repeated during the next season.

Walter Damrosch had been one of the three judges who selected *Mona* for the award.

Shortly afterward he came to Gatti and asked him and Toscanini to come to his house one evening to hear an opera he had composed eight or nine years before and which he had recently revised.

This was *Cyrano de Bergerac*.

The libretto, in English, was by William J. Henderson, now music critic for *The Sun*. In it he had followed closely the outlines of Rostand's famous play, which Walter Hampden later produced on Broadway.

Gatti and Toscanini heard Damrosch play the score through. They asked him to rewrite the Fourth Act, and when that had been done, Gatti accepted *Cyrano* for the Metropolitan.

'You will sing Roxane,' Gatti said to me. 'Amato will sing Cyrano, and Martin the tenor rôle, Christian.'

The première was set for February 27, 1913.

I remember when the rehearsals began, we all groaned over the length of the piece. The rehearsals lasted from five to five and a half hours.

'Starting at eight, that will bring the final curtain down at 2 A.M.!' I said to Gatti. 'Fine and dandy. You know nobody will stay in the opera house after eleven o'clock. We'll be singing the last two acts to empty seats.'

Persuading Damrosch to make the necessary cuts was not accomplished without protestations and objections and argument. Finally, the opera was reduced to a more reasonable length. These cuts, which were marked in pencil on our scores, created a certain amount of confusion at the rehearsals. Especially as certain portions of Mr. Damrosch's music had an elusive familiarity about it that brought up vagrant memories of too many other scores one had heard.

We were rehearsing one day. I had just finished my first duet with Amato. The pencil marks on my score were misleading.

'Where do we go from here?' I asked Amato.

Before he could reply, Hageman, the assistant conductor, who was rehearsing us, spoke up:

'From Gounod to Meyerbeer.'

In fact, the number of familiar passages we found in *Cyrano* began to be more or less of a joke with us artists.

Nor shall I ever forget during another rehearsal, I was sitting in the stalls when I saw Pini-Corsi, who sang the part of a monk, standing at the side of the stage alone and quite grave. He held his hat in his hand. As the opera went on, now and again he placed his hat over his heart and so holding it, made a courtly bow.

To no one.

I watched him do this three or four times, then my curiosity couldn't stand it any longer. I got up and went over to him.

'Whatever are you doing?' I asked, speaking in Italian.

'I am saluting the spirits of the dead masters,' he gravely replied.

But as far as press notices and society's approval went, *Cyrano's* première was a success. I remember Amato and I took nine curtain calls after the First Act. And after the balcony scene, which was romantic and very appealing, there were calls for the author, who came forward and made a little speech of appreciation.

We had sung two or three performances of *Cyrano* and were to sing a fourth. In the middle of the afternoon about three hours before I expected to go to the opera house to make up for Roxane, Gatti telephoned me.

'I have just heard from Amato. He is ill. He cannot sing to-night.'

'What are you going to do?' I demanded.

'Immediately I heard the news, I rang up Caruso. You and he shall sing *Bohème* in place of *Cyrano*. That is the best thing I can think of to do.'

'It suits me,' I told him.

And it did.

Apparently, too, the audience which had come to hear *Cyrano* did not object to listening instead to the wistful love story of Mimi and Rodolfo — as interpreted by Puccini.

But a story went around the opera house that Mr. Damrosch, coming in that night to hear his opera, and knowing nothing of Amato's illness, sat for awhile, then inquired:

'Who changed my scenery?'

Cyrano did not live for more than that one season.

The next September, while Gatti and I were in Paris, I received the following letter:

Hotel de la Trémoille,
Rue de la Trémoille,
Champs Élysées
Sept. 15/13

DEAR MADAME ALDA:

I am so sorry not to have found you at home this morning and as you are leaving Paris and we sail on the 24th, I shall not see you until you return to New York.

Mr. Gatti gave me the mournful news that *Cyrano* is not to be given this winter.

Naturally I am sorry, but suppose its success was not great enough to warrant a reproduction.

However, you made an undoubted success of Roxane and deserved every bit of it and more, too, and I wish you lots more of it for the coming season.

Very sincerely yours,
WALTER DAMROSCH

The Metropolitan made one more attempt at giving American opera in English — the next season when Gatti produced Victor Herbert's one-act *Madeleine*, in which I sang the title rôle.

The story had been adapted from the French. It dramatized an opera singer, a spoiled darling (are there opera singers like that, outside the pages of romantic drama? I doubt it) who tried in vain to get either her lover, his rival, a humble friend of the singer's own humble childhood days, or even her own maid to spend New Year's Day with her. Each one has promised to spend the holiday with his or her mother. The example of so much filial piety recalls to Madeleine Fleury memories of her own mother, and the play ends with the heroine kissing her mother's portrait.

Sentimental — of course.

But when did sentimentality ruin a play?

As for *Madeleine* being grand opera, no one, not even its composer, pretended it was.

It wasn't the sentimentality that oppressed me in the rôle of Madeleine. It was the fact that the part, as originally written, gave me yards of recitative, but nothing to sing.

I complained of this, to Gatti. Loudly.

'What's the use of your paying me to sing a rôle that hasn't any singing in it?'

And I reminded him of what he knew very well: that my whole art, if art I have, is to sing singable music.

'I've got to have *legato*.'

'Now, now, try not to get mad, *tesoro mio*.'

Gatti, in the double rôle of husband of a prima donna who was being very *exigeante* and director of the opera company that engaged her, and looking very unhappy in both, tried to override my objections to playing Victor Herbert's heroine.

At last I got it across to him. It wasn't just my *amour propre* that was offended by the sentimental innocuousness of Madeleine. But how could any director expect an audience who knew me in rôles of dramatic passion, like Manon Lescaut, and who were used to hearing me sing Mimi and Marguerite and Desdemona, to find me commendable in a milk-and-water part?

It just didn't make sense.

It was I — not Gatti — who put it up to Victor Herbert when we began to rehearse.

'I *must* have something to sing.'

Herbert drew his brows together, frowning, as he considered my objection.

'Give me until tomorrow,' he said.

The next day he came to see me. From his pocket he produced some sheets of paper on which was written, in pencil, an aria.

'Try this.'

He sat at my piano and played it through for me. It was charming.

I sang it, and it suited my voice perfectly.

It was the one bit of music in *Madeleine* that won real applause from the house when we gave the opera.

If there's a moral to be found in this story, it must be that sometimes it is not only worthwhile, but absolutely imperative to register one's objections, and with no doubt concerning the force of them.

It was while the Madeleine controversy was still an issue between Gatti and me — before the little aria was written — that Gatti telegraphed me (I was away on a concert tour).

'I am going to give you a performance of the *Tales of Hoffmann*. You shall sing Giulietta.'

In many opera companies it is usual for one soprano to sing the three 'heroines' of Offenbach's fantasy: the Doll, in Act One; Giulietta, the Venetian courtesan in Act Two; and Antonie, the delicate young girl who is the heroine of the Third Act.

Naturally, it is seldom that one artist can play these three entirely dissimilar rôles with distinction.

Gatti had cast Frieda Hempel for the beautiful but unresponsive Doll, and Bori for the fading Antonie. Between these two 'loves' of the poet Hoffmann, in the exotic Venetian scene whose theme is found in the languorous, amorous music of the gondolier's song — the well-known barcarole — I was to appear.

Hempel, Bori, and Alda. In one performance. With Carl Jorn singing Hoffmann.

Oh, Gatti was shrewd! No opera director knew better than he how to fill those tiers on tiers of loges and seats, up to the topmost gallery sacred to ardent music-lovers and students — many of them in a city like New York, foreign-born and with nostalgic memories of La Scala and opera houses in Warsaw and old, imperial St. Petersburg, and Rome and Buenos Aires.

I had not sung Giulietta at the Metropolitan before. But I remembered, soon after I came, seeing Fremstad in the rôle, and feeling that the artist who reached great heights as the temptress in Parsifal failed in the part of the mondaine Venetian courtesan.

The day of the dress rehearsal came. Hempel, rotund and flaxen-haired, was perfect as the German 'doll.' I wore my gorgeous Venetian costume of cloth of gold with a wig of long auburn hair twined with pearls, and knew that at least I looked like one of Casanova's memories, in the days of the Venetian decadence.

But when the curtain for the Third Act went up, still in my make-up, I was sitting in one of the orchestra stalls with some invited guests. At sight of the costume that had been made for Bori to wear, the women among us made that little tch-tch tongue sound of dismay.

The dress itself was not pretty, which was too bad. But what was worse, the cut and color were fatal to Bori's ethereal style.

I suppose only a woman who has been on the stage for more seasons than she cares to count fully understands how an unbecoming costume affects the audience's judgment of an artist. Some of the women in the house may be conscious of exactly what is wrong. In their estimate of the performance, they may be able to distinguish between the singer's voice and her interpretation of the rôle, which may be exquisite, and her costume, which may be appallingly ugly.

But not all the women present will be so subtle in their understanding. And practically none of the men in the audience will know any more than that they reacted unpleasantly to that particular singer that night.

'Bori? Oh, I don't think much of her,' would be their appraisal.

Knowing this, all the while the rehearsal of Act Three went on, I studied Bori in the rôle.

Antonie is young and sad. The shadow of her approaching death is already upon her. One senses, in the music, that this third love affair of Hoffmann's is destined to end tragically. Is not the whole opera meant to portray man who is forever thwarted by an enemy — which is himself? Who is forever robbed of the happiness he seeks?

Antonie, I thought, ought to be dressed in grey — a color which is neither young nor old, but belongs to all ages. The cut of the dress should be youthful and demure and chaste.

Grey chiffon, I decided. Made to the ankles and full. With a delicate fichu crossed over the breast to tie about the waist in back. And a white lace cap — a filmy cobweb of a cap — to enhance the exquisite childlike loveliness of Hoffmann's love, coming after his experiences with the Venetian courtesan. Such a costume would not only express Antonie but would be extremely becoming to Lucrezia Bori and show her at her very best.

Directly the rehearsal was over, I went back to my dressing-room and sent for the wardrobe mistress. I explained to her my idea.

'Will you make a costume like that for Miss Bori?'

'Madame!' She threw up her hands in consternation. 'The performance is only two days off. Impossible!'

'Impossible, nothing,' I retorted.

That word 'impossible'! It does something to my metabolism or blood pressure or subconscious, or whatever portion of our anatomy or psyche the latest fad says registers indignation for us. Isn't the so-called 'impossible' the only thing worth trying to do?

It is for me; I know that.

I've done the impossible most of my life, and triumphed in it. My failures have not been there, but in the realm of the easily possible, in which women with one third my energy and courage and capacity succeed every day.

So the wardrobe mistress's dictum that it was too late to make a new costume for Bori was just the extra fillip my inspiration needed to ensure getting it done.

No matter now what threats or bribes or cajolery I used. The wardrobe mistress went away shaking her head dubiously. But, after all, I was the wife of the director.

When the night of the performance came, and Bori arrived to make up for her part, there in her dressing-room hung, not the costume in which she had sung at the dress rehearsal, but a new one, of pale grey chiffon, with the lace fichu and cap.

And no explanations as to how it got there, or who had ordered it.

She looked exquisite and charming in it.

No one who saw her that night, and at the two or three subsequent performances of the *Contes d'Hoffmann*, was happier than I in her success as Antonie.

Bori was one of the members of the company — almost the only one among the women artists — whom I really liked a lot.

No one felt more troubled than I when because of illness that affected her voice she had to leave the Metropolitan in 1915. And no one was more eager than I to welcome her back when she returned, cured, four or five years later.

Those years of illness — and enforced silence — cost Bori heavily. I remember, she was frequently worried about her financial future.

'If only Gatti will keep me on for a few years,' she confided to me when she rejoined the company.

'He'll keep you,' I promised.

And he did.

Except for the *réclame* she had in *L'Amore dei Tre Re*, which Gatti produced in 1914, Bori's popularity as an artist did not come until those later years — the last five or six years of Gatti's directorship.

In view of so many experiences shared, so many friends and acquaintances held in common, so many confidential hours together, I confess I was at a loss to understand something that happened when the 'Save the Metropolitan' campaign was launched.

As part of the publicity attendant on that campaign, Bori organized a Gala Benefit Night at the Metropolitan. At this every singer of any note who had ever been a member of the company — and who could limp or hobble in at the stage entrance and still sing a note — was invited to take part.

Except Frances Alda.

Why?

I had only left the company two years before, and at the time was broadcasting twice a week from New York. My home at Great Neck, Long Island, is within forty-five minutes' motor-drive of the opera house.

It is true that before that time Gatti and I had been divorced, and he had since married Rosina Galli, the mistress of the ballet. But it is also true that we have remained the best of friends, consulting one another whenever necessary. It is a fact that the day before Gatti sailed from America he spent at my house in Great Neck.

Did Bori believe that it would be too embarrassing for me, or for Gatti, who as retiring director was very much in the limelight on the night of the Gala — or even, perhaps, for Rosina, the 'second Madame Gatti-Casazza' — for me to be on the stage that night with Sembrich, and Farrar, and Frieda Hempel, and Bori herself, and many, many other artists who had made Gatti-Casazza's directorate famous?

But she did not ask me. Nor did anyone ever explain to me, or to the public, how it happened that the singer whose engagement with the company had been longer than that of any other prima donna, with the exception of Sembrich, alone of the Metropolitan's artists, was not there for the Gala Benefit organized to 'save' the opera house where she had sung many hundreds of times.

That evening, at Casa Mia, I turned the radio dial until I picked up the broadcast coming from the Metropolitan. I heard the various voices so familiar to me. I heard Hempel sing 'The Last Rose of Summer,' that exquisite song which I had sung dozens of times in Flotow's *Martha*. I heard Grace Moore sing 'Home, Sweet Home.' Patti sang it years ago when she was at the Academy of Music, before the Metropolitan Opera House was built. When the old Academy of Music was to be torn down, there was a special memorial concert at which I was chosen to impersonate Adelina Patti and sang 'The Last Rose of Summer' ...

A thing like that hurts. There's no use pretending it doesn't.

Didn't I say somewhere awhile back that there was going to be no pretense in this book? It was going to be about me as I was and as I am; sometimes with my make-up on, but more often without it.

Now you see me without it; wondering, as the radio brought the songs and the speeches and the applause to me, what there is in the atmosphere of the stage and opera house that is so fatal to the quality we call gratitude.

Fortunately, for those of us who are sensitive to lack of this in someone to whom we have tried to be hospitable and kind, there are other souls, really great ones, in whom gratitude for even very small favors springs eternal.

They are the true friends.

And in this connection I would tell a story of Harrison Williams. Everybody knows who he is. But back in the years before the Great War, when he first came to New York from the Mid-West, very few people knew him.

In those days he came to call on me — with a note of introduction from some friends with whom I had stayed a few days in Cleveland. They asked me to be nice to him.

To be nice to anyone as young, as interesting, and as attractive as Harrison Williams was the easiest thing in the world. I don't recall that I did anything except ask him to dinner a few times, when there would be present older men of importance in the business and banking world. Nothing more. But Harrison Williams and I became friends. Best of all, we remained friends. Even after he himself became one of the powers 'Downtown' and a very rich man. Occasionally, he would ring me up, or drop in at my apartment at teatime to give me a word of shrewd advice about my investments.

Those words made money for me.

When the Crash came — on that day of 1929, when everyone's securities began tobogganing out of sight, and everyone's security went soaring over the top of the newly-completed Empire State Building, I, like several million others, stood gasping for breath. No use for me to try to recapture the spirit of those first days. The first time I went to San Francisco, people I met there described to me their experiences during the earthquake and fire. When the Boom exploded, I underwent all the sensations my California friends had described so graphically.

Sometime during the first week of horror I wrote a note to Harrison Williams. I described my immediate situation in regard to a large bank loan, and asked him to telephone me his advice.

Scotti, Alda, Caruso

Elsa Maxwell at the Lido

A fishing bet with Charlie Chaplin

Alda and Mary Garden

I heard nothing for twenty-four hours.

Then I had a message from the bank. The managers informed me that they had received from Mr. Williams a number of securities to be placed against my account, which redeemed my waning credit many times over.

Feeling weak in the knees, as one does when the relief from anxiety touches one more acutely than the anxiety itself, I sat down and wrote Harrison a note of thanks.

Next day, I had this in reply in his own handwriting:

> DEAR ALDA:
> When I first came to New York you did me a favor. I don't forget.
>
> HARRISON WILLIAMS

In all my experience, that note and the writer's act of friendliness stand out as the height of gratitude and generosity.

Busy years.

Now, looking back over them, they seem like a kaleidoscope, one of those painted metal cylinders filled with flecks of colored paper. My grandmother used to get one for me every Christmas because I loved them and played with them so much that one year's Christmas toy never lasted into the New Year. You shook the box and then squinted one eye to look with the other through the peep-hole at one end of the cylinder. And lo! a pattern, magically achieved. You shook the box (how vigorously I shook it!) and looked again. A different pattern this time.

Let us shake the box.

Now look.

It is no longer New York, no longer the Metropolitan Opera House. It is Paris, and the boat train from Cherbourg is arriving at the Gare St. Lazare.

And it is May, 1914.

All the way across Normandy, the historic land of Calvados. with its apple orchards a rosy bower about the old, brown stone farmsteads and *manoirs* that are so much more English than are many things in England, I have been staring out the carriage window. I have been scarcely conscious of the scenery, though I love that corner of France.

On the opposite seat, Gatti has sat ever since the train started, with his nose buried in one after another of the stack of French newspapers bought in Cherbourg immediately upon landing.

Occasionally he sniffs. Disapproving, I surmise, this or that policy of Briand's. Once I hear him groan.

'That'll be Clemenceau,' I think. 'Wonder what the old boy is up to now.'

But my interest in the French political scene passes as lightly as my interest in the blue-painted farm carts drawn by chunky Norman mares, and driven by blue-bloused farmers with uncovered round Norman heads who halt at the road crossings for the *rapide* to pass.

My mind is already in Paris. It has run on ahead of me to a house where I have never been but which is to be 'home.' It is busy wondering what delicious surprise is in store for me when the door of that new home is opened and I cross its threshold.

To explain, I must flash this story back one year. Whilst Gatti and I were in Paris during 1913, he introduced me to some old friends of his, Count and Countess Trotti. The former was then one of the greatest collectors and connoisseurs of antique furniture in the world. At that time I was finding my old apartment in the Avenue Bugeaud too small and too crowded for Gatti and myself.

'We must move,' I declared. 'We must find a larger apartment and furnish it.'

I said this once in Count Trotti's hearing. His eyes began to sparkle.

'Let me find an apartment for you,' he suggested. 'You have not the time to go seeking a place. Tell me what you must have in the number and arrangement of rooms. And what rent you will pay. Then leave the rest to me. And leave the furnishings to me. I know your taste, Signora — Louis Quinze and Seize. And now and then something Italian of the same period. As though an eighteenth-century French exquisite had travelled in his coach across the Alps and down to Milan and to Venice, and returned, bringing back with him — memories. I will furnish the apartment completely. My wife will engage the servants. When you return next year you will have only to open the door and be at home.

'And whatever you do not like that I choose — you will not have to keep. There will be a tag on everything in the apartment, telling its period, its maker, and the purchase price. Those pieces you do not want to keep, you may send back to me.'

Well, what would one say to such an offer as that?

Only that fairy tales *do* come true sometimes.

All that winter in New York between rehearsals, performances, concerts, social engagements, and hours of practising, I had felt my anticipation growing like a hothouse plant. Now, with the soil of France actually, if not under my feet, at least under the wheels of the railway carriage, that anticipation was rapidly getting out of control.

Then came a curve of misty grey river, and across it a sudden vista of roofs, chimneys, church spires, the skeleton *Tour Eiffel* —

Paris!

I pulled at the newspaper that enshrouded my sphinx-like husband.

'Gatti! We're there!'

It was like a fairy-tale adventure, driving through the city that, no matter how often I come back to it, always holds a thrill of wonder and happy expectancy for me, to the address on the Champ de Mars.... Giving our names to the bowing concierge ... going up, up in one of those extraordinary self-sufficient lifts one finds in France.... Ringing one's own doorbell ... having Paul, one's own butler (though you never had seen him before that minute), throw wide the double doors into what seemed to me a treasure house of beautiful, rare, old things.

And then the fun of going about from room to room examining, studying, exclaiming over this and that perfect piece of furniture, or silver, or brocade or *petit point*. Discovering, on a second visit to the room, something missed the first time.

'What will you keep?' Gatti asked me anxiously.

'Everything' was my enthusiastic reply.

I did, too — almost everything. I went through all the agonies of trying to be economical. (Authentic eighteenth-century French furniture comes high. There were two *bergères*, covered in *petit point*, rich yellow and blue, whose cost, estimated in American currency, was two thousand dollars each!)

I succeeded only so far as to send back half a dozen or so pieces. Among them was a little satinwood table whose tag read 'Fs 5000.' (This was two months before August, 1914, remember, and the francs, like the Dionnes, were arriving five to a dollar.) But I've never ceased to regret that little table and the impulse toward prudence and economy and self-denial that prompted me to send it back.

Those virtues are awfully hard ones to keep in their right place, I find. They have ways of creeping upon you when you least suspect them, and of suddenly taking the stage and the conductor's desk and the prompter's box and directing you to play a part you don't want to play and which you don't play very well.

But I loved that apartment on the Champ de Mars with all the lovely remembered things from the Avenue Bugeaud and the new treasures Count and Countess Trotti had added.

When Gatti talked of our going to Italy I held out. I didn't want to go.

'We can come back about the first of September,' Gatti promised me. 'And you can have six weeks here in Paris before we sail.'

'*Va bene*,' I agreed, and I chalked that promise up where I could see it mentally every day.

We went to Italy. It was the twenty-eighth of June. Midsummer. When we left the train at Milan to spend the night there before starting next morning for Ferrara, I remember some men with stacks of freshly printed newspapers passed us, hurrying to the station bookstalls.

Gatti pulled one of the men's sleeve to catch his attention, then held out a few centesimi. The man flipped a paper from the pile he carried and handed it to my husband, then went on.

Gatti unfolded the sheet.

Black headlines ran across the top of the front page. Below were photographs of a man and a woman.

'What's happened?' I demanded.

'Austrian archduke murdered,' he replied laconically.

'Oh, if that's all ...'

My attention went back to my maid and Gatti's valet, who were directing the procession of porters with our luggage.

All ...

Well, that is how most people felt about it that July of 1914. Though Gatti pursed his lips and shook his head and read every newspaper he could get his hands on, and talked interminably with some of the men we met at Monte Cattini.

It seemed to me they were making a most unwarranted fuss over the loss of one archduke — not very fine-looking, either — and his morganatic wife.

Europe had so many archdukes in those days.

We were still at Monte Cattini when the various countries began to mobilize — Serbia, Russia, Germany, France — Belgium invaded ... England declaring war ...

The thing didn't make sense.

'What's going to happen?' I asked Gatti when he came into my room one morning.

'It has happened,' he replied. 'It's the war everybody has known for years was coming. Now it's come ...'

'What'll we do?'

He shrugged. 'Go back to America, as fast as we can get there.'

'But I'm going to Paris,' I objected.

He spread a bevy of newspapers over the bed in which I was lying.

'Look...'

I read that France was mobilizing, Paris was an armed camp; foreigners and tourists were fleeing like locusts before a storm.

I think then the gravity of the situation dawned on me.

'But the apartment in the Champ de Mars!'

What a prophecy there was in that address!

'And all my lovely things! Giulio, I've *got* to go back.'

I threw off the coverlet, sending the newspapers helter-skelter. I sat up and thrust out my feet for my slippers.

'When is the next train to get out of here? How soon can I get to Paris? Get me a telegraph blank so I can wire Paul that I am coming.'

But the wire to Paul brought the reply that he had been mobilized. The other menservants were gone, too. The railway officials didn't encourage our trying to cross the border into France. They reported that the French railways were filled with troop trains.

So I did not go back to the Champ de Mars. I never saw the apartment again. By telegraph we arranged to have it padlocked and sealed. Then Gatti and I went to Naples. Gatti had wired all the members of the Metropolitan Opera Company who were summering in Europe to start at once for Naples and the S.S. *Canopic*, on which he engaged all the space available.

'The Metropolitan Noah's Ark,' the papers called that ship when she docked in New York bringing nearly a score of artists whose contracts compelled them to be in New York for the rehearsals before the opening of the opera season.

Soon after we reached New York, I had word that Paul had been killed in the very first week he was at the front.

'How long do you think the war will last?' I asked my husband.

'Three years,' he replied.

'Three years! It's impossible. Three months maybe.'

Well, you know which one of us was right that time.

Even though I didn't agree with Gatti about the amount of endurance of horror and suffering that the world could show, I thought I knew how accurate his judgment of European political conditions was. So I considered his prophecy carefully.

Up to this time, we had been living in hotel suites, as so many artists do live. That arrangement was satisfactory for the seven months of the year we were in New York, both of us intensely busy with our work, and I away a good deal on concert tours. When I began to feel myself without roots, I could think of the apartment in Paris which was 'home.'

But if Gatti was right, and the war should last three years, during which time we would not be able to go to Europe, then we should need a home in America.

I thought about it a good deal, without saying anything to Gatti. Then I went out and began looking for an apartment.

The one I ultimately took was on West Fifty-Eighth Street, at the top of the house with a superb view over Central Park. In any place I live, I have to be able to see out and away from me. The apartment had sixteen rooms and six baths. After consulting with the manager of the building and his architect, I got them to open a stairway from my apartment to the servants' rooms on the floor above, so that my household staff could go up and down without using the lifts or the public hall. One room I had made into a conservatory. Another I ordered lined with bookshelves to hold Gatti's three or four thousand books which were tumbling about his office at the opera house and his rooms at the hotel. He had collected books, and many of them rare volumes, for years. But he had no system of arranging them. They were heaped in the corners of his bedroom and his office at the opera house — everywhere. I gathered them together and had many of them rebound, beautifully.

When the lease was signed, I cabled Maples in Paris to dismantle the apartment on the Champ de Mars and to send the furniture to the address on Fifty-Eighth Street, New York.

This was during the late winter of 1915. The war was raging. German Big Berthas were hammering away at Paris; French regiments were feverishly burrowing trenches around Verdun; floating mines and vicious submarines infested the Channel and the waters of the Atlantic.

But the six vanloads of my precious French furniture, crated and packed by the redoubtable Maples, crossed the Atlantic in a ship's hold, passed the United States Customs, rolled up Seventh Avenue to the corner of Fifty-Eighth Street, and were carried upstairs, unpacked and set in place, almost exactly as Count Trotti had originally arranged them in the Paris apartment.

And all this without one precious delicate table leg, or one mirror, being broken. Without the loss of even one drawer knob!

Whilst all this was going forward, Gatti, with his nose buried in the Metropolitan's affairs, was entirely unaware that his wife, aided and abetted by the firm of Maples, was circumventing all the restrictions imposed by the War.

On a smiling March morning, I drove to the opera house and presented myself at Gatti's office. He was seated at his desk busy with some reports.

'Come, Giulio,' I said. 'We have a luncheon engagement.'

He looked up at me, surprised.

'I know nothing of an engagement for today. I am not going.'

'Oh, you must go,' I said. 'It's the Y——s (inventing a name). They live on Fifty-Eighth Street.'

He demurred some more; but as much as he demurred, I insisted. Finally, he came with me. We drove up to the door of the apartment house and went in. We entered the elevator and were whisked up to our own door. It was opened by Campbell, who stayed with us seven years, and was the perfect butler.

Within the hall, as we entered, was a long, carved Italian

chest. On the wall above it hung an antique cope of rosy red brocade. They were the furnishings from the hall in the apartment in the Champ de Mars.

Gatti gave me one look.

But he said nothing.

Only, following a step behind me, he went from the hall to the salon, to my boudoir and bedroom, both arranged as I had had them in Paris; through the conservatory, which was filled with flowering plants, and the dining-room with the furniture Beppino had had made for me in Venice, reproducing exactly the style and decoration of an eighteenth-century painted sideboard and two chairs which he had discovered and bought for me. Then into the library, through Gatti's own suite, through guest rooms and back to the hall.

There he sat down on the long chest.

He spoke. It was the first and only comment he had made since we arrived in the taxi.

'What a pity the ceilings aren't higher!'

Well!

What would you have done?

I burst out laughing.

Was that all he could think of to say? Did he find nothing extraordinary in the fact that six vanloads of antique furniture had been brought from Paris and across the Atlantic in the midst of the most devastating war in history? And all this without one moment of worry or annoyance to him?

He patted my arm.

'But, of course, you're an intelligent woman, *tesoro mio*. I know that. I know it. Of what use to say more?'

And that was that.

TIME and again Gatti would come home to the apartment to lunch (he always *did* come home to lunch) a thundercloud.

'What's the matter, Giulio?' I would ask.

Vague murmurings in Italian that could mean only one thing: something had offended him.

I would catechize: Was it the stage hands? Was Farrar having a new excess of 'temperament'? Were box-office receipts falling off? Had Mr. Kahn discovered a new Russian dancer he wanted to promote?

Shakes of the head to all of these.

Ah-ha!

'Was it Toscanini?'

'Ah...'

Immediately a torrent was loosed.

That *maestro* ... couldn't he understand that an opera house had to be run so that it would pay? Couldn't he grasp the significant fact that so many seats sold at so many dollars a seat amounted to so much? And equally, that so many stars at two thousand, and fifteen hundred, and even twenty-five hundred dollars a performance, and so many choristers at forty-five and fifty dollars a week, and so many musicians at so much, not to mention stage hands, carpenters, scene-shifters, and the like, would amount to a sum equal to or even in excess of that produced by the sale of seats? And yet he wanted them all. There were never enough singers or those fine enough, to satisfy him.

That was a perpetual quarrel between Gatti and Toscanini.

Gatti contended that an opera house, like a soup factory, existed to make money for its shareholders. Toscanini held that it existed as a place in which the best opera could be given. And that unless the best was given — with the best musicians and singers available — then the opera house, whatever the box-office receipts amounted to, was a flat failure and a disgrace. They would wrangle about it for hours.

Gatti would quote Verdi, 'An opera house exists to be filled,' and tell the story of the composer's reply to the telegram sent him by the director of La Scala after one of his operas had been given there and was acclaimed a great success.

'Very nice,' Verdi had wired in response, 'but please inform me of size of receipts at following performances.'

But always Toscanini has been too completely an artist to comprehend this decidedly mercenary point of view. He is one of those who are obsessed all their lives by an insatiable passion of perfection. His devotion to art was so ardent, so whole-souled, that he could not — it was not simply that he *would* not — agree without vehement protest to any presentation that was less than the best that could be achieved.

It was this wide difference between their points of view that caused the final break between Gatti and Toscanini, and Toscanini's resignation from the Metropolitan in 1915.

When he and Carla and their children said good-bye to me before sailing for Italy — not, as in other years, to return to the opera house a few months later — I felt that one of the ties that bound me to the Metropolitan had been broken. Our interests and our fortunes had been bound up with the same enterprise. But, more than this, we had been friends.

Sometimes, when I would be away from New York on a concert tour, Toscanini would write me a funny little letter in English like this one:

New York, *Oct.* 29

Many thanks for your kind letter which made me so happy as you cannot imagine. Presently I am feeling a little better but not yet quite well are you always satisfied with your concerts I congratulate you very much I am often thinking & speaking of you though you are out of sight you are not out of mind. Come back quick your affectionate friend

TOSCANINI

I have, too, a post-card picture of himself sent through the mails on which he pencilled:

> My dearest Alda — Are you still in Venice? May I remember me to you most affectionately. I was in Venice long past and I hope in future. I am here alone I have undertaken a treatment of my eyes.
> My family is at Viareggio. When do you start for America? Do you enjoy yourself? I love you in your health — your cheerful spirits. Happy? I send you a big kiss.
>
> TOSCANINI

I have told how he taught me the rôle of Louise, and that of Mimi in *La Bohème*. Often, when I would be practising in the mornings or in the late afternoon, Toscanini would come to see me.

Then he would wander about my boudoir, stopping to take down from the shelf the little leather-bound music books that once belonged to Marie Antoinette. (Brentano's in Paris collected them for me.)

'Give them to me,' Toscanini would beg.

'But, of course, any little thing like that,' I'd say.

Then he would sit down at the spinet and play for me some of the quaint, tinkly little songs that are written in the books, songs Marie Antoinette and her ladies used to sing and dance to.

Another possession of mine he always coveted was my canary.

It flew in the window of the apartment one day. We advertised in the papers but no one ever claimed it.

It was mine.

I have had many birds, but never one so quick to learn as this one. Very soon it would stand on my shoulder and eat crumbs from my lips. And it loved to perch on the top of the music rack when I sat at the piano and sing with me. Always it kept on the pitch. I would change from one key to another, and the bird would change with me.

Toscanini was crazy to have it.

How I wished, later, that I had given it to him.

Is it a piece of the life-stuff that anything so perfect should find tragedy at the end?

One evening, Mrs. William Randolph Hearst gave a party for me. The supper room was hung with singing birds in cages.

'Choose one, Alda,' she said.

I chose the bird I liked best and took it home. When my own bird saw the newcomer, he hurled himself against the bars of his cage in a frenzy of jealousy. I put the stranger in another room of the apartment where I was sure that his singing would not be heard.

But two days later my first pet was dead, of a broken heart.

'*Senti*, Aldina, you should have given it to me,' Toscanini chided me.

Last winter when Toscanini played his farewell concert at Carnegie Hall I sat with Carla Toscanini in her box. I watched him — grey now, as he was not when he heard me at La Scala and mimicked my Italian.

But the fire in him still undimmed.

Two days before, at one of the big motion-picture theatres, I had watched a conductor who has gained a measure of renown. Such twistings and writhings! Such tossing of head and hands and hair! Such grimaces! Toscanini barely moved a muscle. He kept his eyes closed. No need for him to read the score, since it is all printed indelibly on that prodigious memory of his. Just the lift of a finger, the slightest wave of a hand to quiet the violins, and the music came into its own.

That was the night when the reporters and news photographers overrode Toscanini's request to be allowed to conduct his last concert undisturbed. As he was bowing to the tremendous applause one photographer suddenly took a flashlight. The explosion hurt Toscanini's eyes and he dashed from the stage.

Afterward, I said to Carla:

'I'll go behind and congratulate him.'

'Don't,' she said. 'He's in a very bad temper, anyway. And all this will have made him worse.'

'Don't I know his tempers?' I retorted.

And I do. I've lived through them. Days when he would refuse to speak to anyone, even to Gatti. When he would conduct a whole performance without once raising his eyes to us on the stage. Once, I recall in Philadelphia, thanks to his refusing to look at what we were doing, we finished the matinée twenty minutes ahead of schedule!

However, despite Carla's warnings, I did go round to his dressing-room that last night at Carnegie Hall.

'Alda!'

He grabbed me by both hands and kissed me on both cheeks.

There were tears in my eyes. I know there were in his, too.

In our years together at the Metropolitan, we had both seen so many 'Farewells.'

PART
VI

A PRIMA DONNA ON WHEELS

'*Ave Maria, piena di grazia* . . .
. . . . . .
Prega per chi adorando
A te si prostra,
Prega pel peccator
Pel l'innocente,
E pel debo le oppresso
E pel possente
Misero anch esso
Tua pieta di nostra . . .
. . . . . .
Prega per noi,
Prega per noi,
Prega!
Ave Maria!'

OTHELLO

VI

I N THE seven years I had spent in America, a new amusement had been born — motion pictures.

The first of these I ever saw was in Paris, when I was studying
under Marchesi. Five or six of us young people went one evening
to a tiny music hall in Montmartre to watch an indiscriminate
flicker of figures and captions across a sheet.

'*Tiens! Comme c'est bizarre, ça!* '

None of us was much impressed, as I remember. Certainly I,
for one, did not imagine I was witness to the infancy of the
greatest rival the legitimate stage has ever had.

In New York, in those years between 1908 and 1915, people
laughed about 'the movies,' though every year saw more cine-
mas opened and hundreds of thousands more persons dropping
their nickels and dimes into the coin-boxes in the lobbies where
the mechanical pianos kept up a constant stream of the new
'ragtime,' 'Alexander's Ragtime Band,' 'Oh, Oh, You Beautiful Doll,' 'Everybody's Doing It.' Songs that started Irving
Berlin on the road to fame.

Would 'the movies' ever threaten the prestige and the
popularity of grand opera?

'Impossible,' I should have said then, not visioning a Roxy's
or a Radio Centre, or the existence of enormous ornamental
palaces devoted to 'talkies,' palaces far more elaborate and
luxurious than any opera house in the United States.

Talking pictures ... singing pictures. ... dramas with theme,
songs and choruses and colored lights and operatic numbers.
... Not even Gatti, who knew so accurately what the stage could
be made to do and what the public liked to see, had thought of
these possibilities, I am sure.

But already there was Hollywood, that amazing *papier-mâché* universe where Mary Pickford and Doug Fairbanks and a screamingly funny little English comedian named Chaplin, who did tricks with custard pies, and Mr. and Mrs. Sidney Drew, and Pearl White, the famous heroine of *The Perils of Pauline*, were working hard, and believing they would some day make money.

Most of the successful actors and actresses sneered at 'movie actors.' The opera singers, most of whom knew well enough that their acting was endured for the sake of their voices and art of singing, scarcely gave Hollywood a thought.

Then, sometime late in 1915, we at the Metropolitan heard that Farrar had gone to Hollywood and was making a picture of *Carmen*.

Carmen was one of Farrar's most popular rôles, and one in which the 'gerry-flappers' in the audience most ardently admired her. She sang it frequently during the 1914–1915 season with Caruso or with Martinelli. After her return from Hollywood, Gatti scheduled a *Carmen* for her.

In that performance I sang Michaela.

The part of Michaela, the innocent young cousin of Don José, is one of the principal lyric rôles. In the midst of music tumultuous and passionate it is limpid *bel canto*. Michaela is pure singing. If it isn't sung purely, it's nothing. Nowadays the rôle is usually given to some second-rate artist, for economy's sake. But as a matter of operatic history, every big soprano has sung the rôle. When Calvé sang Carmen, Emma Eames sang Michaela.

The night of the performance came, and the First Act. During the scene with the cigarette girls, Farrar suddenly shook one of them so realistically that the rest of the chorus gasped.

'Hollywood tricks!' Caruso snorted to me. 'What does she think this is? A cinema?'

If there is anything an artist resents — and rightly — it is for another artist to bring forward a bit of *mise en scène* which draws the attention of the audience away from the action or the actor that the author intended to be at that moment the centre of attention. Every singer who has sung Marguerite in *Faust* has been told this story of Calvé: at one performance, during Valentin's death scene, while the company is gathered about him, and he sings his dying accusations of Marguerite's falseness, Calvé as Marguerite suddenly got up and walked across the stage, simulating madness. It was a piece of superb acting. But it was entirely out of place, because it deflected the attention of the audience from Valentin, and the singing of the villagers who have heard Valentin's last words.

Our performance of *Carmen* went on, with no more innovations introduced by Farrar until later. Then, in her struggle with Don José, she fought so vehemently, writhing and twisting about the stage during Caruso's singing, that he suddenly gripped her by the wrist to hold her still.

Just for a moment.

She turned in his grasp, bent her head swiftly, and bit the hand that held her.

Caruso, furious and bleeding, flung her from him.

She went down, smack, on her btm!

I stood staring, my mouth open, entirely forgetting my cue, until called to my senses by a sharp rap of the conductor's baton.

Then curtain.

Immediately the heavy velvet folds hid the stage from the audience, Farrar was up on her feet, and she and Caruso were having it out between them, whilst I tried to soothe them both.

The applause from the other side of the curtain was tremendous and insistent. There was no denying those calls. Hand in hand, smiling, the three of us would come forward to bow; then retire behind the folds where the row was immediately on again.

There were headlines on the front pages of the New York papers next day. 'Miss Farrar a Very Rough Carmen.' The reporters made good copy of it.

Through those years 1915 and 1916 the cataclysm in Europe was jarring America out of smug complacency. Young men were going up to Canada to join Canadian regiments going overseas, or to France to offer their services. I read every news bulletin I could get hold of for reports from the Western front.

After all, I was British. Every drop of Davies blood in my veins felt the challenge of those bombing planes flying over London. France, my grandmother's country, had been my second home after I left Australia. The sons and grandsons and the husbands of those families in Paris in whose homes I had been entertained and where I had sung were dying in the trenches around Verdun.

Brussels, where I had been fêted and made much of — was occupied by the German armies.

I was ardently, vehemently, terrifically pro-Ally.

How could I be otherwise?

But I could not stretch my patriotism to the extent of hating all German music and wanting to have it banned from the opera house or the concert stage.

Can any race or nation lay hold on art and claim it for their own?

It doesn't seem to me that they can.

Beauty has wings. Inherent in beauty is its complete freedom from possession. I couldn't agree with the fanaticism that hissed Wagner during the Great War, any more than I can agree with the Nazi's vicious antagonism to Jewish musicians and scientists today.

However, I suppose it was inevitable that the war fever and the hatred it fostered should have its effect on the popularity of German opera and German artists in America.

In those seasons, and indeed until several years after the Armistice, Italian and French operas led the list at the Metropolitan.

But the war brought a new interest to America. This was the vogue for art, music, and dancing out of Russia. The Russo-Japanese War had given America its first faint cognizance of the fact that the barbaric empire of Peter the Great and Catherine 'the Greater' had a descendant in the empire of the czars. But in 1914 and 1915 Russia leaped to first place as 'news.' What was Russia doing? What could Russia do? What was Russia like?

Very few persons in the world, and practically none in America, could answer those questions, that were on everyone's tongues.

New York audiences had already had a taste of Russian opera in Moussorgsky's *Boris Godounow*, sung two seasons before by Didur and Homer, with Toscanini conducting. Now, subtly aware of the increased interest in all things Russian, Gatti determined to produce *Prince Igor*. Borodin had left the work uncompleted at his death; it had been finished by Rimsky-Korsakoff.

The cast of *Prince Igor* included Amato, in the title rôle; Didur, Luca Botta, de Segurola. And myself, as the Princess Jaroslavna.

We gave the première performance during the Christmas holiday week. Dressing before the performance, in my stiff mediaeval robes of gold brocade, with a Nattier blue veil and a high jewelled headdress of stage emeralds and sapphires, I felt myself like one of those richly gilded ikons one used to see in old Russia brought out during the Christmas feast.

When the curtain went up, revealing me standing very stiff and straight and still against the dark heavy door of the cathedral, I knew the effect I had striven to achieve by the costume had gotten across the footlights to the audience. There was a gasp, then applause.

Lovely? Yes.

But what that applause did to me was just too bad.

Borodin's and Rimsky-Korsakoff's music was beautiful, but difficult to sing. And after the curtain rose I had to sing unaccompanied by the orchestra.

Studying the rôle, I had found the Slavic music difficult. But when the applause broke in between that opening chord and the moment when I was supposed to open my mouth and sing, I felt the most acute terror I have experienced in my stage career.

Was I on pitch?

Was I off it?

I couldn't for the life of me have told you. I waited for the moment when the orchestra would come in, supporting me, with anguish. Not knowing whether it and I would meet harmoniously, or in such a discord that even those in the audience who thought all Russian music was composed of ear-splitting combinations and nerve-racking dissonances would know this was something even Rimsky-Korsakoff had not intended.

I never did get over that fear, all the seasons that we sang *Prince Igor*.

Jaroslavna, who appeared so stately and commanding and assured, was quaking inwardly until after she and the orchestra had met, and as it were, embraced.

The success of this Russian opera gave Otto Kahn the idea of bringing over Diaghileff's Ballet Russe for a season of three weeks after the Metropolitan closed the first of April.

'Kahn is terribly enthusiastic about this ballet,' Gatti told me.

'And you?'

'No, no ...' He shook his head. 'It is terribly expensive. Americans are not going to pay for a whole performance of nothing but dancing. But Kahn won't listen to me. What can I do?'

The Ballet Russe introduced Nijinsky to New York.

What an extraordinary artist he was! Superb in the poetry of his motions; using his body as exquisitely as a singer uses his voice to convey meaning and emotion.

I sat in my box watching those performances, enthralled.

But New Yorkers *en masse* were not readily responsive to dancing in which they themselves did not take part. The young men and girls who 'bunny-hugged' and 'grizzly-beared' and 'bostoned' to the strains of the British Tommy songs that everybody here, as in England, was beginning to sing, would not pay the admission prices.

Artistically, Mr. Kahn's adventure was noteworthy. Financially, as Gatti foretold, it was a real disaster.

'I hope that buries the Diaghileff affair,' was Gatti's comment.

More successful in every way was Gatti's staging of Rimsky-Korsakoff's *Coq d'Or* a few seasons later. The rôle of the Queen was sung by Maria Barrientos, and in the pantomime, which parallels the action of the opera, the same rôle was danced by Rosina Galli.

There would seem to be an ironic gesture of Fate in casting for the same part Barrientos, who had at one time been engaged to Gatti-Casazza, and Rosina Galli, whom he married after I divorced him.

Galli had joined the Metropolitan Company in 1914. She was a very finished artist, having fulfilled the promise she showed when I saw her dance at La Scala six years before. Like me, she had a rather pretty face but too fat a figure.

Isn't there, in every active life, a year or two of high tide?

In such seasons it would seem as though the Fates that sometimes smile and sometimes frown have suddenly taken it into their heads to give you all the things you've wanted. To make all your efforts successful, to open every way you feared was closed.

So wonderful is it that you feel you must walk delicately, scarcely breathing, lest, by a breath, you break the spell.

The years 1915 and 1916 were like that for me.

High tide and midsummer.

The summer of 1916, Gatti went alone to Europe to see his parents and on business for the Metropolitan. I rented a house at De Soris' Point, Long Island, the old home of Charles Dana, and there I spent happy days, swimming, sailing, playing tennis, yachting with old Captain Delamar, whose daughter Alice was one of my best friends.

'What do you do with all your money, Alda?' he asked me one day.

We were out on the Sound in his yacht at the time, running before a stiff west wind. I felt gay and carefree.

'I spend it,' I said.

'All of it?'

'Listen,' I told him. 'I was brought up by a French grand-mother. Doesn't that tell something?'

He grinned.

'The next time you feel like spending, don't buy a sable coat or another string of pearls. Buy X——' — he named a stock which was then in the market news. 'And don't tell anybody else I told you to buy it, either.'

The next morning, at exactly nine-fifteen, I rang up my broker.

'Buy me three thousand shares of X——,' I told him.

And then I sat back and watched the papers each day. Presently X—— began to move upward. Every evening there was a plus 3 or plus 4 after it in the quotations.

One day Captain Delamar took me sailing again.

'Done any shopping lately, Alda?' he asked.

'I spent so many thousand dollars the day after I went sailing with you before.'

'Oh, you did. Well, when X—— reaches 79, sell out. And don't tell anybody I told you to, either.'

'Very well,' I replied.

And followed instructions.

That summer I made fifty thousand dollars in the market. And I lost twenty pounds. I don't know which of these two achievements gave me the more happiness. I would look at my banker's statements and feel good. And I would look at my slowly diminishing figure, as reflected in my long mirror, and then I would go downstairs and study the rôle of Francesca in Zandonai's opera, *Francesca da Rimini,* which I was to create at the Metropolitan with Martinelli during the coming opera season.

The première was to be very much of an occasion, with the Italian ambassador coming on from Washington, as Otto Kahn's guest in the Morgan box, in honor of the composer and of d'Annunzio.

My vivid memories of Duse in the rôle influenced my interpretation of Francesca in even more ways than in making me insist on having a column against which to rest my outstretched hand, as I sang.

When it came to the costumes for Francesca I had an idea that seemed to me stunning. I designed and had made to wear in the Second Act a gown of purple and scarlet. It was a trailing mediaeval dress, frankly copied from those worn by the ladies in the frescoes of one of the old churches in Florence. I loved it. I knew it was becoming to me. And I felt confident of the success it would be on the stage.

Until the final rehearsals, when I saw the scenery for that act.

The set for Act Two was all bright reds and yellows. When I came on the stage in my purple and scarlet, the effect was that of all the wind instruments in the orchestra being played off-pitch.

'You'll have to change the sets,' I told the stage director.

'Impossible,' Gatti rebuked me. 'You must change your costume.'

Give up my purple and scarlet? Only a man would see that as the solution of the dilemma. In the end, I wore the costume, but in another scene when I would appear against a less flamboyant background. Meanwhile, Celia and I hastily contrived a new costume for Act Two.

After one of the performances of *Francesca* that winter, I had this letter:

Feb. 1, 1917

DEAR MADAME ALDA:

Last night at last I was able to go to hear your beautiful rendering of Francesca.

I followed the whole performance with interest and admired how well it was given.

You sang beautifully and the voice sounded splendidly! And of course you looked lovely in your gorgeous costumes.

Thanking you for offering us the pleasure of hearing Figaro and the Trilogy in your box, and hoping to see you there, I am, with much love,

Affectionately yours,

MARCELLA SEMBRICH

Celia...

I could not write the story of my life, especially the story of those years at the Metropolitan, without giving a place in it to Celia, who was my theatre maid for fourteen years.

Soon after I came to the opera house, while I was dressing for a performance one evening, there was a knock at the dressing-room door.

'Come in,' I said.

The door opened to admit a short, fat, rosy-faced smiling little Italian peasant girl, who carried one of my costumes over her arm. She worked in the wardrobe and was bringing back my dress after pressing it. That night my own maid was ill and not up to helping me. I sent her home and kept Celia (the sewing girl told me this was her name) in her place.

The next day I said to Gatti:

'I want Celia.'

'Who is Celia?'

I explained. 'I want her for my own theatre maid.'

'*Mai, perche...,*' he protested.

But I stuck to it. Moreover, I saw to it I got her.

Everybody who knew me well enough to come round to my dressing-room on the nights I was singing came to know Celia and to marvel at her deftness, her amazing memory that extended to every last ribbon, buckle, petticoat, veil, cap, handkerchief, fan, and jewel of every costume in every one of the many operas I sang at the Metropolitan.

I never knew her to make one mistake.

I never knew her to be anything but calm, practical, sure, eager, smiling.

No bursts of temperament or tired nerves ever upset Celia. '*Madama e nervosa*,' she would say consolingly, nodding her head at me kindly as to a child. Then, having done all, she would tiptoe away, to come back the next time I went to the opera house, as unruffled as ever.

Blessed Celia!

When I left the Metropolitan she wept. Big, fat tears that ran down her round rosy cheeks, inappropriately, one felt.

'Don't cry, Celia,' I told her. 'You're such a marvellous maid, some one of the artists will grab you the minute I take my hands off you.'

'Oh, madama,' she sobbed. 'I'm not staying on at the opera house. I am going to get married to Jean.'

I knew who Jean was. He, too, had worked in the wardrobe department. Then he and his partner kept an Italian restaurant. He had been wanting Celia to marry him for years.

'So you're going to marry Jean at last,' I exclaimed. 'Then what are you crying for?'

'Oh, madama, it will not be the same.'

True, it is not the same. But Celia — Jean, restaurant, and all the rest — is still part of my life. I know she will be until she, or I, die. Whenever I move, go to Europe, rent my house, or go away for the summer, I send for Celia. I see her trotting up and down stairs with curtains, rugs, *bibelots*, clothing, linen; putting things away, still eager, rosy-cheeked, and smiling.

And still without making a mistake.

'*Madama e nervosa*,' she says to me soothingly when the many telephone calls, mishaps, and stupidities happen all at once, and my patience flies out of the window.

And she nods her head, understandingly.

Celia is the one person I have ever known who completely understands a prima donna's temperament and how to deal with it.

The other person who played a constant part in those crowded years of opera engagements and concert tours was Boo.

Margaret Evans was her real name, and she was my secretary.

But I never called her anything but 'Boo,' which was her name when I saw her first, the middle one of the three little daughters of the rector of the English church in Brussels. I had met Mrs. Evans at a reception at the British Embassy. Later she wrote me, inviting me to tea at the rectory.

I went. Whilst we were having tea, the drawing-room door opened and a prim English governess came in with three little girls. The three were dressed alike in white piqué frocks under scarlet reefer coats, and round black beaver hats. Presented to me, they courtesied in unison.

The middle one kissed my hand.

Later, I was taken upstairs to see the house. In the nursery were three little white beds. Just alike. But over the middle one was the most amazing array of photographs I ever saw anywhere.

They were all of Alda.

Alda as Manon, as La Traviata, as the Queen in *Les Huguenots*, as Marguerite and Juliette and Madame Chrysanthème.

'Whose are these?' I asked.

It came out then. The photographs were 'Boo's' (Margaret's) prized possession. She spent all her pocket-money buying every one that came out. By a system of espionage and bribery that would have done credit to Scotland Yard, she had even secured some wisps of straw from the pallet on which as Marguerite in *Faust* I died weekly.

Her sisters told me this whilst Boo stood silent and blushing and abashed.

Of a sudden I was back seven, eight years. At Miss Brown's in Melbourne. And before my eyes was a fat little girl in a short white linen frock carefully pasting photographs of Cora Brown-Potter on the inside of the screen about her bed in the dormitory — cherishing under her pillow every night a letter from the actress who was her idol. I bent down and put my arms about the little girl called 'Boo,' I heard Cora Brown-Potter's lovely voice saying, 'You must come and see me in England some day, Francie dear. . . .'

'I'll tell you what, Boo darling,' I said. 'When you get big enough you must come and be my secretary. We'll travel all around the world together.'

She put her face suddenly against the soft chinchilla coat I was wearing. What I kissed was the tip of one ear.

As I have told, Brussels gave place to Milan, Warsaw, Buenos Aires, New York. The years passed. In May, 1914, during the brief weeks Gatti and I were at the apartment in the Champ-de-Mars, Boo came to see me. She was grown up . . . pretty . . . chic.

'I'm ready now to be your secretary,' she told me.

She came back with us to New York that winter. All through the war years and until after I returned from the Metropolitan she was with me.

How much longer could America stay out of the war?

Not much longer. Already the chief interest of New York centred about relief work for the cause of the Allies.

Would I sing for this war charity? At this hospital benefit? Whenever I possibly could, I did.

All these activities were bringing to New York the greatest French and English artists. Bernhardt, lame, old, and crippled, but still marvellous. There was something in her face that did things to you. Ellen Terry came, sad and *fanée*, but still lovely. And inimitably woman.

At a concert entertainment at the Plaza shortly before America entered the war, I remember I sang a group of Russian songs — in Russian — with a *balalaika* orchestra, wearing my famous costume from *Prince Igor*.

At the Metropolitan, the old idea of opera in English had been revived. Gatti had promised to produce Reginald de Koven's *Canterbury Pilgrims*.

'De Koven wants you to sing the Wife of Bath in his opera,' Gatti told me.

My eyebrows went up.

'You will?'

'I won't,' I said flatly.

'Why not?'

'You know why not.'

I thought the whole matter was ended right there. I was un-prepared for Mr. de Koven's coming round to my dressing-room at the opera house one night when I was singing, to beg me to change my mind and agree to sing the leading rôle in his opera. Had he forgotten that when I made my début in New York he, as one of the musical critics, had written for all to read that as a singer I fell far below the standard of the Metropolitan? And that it was difficult to understand why I should have been per-mitted to appear at all?

'But how spiteful of you to remember that, all these years!' he exclaimed.

It didn't seem spiteful to me. It seemed just. And I couldn't help it.

Theoretically, I knew, I was grateful for that dash of cold water that had waked me out of my rosy dream into a world of intense reality and endeavor. But I could no more forget the experience than I could forget my grandmother's death, or my first appearance at the Opéra Comique, or the night I cracked on the top note singing the Queen's aria in *Les Hugue-nots*.

When the *Canterbury Pilgrims* was produced early in March, 1917, Marguerite Ober sang the Wife of Bath.

She was singing it on the night of April 5, 1917, when the news went out to the world that President Wilson had declared war on Germany.

The report reached the opera house just before the curtain rose on Act Three. A wave of intense excitement spread through the house. Bodansky rapped with his baton, and suddenly the orchestra was playing 'The Star-Spangled Banner.'

The whole packed house began to sing it.

James Gerard, who had been Ambassador to Germany, stood up in his box and called for cheers: for the Army and Navy; for the President; for the Allies. Our Allies, now. Tears ran down people's cheeks. Perfect strangers, finding themselves shoulder to shoulder, embraced. Behind the scenes, Ober fainted.

The *Canterbury Pilgrims* were completely forgotten.

The first American casualty after the United States was officially at war was de Koven's opera!

But in those months of April and May, 1917, America was tremendously alive.

And singing. I know I was.

Briefly put down, my record of engagements during those first weeks runs as follows:

March 12	War Thrift Concert
April 8	Benefit Junior Patriots of America (Hippodrome)
April 14	Italian Benefit (Metropolitan)
April 15–22	Atlanta Music Festival
April 27	Concert, Charlotte, North Carolina
May 5	Canadian Club Concert (Hippodrome)
May 20	Italian Benefit, Washington, D.C.
May 24	Italian American Fête (Metropolitan)
May 26	British Empire Day Celebration (Carnegie Hall)
May 27	Red Cross Benefit
June 10	Navy Festival (Metropolitan)

The Navy Festival was arranged to raise a fund from which to supply the men on the ships and at the naval training stations with music and musical instruments. Mrs. E. T. Stotesbury, who was Chairman of the Department of Navy Recreation, wanted some of the money we raised set aside to buy hymn books.

In my official capacity as National Chairman of the National Committee on Music of the Department of Navy Recreation, I stood my ground.

'No hymn books,' I protested. 'Pianos, mouth organs, cornets, saxophones, accordions, ukuleles. Anything you can play a tune on. But not one single hymn book.'

Let the reader guess which one of us carried the day.

That Benefit Concert held at the opera house brought together the five greatest tenors in America: Caruso, Muratore, John McCormack, Luca Botta, and Martinelli. Rothier, de Segurola, and Didur sang too. Mischa Elman played, and Harold Bauer. Of the women singers from the Metropolitan, we had Anna Case, Mabel Garrison, Sophie Braslau, Kathleen Howard, Leonora Sparks, and myself.

Martinelli and I sang together the duet from *Madame Butterfly*. Caruso sang an aria form *Pagliacci*; John McCormack gave a group of Irish ballads.

And how he sang them!

Sentimental, I agree. But also art of its own special kind. And perfect of its kind.

But our program wasn't all art. Elsa Maxwell wrote a song for the occasion: 'Help the Navy Here Over There' — and we sang that, too!

We had the Metropolitan's orchestra and John Philip Sousa with the United States Marine Corps Band and three hundred seamen from the Pelham Bay Naval Training Station who could sing.

And did they sing!

Shrewdly combining singers and actors and society people, we had Ethel Barrymore in a recitation, and tableaux posed by Ben Ali Haggin in which appeared twenty society women, including Mrs. Lydig Hoyt, Mrs. Oliver Harriman, Mrs. Charles de L. Oelrichs, Mrs. Sidney Breeze, Mrs. Charles de Rham, and a lot more.

And we had all the season's prettiest, most popular débutantes to sell programs.

Every seat in the house was sold out. A few moments before the curtain was to rise, Mrs. Stotesbury made a regal entrance, wearing a diadem of jewels. She passed down an aisle formed by sailors standing at attention, and followed by Lady Lister-Kaye and my friend, Bridget Guinness, who must have had a twinkle in her eye.

That night we netted over forty-seven thousand dollars for the fund.

Sixteen thousand dollars of this amount was the price paid for an autographed program which I auctioned off from the stage. Afterward, I received the following letter from Franklin D. Roosevelt, then Assistant Secretary of the Navy:

THE SECRETARY OF THE NAVY.
WASHINGTON.

JJ410-55

6 May 1919.

My dear Madame Alda:

        My attention has been called to the work done by you for the Navy in supplying musical instruments to many of our Ships and Stations. These instruments have brightened the lives of thousands of our sailors, and have contributed much to the morale of the men.

        I wish to thank you for this on their behalf and also on behalf of the Navy Department.

Sincerely yours,

Franklin D Roosevelt

Acting

Madame Frances Alda,
15 East 40th Street,
New York City.

Every cent of the forty-seven thousand dollars, except for an almost infinitesimal amount needed for postage and printing, we spent on the men themselves.

The letters they used to write us:

> *'Do you think you could get us a second-hand piano that could go down in a submarine?'*
> *'I used to play on the banjo. Can you ladies supply me with same so I can practise up and play for the wife and the kid when the War is over?'*
> Telegram: *'Please send three hundred harmonicas, twenty trombones and four snaredrums.'*

If America was going to win the war on noise, we were doing our bit to supply it!

Would Madame Alda appear on a program with Madame Sarah Bernhardt and Ignace Paderewski at a benefit for the War?

Would Madame Alda dress like Columbia and stand on the steps of the Public Library during the Liberty Loan Drive and sing 'The Star-Spangled Banner'? Would Madame Alda appear on the Hippodrome stage along with Ex-President Theodore Roosevelt and sing 'The Star-Spangled Banner'?

Getting into the white satin costume over which could be draped any flag the song called for (I had that costume made and repaired and remade half a dozen times before the Germans called for an armistice), I used to think:

'If this War can be won by singing the top of your head off, I'm winning it.'

That was the winter I was in love with Robin Innes-Ker.

I have no intention of emulating Frank Harris, whom I once met, by telling over the toll of my kisses. But no more do I intend to pretend that I have not been in and out of love a number of times in my life.

My marriage to Gatti was frankly, on my part at least, a marriage after the European pattern; a sensible arrangement between a man and a woman who liked and respected each other and who would be mutually benefited by sharing the same name and the same home. We had no children. In the eight years we had been married, our interests had been directed along the same channels by his work and mine at the Metropolitan. But a man and a woman do not fall in love with each other because their careers lie side by side.

And no one, no convention, no exchange of promises can prevent a woman from falling in love when a man who stirs her deeply comes along.

Winter of 1918. Enter Lord Robin Innes-Ker.

He was young, six feet tall, and magnificent in his Guards' uniform of grey and scarlet, when I first caught sight of him across the dining-room of the Ritz. He was with Ella Widener.

But he was looking at me.

All through luncheon, neither the Guardsman nor I paid more than cursory attention to our own parties.

Who was he?

New York was full of foreign officers in horizon blue, and olive grey and khaki.

I was still wondering about my Guardsman next morning, when the telephone rang before I was out of bed.

I reached for the receiver.

Ella Widener's lisp came over the wire:

'Alda darling, won't you come to dinner tonight? I want you to meet Wobin Innes-Ker. He's just *cwazy* to meet you.'

So that was his name! I knew then who he was. A younger brother of the Duke of Roxburghe, who had married May Goelet. I guessed he was in this country on recruiting service. I could guess, too, that his good looks and debonair charm were raising no small havoc among New York's society women.

'I'd love to come to dinner, Ella,' I told her. 'Tell Wobin I'm *cwazy* to meet him, too.'

That's how it began.

In a week we were seeing each other every day; he was sending me flowers, notes; I was recklessly ordering new frocks and hats calculated to light up his blue eyes.

Of course, people knew about it.

People always do.

Old Mrs. Goelet smiled and patted my arm.

'Why don't you divorce Gatti, my dear? And marry Robin?' she whispered.

Why didn't I?

I think two other beaus of mine got to feeling that I might. They began to be even more attentive, more solicitous, more eager to take me out and do charming things for me.

'Lunch with me today, Alda?' one of them telephoned to ask me, one day.

I said I would. I was terribly fond of him.

But not the least little bit in love with him. Ever.

Still, I wore that day a gown and a hat that I knew were his style. And we had an enjoyable luncheon à deux.

As we rose from the table, 'Let's walk in the Park,' he said. 'I have something terribly important I want to talk over with you.'

I couldn't tell him that I had already promised Robin to walk around the reservoir with him that afternoon. Or that I knew Robin was probably at that very moment waiting in my salon for me to come home so we could go out together.

By nature and by preference, I speak the truth as I see it.

But this day I lied: 'I have to go to a rehearsal. I'm terribly sorry.'

He kissed my hand as he saw me to my car.

'Some other day, then?'

I waved my hand to him from the car window.

Just as I thought, Robin was waiting. Not very patiently. Handsome Guardsmen aren't used to being left to cool their heels while the ladies they fancy are lunching tête à tête with someone else.

'It's good for Robin,' I thought, as I left him, to go and change to sports shoes and tweeds and a felt hat.

I took my time about it, too.

Presently Robin and I started out, past the Plaza, and in at

Princess in *Marouf*

Marguerite in *Faust*

'Si, mi chiamino
Mimi,' *La Bohème*

With Mrs. Harriman in a War
tableau

the Park gate. We walked briskly up to the reservoir and along the path that encircles it.

It was a crisp, sparkling winter day. Glorious!

We were too absorbed in each other to notice particularly the other couples we met or passed. Still, I felt, there was something very familiar about a man I saw coming along the path toward us. He was walking with a handsome woman.

Well, he ought to seem familiar.

It was the man I had lunched with an hour and a half before! The joke — if there was a joke, and I think there was — was on me that time.

Well, someone won the War. At least, it came to an end. The horror and the bloodshed and the fear and the hate, and the ghastly unreasonable waste.

And with it came an end to the hysteria and the publicity-seekers and excitement that had gripped us all.

On the night of November 24, 1918, at the Hippodrome, at the Victory Peace Festival for the French Wounded, I sang three songs. Among them, 'Ring Out, Sweet Bells of Peace' and 'When the Boys Come Home.' During the second verse of this, Raymond Hitchcock, who was master of ceremonies, pranced out on the stage and acted in pantomime the words I sang.

As part of the ceremonies, he presented me with a gold medal for my work on behalf of the orphaned children of France. Another medal was given to Rothier, whose singing that night of the 'Marseillaise' brought the tremendous audience to a high pitch of enthusiasm.

Singing for these war benefits had not cut into my work at the Metropolitan, where we gave the première of *Marouf* that season. I had seen the opera in Paris, several years before. Its composer, Henri Rabaud, was then conductor at the Opéra Comique. Later he conducted the Boston Symphony Orchestra. I persuaded Gatti to produce *Marouf* in America.

De Luca was cast to sing Marouf, and I the Princess who dons boy's attire, runs away, and has amazing Arabian nights adventures in the streets of Cairo.

That quick change from my harem dress to the disguise as a boy! I had less than two minutes to make the change and reappear on the stage. Not even time enough to get to my own dressing-room and back again.

And there I blessed Celia.

Every night I sang Marouf she stood in the wings with my boy's costume in her hands, held the way the harness used to hang over the backs of the firemen's horses.

I would make my exit. Then zip, bing! Off went my slippers, snap went the snappers that held my harem costume.

The doublet, hose, and shoes of the boy's disguise, Celia had cleverly sewn together. I stepped into them, gave a jerk, a wriggle. Celia fastened one hook. I pulled my tasselled cap down on my head. And made my entrance on my cue.

Just before the dress rehearsal of *Marouf* there was another contretemps over the costume the wardrobe mistress had made for me to wear in the First Act.

It was hideous.

'I won't accept it,' I said.

I knew there was no surety that she could contrive another that would be any better.

What to do?

Then I remembered that Morris Gest had bought a lot of properties and costumes in Paris for a gorgeous Oriental production he was going to put on — *Sumurun*.

I rang him up.

'Have you a costume I can buy, borrow, or steal?'

He thought a minute.

'There's a dress we had made for Ida Rubinstein,' he said. 'It's magnificent, really. I'll sell it to you for *Marouf*, for five hundred dollars.'

'Fine and dandy,' I said. 'Only Ida Rubinstein is tall and as thin as a rail. I'm short and forty pounds overweight.'

He chuckled.

'Don't waste time laughing,' I retorted. 'Send me the dress. Thank God for scissors, an extra yard or two of chiffon, and for Celia.'

That's how I achieved my Oriental costume for *Marouf*. The press commented on it. No wonder. It really was the most gorgeous thing; after what Celia cut off the length of the long, full, harem trousers and pieced out the back to fit my figure.

Meanwhile, I wondered what would become of the costume made for me which I had refused. I knew the orders from the Director's Office would be that it must not be wasted.

On the day of the dress rehearsal I found out.

Out in the hall beyond the dressing-rooms the most awful row was going on. First the voice of the wardrobe mistress. Then that of Rosina Galli, the première danseuse:

'What do you mean, bringing me a dress like this? How do you expect me to dance in such a thing? It's impossible. I won't wear it. I'll complain to Mr. Gatti.'

'Do, my dear,' I thought to myself.

Eventually, the despised dress turned up as part of the covering of the divan which was brought on the stage for me to recline on. After all, budgets must be met in spite of the temperamental tastes of prima donnas and première danseuses!

The Metropolitan needed new voices.

It seemed to me sometimes the great dingy brown brick building was like a machine devouring all that was poured into it, and clamoring always for more.

Sometimes, away on a concert engagement, I heard some singer who seemed to me so good that I wired at once to Gatti, recommending that he arrange to hear him or her. I remember going to Utica, New York, to sing Aïda in concert form, under the direction of Walter Damrosch, and hearing there, at our rehearsal, one of the finest bass voices I ever heard.

The singer was Arthur Middleton.

Gatti, at my instigation, engaged him for the Metropolitan.

Arthur Middleton could sing, but apparently he could not reduce his figure, which was too fat for stage appearances. He stayed with the company a few seasons; then, as his girth increased, instead of lessening, he was not re-engaged.

It was I, too, who heard the young American tenor, Orville Harrold, at Hammerstein's and spoke to Gatti enthusiastically about him. Harrold had been famous for years as a boy singer. Hammerstein heard him somewhere, engaged him, and taught him to sing grand opera.

'You ought to get him,' I told Gatti.

He was not terribly enthusiastic about Harrold when he first heard him sing but, whatever else might happen, Gatti seemed always to trust my judgment about voices and a singer's art.

He engaged Harrold for the Metropolitan. But he cast him in only small unimportant rôles, despite my reiterating that I was confident Harrold had it in him to sing the big tenor parts.

Then one day at the Metropolitan there was a performance for some charity. Harrold had a strong rôle to sing, and sang it so well Gatti could not refuse to agree with me that he was good.

'You see,' I said.

'Well, if he's as good as all that, he can sing *Bohème* with you at the Academy in Brooklyn on the twenty-eighth,' Gatti decreed.

'The twenty-eighth' was the twenty-eighth of November, 1918. On that night there was to be a gala performance at the Metropolitan in honor of Edward, then Prince of Wales, who was making his first visit to the United States after the War.

The Prince of Wales's visit to the Metropolitan was the most brilliant and socially exciting event the opera house saw in all the years I sang there. The Prince was the most important foreign visitor to New York since the state visit of Prince Henry of Prussia early in the century. He came attended by his own aides, Admiral Halsey and Lord Viscount Grey, and by the United States Assistant Secretary of War. Otto Kahn and

Clarence Mackay met them at the entrance and escorted the Prince to J. Pierpont Morgan's box.

The program for the Gala included scenes from various operas, sung by the Metropolitan's finest artists. Caruso and Amato were to sing the First Act of *Pagliacci*. There were to be two ballets. Finally, at the close, I was to be whisked over from the engagement in Brooklyn to come on the stage and sing 'God Save the King' and 'The Star-Spangled Banner' in honor of England's heir.

I was feeling considerable chagrin that whilst all this marvellous program was going on at the Metropolitan, I should be singing in Brooklyn. At least, I felt so, until I actually heard Orville Harrold sing his first Rudolfo. Then the beauty of his pure tenor voice so enthralled me I forgot about the Prince and the glitter across the Brooklyn Bridge. I forgot my anxiety about getting to the opera house in time to change from Mimi's to my Grecian costume of white *crepe de Chine* draped with the flag, in which I always sang the national anthem.

I could only realize that here was a marvellous voice and a marvellous singer. Brooklyn realized it too that night. The audience gave Harrold a tremendous ovation after his aria in the First Act, before I began to sing. It was sincere and genuine and touching. Best of all, it was deserved.

Three quarters of an hour after it was all over, and dressed in my white dress with the Union Jack draped from my shoulders, I stood in the wings of the Metropolitan ready to go on the stage to sing 'God Save the King.' I found Gatti and Otto Kahn standing beside me.

'How did it go in Brooklyn?' Gatti asked.

I told them both, in no uncertain phrases.

'Harrold had the biggest ovation any tenor ever had. Even Caruso.'

That opened their eyes. Several days later, Harrold sang a Monday night performance of *Bohème* with me, and the applause given him lasted for minutes.

Immediately after that, Gatti began giving Harrold all the big tenor rôles to sing. Even *Parsifal.* I protested. 'You're pushing him too hard. No voice can stand it.' But my protests counted for nothing beside the facts and figures on the book-keeper's ledger. Harrold did not command as high a fee per performance as some of the other tenors received. And he drew the crowds. The box-office receipts swelled.

What happened was one of the great tragedies that can happen to a young singer who has not had the shrewd advice of a Maman Marchesi. He sang too often, and in rôles that were still too heavy for him. After a few seasons his glorious voice began to show the strain; the critics first, then the public noticed it. Harrold's popularity waned. His career as a great tenor was over.

SIGNIFICANTLY enough, as I see it now, that Gala for the Prince of Wales occurred not long before Caruso's — the greatest voice of our times — was hushed forever.

Eleazaar in *La Juive* was the last rôle Caruso studied. And of all the thirty-six rôles he sang in New York, it was his finest. He sang it with Rosa Ponselle and Orville Harrold and Rothier on Christmas Eve, 1920. It was his last performance.

Two weeks previous to this he had strained his side whilst singing 'Vesti la giubba' in a performance of *Pagliacci* with Emmy Destinn. The doctors pronounced his illness 'intercostal neuralgia.' They strapped him, and three days later he sang a performance in Brooklyn. Before the First Act of the opera (it was *L'Elisir d'Amore*) he began to cough. A trickle of blood appeared at the corner of his mouth.

He should have cancelled the performance at once, of course. But he wouldn't. He sang the First Act through, sang it marvellously — though the bleeding went on continuously. Members of the chorus kept passing him fresh handkerchiefs as he sang. Caruso wiped his lips, then threw the bloody pieces of linen in the well, which was part of the set.

It was one of the greatest feats of heroism the stage has ever seen.

During the entr'acte Swin, the Brooklyn manager, telephoned Gatti in New York for advice. Then he informed the audience of the tenor's illness.

'He says if you wish, he will go on with the performance.'

'No! No!' the house cried.

Caruso was taken home to the Vanderbilt Hotel and put to bed.

But he, and his doctor, thought him well enough to sing on Christmas Eve. It was his six hundred and seventh performance at the Metropolitan. He sang it through, but next day he was terribly ill. We all realized that he would not sing again for a long time. If ever.

The last time I saw him was shortly before he sailed for Naples. The illness had affected one of his hands so that he kept it covered with a glove. I remember he sat down at the little white upright piano in his suite at the Vanderbilt Hotel and played and sang for me — but softly — a passage from *La Bohème*.

'You see I'm all right,' he insisted. 'I'll sing *Bohème* with you again next season.'

I never saw Caruso again.

Three days after Dorothy had cabled us the announcement of his death, the mail brought Gatti a letter written in Caruso's own hand and full of his old playful spirit — with messages to me. It was, it seems likely, the last letter Caruso ever wrote.

I had many from him in the twelve years whilst we were both members of the Metropolitan; witty, ironic little notes, written half in Italian, half in French, and with a quickly executed, amazingly clever caricature of himself, of Gatti, or Toscanini or me. But notes full to the brim of genuine affection and deep friendliness. There was never any doubting Caruso's sincerity. In my autograph book he wrote:

> Vorrei poter con la mia penna cantar le lodi me a voi m'addicono mia cara e buona Signora e amica ma essa e povera e non mi resta che dirvi che in me avete un cuore un anima un ammico affectionato e devoto
>
> ENRICO CARUSO [1]
>
> 5/9/14

No eulogy or tribute in that little volume means more to me than these lines.

The Metropolitan without Caruso! How strange it seemed! How empty! Gatti was frankly anxious about the box-office receipts. What could he produce for the insatiable public to compare with those magnificent *Aïdas* with Caruso, Destinn, and Homer? The *Bohèmes* with Caruso, Scotti, de Segurola, and myself? The *Manon Lescauts* and the *Toscas* in which Caruso had sung so gloriously?

During the 1919–1920 season Gatti had produced another American opera, Henry Hadley's *Cleopatra's Night*. The story, of course, was Théophile Gautier's, and the gorgeous sets were designed by Norman Bel Geddes.

I had sung the Queen, and in the first three performances Orville Harrold sang the tenor rôle. Something funny happened at the dress rehearsal — in fact, two funny things happened, which hugely delighted the special 'Dress Rehearsal' invited audience.

The first of these laughs was occasioned by Jean Gordon, who sang the rôle of one of my slaves. In one scene, she was supposed to stab herself and fall dead on the steps at my feet.

The stabbing went according to stage directions. But instead of falling at my feet, she tumbled down the steps, ending in a tangled heap of chiffon, most of it over her head! Had she

---

[1] 'I wish I were able to sing with my pen, the praises I would address to you, my dear and good lady and friend, but it is poor, and nothing remains for me but to tell you you have in me a heart, a soul, and an affectionate and devoted friend.'

remained in that position, it would have been bad enough, but worse was to come.

Apparently, the fact that she was exposing her legs and a good part of her body to the hundred or more guests in the audience was more than she could bear. Though officially dead, she sat up suddenly, switched down her skirts, composed herself as a modest corpse, and proceeded to die all over again.

The other laugh greeted Harrold when he made his entrance, emerging from the swimming bath. Up he came, only too evidently bone-dry. In place of the leopard skin which was to have been his costume, and which had gotten mislaid at the last moment, there was a Turkish towel tied about him diaper-wise, and fastened with a huge safety pin!

Later, as Gatti began giving Harrold the Parsifals, Lohengrins, Tannhäusers to sing, the tenor rôle in *Cleopatra's Night* was sung by Morgan Kingston.

Cleopatra's Night was the only 'American made' opera that lasted through two seasons. When the program for the next year was arranged, the composer wrote me:

224 West Eleventh St.

DEAR ALDA:

Let me convey to you as best I can, my genuine thanks for your incomparable art as 'Cleo.'

I owe you a great debt, and having heard you three times in the rôle I can only repeat what I said to you in San Francisco. You are superb as the Queen, and your voice gave me the greatest possible joy. I am sending you a souvenir score and when you have a spare hour I want to come and see you. I feel certain that I have some newer songs that you will love.

Last June you said to me that you wanted this opera to be retained in the repertory. I believe that Gatti feels that it got over better than any other American work, and its reception by both press and public was far beyond my fondest anticipation.

Seriously, dear Alda, you cannot know how much I attribute this success to you.

Believe me, in deepest appreciation,

Faithfully yours,

HENRY HADLEY

Feb. 8, '20.

The two or three seasons after Caruso's death saw several new singers make their débuts at the Metropolitan. Galli-Curci was one of these. She had sung in New York with the Chicago Opera Company several years before. Her first performance was a tremendous success. I went to hear her, and told Gatti he should engage her for the Metropolitan. Edward Johnson was another member of the Chicago Company who joined the Metropolitan about this time. And, during the season of 1922, Jeritza made her American début. Whilst Gatti and I were in Europe in the summer of 1912, we went to Munich to hear Maria Jeritza in Offenbach's *La Belle Hélène*. She sang the rôle with a charming, fresh voice; and she was lovely to look at. Gatti engaged her then for the Metropolitan. She was to have joined the company in the season of 1914, but the War interfered, and she did not make her début in New York until six years later.

Galli-Curci and Edward Johnson had sung with the Chicago Opera Company under the direction of Cleofonte Campanini. During several winters Campanini leased the Lexington Theatre in New York and brought his company there for a short season, defying the Metropolitan's monopoly of grand opera in that city. Now, in the season of 1922, the Chicago Company came once more to New York, but this time under the direction of a woman — Mary Garden.

A woman director!

Gatti's expression of horror and disgust at this intrusion on the divine rights of males made me long for Caruso, with his quick pencil and his gift for caricature. Which explains why I did not show my husband the telegram I had one day. It was signed GARDEN:

The message, as nearly as I can recall it now, ran something like this:

> Dearest Alda: Won't you be my guest opening night Chicago Opera Company sit in my box and let us show

the world there are two women opera singers who can be friends.

Mary had chosen Bellini's *Norma* for the first performance in New York under her directorship. It was the first time *Norma* had been sung in New York for nearly thirty years. Rosa Raisa was to sing the title rôle.

I wired Mary accepting her invitation. On the night of February 3, still without telling Gatti my plans, I drove down to the Lexington, and went to the Director's Box.

It was empty. I sat down and watched the audience come in. A good house. Presently the orchestra members began to take their places; the conductor entered. He rapped his baton. Coincident with the first chord of the overture, the velvet curtains of the Director's Box parted, and Mary Garden came in.

Mary, in all her war paint!

Diamond and emerald bracelets from her wrists to her elbows. Diamonds and a bird of paradise in her hair. An enormous feather fan . . .

She swept regally to the front of the box and stood, surveying the house. All eyes were on her. She turned toward me, and beckoned me with her two hands and the fan. In her very throatiest voice, she said loudly:

'Sit forward, Alda, sit forward. Let the people see you.'

Norma began.

When the curtain fell after the First Act, Mary leaned far out over the parapet and clapped and clapped and clapped.

'Bravo! Bravo! Bravo!' she shouted, while again the house turned and craned and stared at her.

Then to me, and without once lowering her voice:

'Bloody opera, Alda, isn't it?'

T HAT year Gatti staged Pierre Lalo's opera *Le Roi d'Ys*, in which Ponselle and I sang the two chief feminine rôles. During the rehearsals, I voiced the same objection to my part of Rozanne that I had found with Victor Herbert's Madeleine: there was nothing to sing. Nothing, until Lalo wrote for me a really charming aria which he interpolated into the opera's Third Act.

On the day after the première I had the following note:

le 5 *janvier*, 1922

CHERE AMIE:

Recevez mes vifs remerciments pour la loge d'hier et le grand plaisir que cela a été d'entendre l'excellente representation du *Roi d'Ys*.

Voilà deux ans que je ne vous ai pas entendue, et il m'a semblé que jamais votre voix n'avait sonné aussi chaude et expressive — Il y avait des moments tout a fait ravissants. Vous étiez une charmante apparition dans vos superbes costumes.

Merci de votre amabilité et croyez-moi affectueusement à vous

MARCELLA SEMBRICH [1]

One tradition of the opera house I had watched develop during the years I was with the Metropolitan — that was the popularity of the dress rehearsal.

It was amazing how many people apparently adored coming to those 'previews.' Usually less than one hundred guests were admitted, but the competition for invitations was keen.

Elizabeth Marbury was one of the dress-rehearsal 'fans.' She would ring me up a week or a few days before the first night

[1] 'Dear Friend:

Please accept my sincere thanks for the box yesterday, and the great pleasure it was to hear the excellent performance of *Le Roi d'Ys*.

It is two years since I heard you, and it seemed to me that your voice never sounded so warm and expressive. There were moments that were altogether ravishing. You were a charming sight in your superb costumes.

Thank you again for your kindness, and believe me,

Affectionately,

MARCELLA SEMBRICH.'

of an opera, and frankly beg for an invitation to the dress rehearsal.

She was one of the most unusual and interesting women I ever knew, anywhere. She possessed real power. Not just the feminine power that woman derives from sex; but the impersonal power that comes of clear, straightforward thinking, and of living, to some extent at least, detached from the prejudices, fears, and ambitions that sway most lives. Not that this lessened Elizabeth's human sympathy or her love of life. I think, on the contrary, these were heightened by the sweeping freedom of her spirit.

I remember after the dress rehearsal of *Le Roi d'Ys*, I was in my dressing-room changing to street clothes to go out to luncheon with Elizabeth Marbury, when suddenly she came barging in.

It was a rainy, sleety January day, and Elizabeth looked like an English duchess in a mackintosh, stout boots, and shapeless felt hat, with an umbrella carried martially under one arm.

She shook the umbrella at me.

'You've too much intelligence for this place, Alda,' she snorted. 'You're wasted here. You belong on Broadway, and I could put you there.' There wasn't any use trying to convince her that, geographically at least, the Metropolitan *was* on Broadway.

'Arty. Too arty,' she sniffed. 'Fol-de-rols set to slow music. You're wasted here, wasted.'

Secretly, when it was a matter of singing *Le Roi d'Ys*, I thought I was, too.

I felt differently about *Marta*, when, the next season, Gatti told me I was to sing Lady Harriet. I flattered myself that here, at last, was really singable music. *Bel canto*. And, at one point in the opera, Lady Harriet sings in English Tom Moore's song, 'The Last Rose of Summer.' How I adored that! Till the rehearsal before the dress rehearsal.

I was standing in the wings waiting for my cue, and humming

softly the plaintive music of the song. Near me stood an assistant conductor. 'You know,' he said casually, 'Patti said that was the most difficult song in the world.'

'What is?' I demanded.

'"The Last Rose of Summer"— I read somewhere she said she was always afraid when she began it.'

Patti!

I remembered her, exquisite and lovely and poised. And her voice that still had the peachlike bloom on it, as I heard her at the concert for *Les Enfants de la Presse,* years and years before. And she, the great Patti, had found 'The Last Rose of Summer' the most difficult of all songs to sing!

I heard my cue. I went on. I began to sing, but dreading the moment when I should have to begin:

'Tis the last rose of summer...'

Through the tail of my eye I saw the assistant conductor vanish backstage, unaware that his lightly spoken words were to influence me for years to come.

For from that day to this, I have never sung 'The Last Rose of Summer' without qualms. I have never ceased to make Patti's anxiety mine. I know that I sang Marta through two seasons before I ever sang 'The Last Rose of Summer' as well as I had sung it before that assistant conductor gave me the jitters.

So much for the power of suggestion.

BUT there was no denying it. The great days of the Metropolitan were waning. Farrar had left in 1922. Scotti celebrated his twenty-fifth anniversary as a member of the company on New Year's Day, 1924, and began to speak about retiring. The new singers who were engaged could not replace the losses. People began to speak a trifle wistfully of 'the good old days.'

It was I who suggested to Gatti that he offer Schumann-Heink a short engagement. Schumann-Heink had left the Metropolitan before the War aroused contentions and bitterness toward certain German singers like Gadski, and even Farrar, whose years with the Berlin Opera Company and whose popularity with the German royal family were held against her.

Possibly no singer who was ever a member of the Metropolitan Opera Company awoke the same response in the affections of the whole nation as did Schumann-Heink. That tremendous motherliness of hers, which unsuited her for many opera rôles, surged like a warm tide over the footlights and engulfed the audiences who flocked to her concerts. Though well on in years, the great contralto was singing in concerts and having a great success. I pointed this out to Gatti.

'She will draw, here in New York.'

If there's one thing everyone who has ever sung in grand opera or had even a finger in the job of directing an opera company knows, it is that the true music-lovers cherish the memory of great musicians and singers they have heard. Bring a great singer back to the stage where she has sung many times, and immediately hundreds of persons will come to hear her out of loyalty to the past. That loyalty and the audiences it creates will probably not endure for more than a very short engagement. But while it lasts, the house is fairly certain to be sold out. The same holds true of the theatre. That was the principle on which Duse and Bernhardt and Ellen Terry made their last American engagements.

It never fails.

Gatti knew this as well as, better than, I.

Schumann-Heink's telegraphed reply to his offer was characteristic of her:

MADAME FRANCES ALDA,
182 West 58th Street.

My beloved blessed friend all is settled thanks to you
I wish I knew how to prove to you my everlasting gratitude
to you and your husband you dear dear daughter of mine.
Devotedly ever your happy old
ERNESTINE SCHUMANN-HEINK

She came and sang several times; always to packed, enthusiastic houses.

But the amazing event of that season of 1925 at the Metropolitan was the début of Marion Talley.

Three years before, during the winter of 1922, an unheralded young girl of fifteen from the Middle West had arrived at Gatti's office for an audition.

I had gone to the opera house for a rehearsal. As I walked across the stage to my dressing-room, I heard a voice singing. I stopped short to listen.

'My God, that's marvellous,' I said, as the clear, pure tones poured out. And to one of the stage hands:

'Go and find out who that is.'

He came to my dressing-room a few minutes later.

'I found out, madame. It's a young girl named Talley.'

'You ought to engage her,' I told Gatti.

What he did was to send her home to study for three years more.

'Then, when you are eighteen, come back and let me hear you again.'

The night of her début as Gilda, in *Rigoletto*, was one of the most fantastic events the opera house ever saw. Crowds of fanatically enthusiastic fellow-citizens from Kansas City besieged the opera house doors and stood cheering outside. Twenty or more special police were needed to preserve any semblance of order or traffic regulations in the four blocks below Times Square. Papa Talley, a professional telegrapher, stood in the wings during the performance tapping out in Morse code his impressions of his daughter's triumph, which the wires carried out to the folks at home in Kansas.

If success is measured by the box-office receipts and the number of persons who are turned away from the doors at each performance, then Marion Talley was the greatest success during all my years at the Metropolitan.

Telling me about it, Gatti ran his fingers through his hair till the ends stood up in excited exclamation points.

'It's astounding. Only in America could such a thing happen.'

'What will you do with her?'

But already I knew what he would do. What he had done with Orville Harrold. Give her as many performances as possible while the public vogue for her lasted, and while her voice was still fresh and true and pure. After all, Gatti was an impresario who had inherited Verdi's point of view: 'An opera house exists to be filled.' He might have added to this, from his own opinions: 'And singers exist to fill it.'

There was no use of my arguing, à la *Maman Marchesi*, as I did, that such a course was ruinous for the young singer. Marion Talley was eager to sing and to appear on the stage as frequently as possible. Much more eager than she was to study, or to learn to conserve her voice, or to perfect her art of singing.

'All I need is coaching,' I was told she said to Sembrich, who offered to teach her. If ever a child had a God-given voice, that girl had it. But intelligence about using it? That's something else again.

A PRIMA DONNA on wheels.
Bohéme in Boston ... a concert in Toronto ... *Marta* at the Metropolitan ... a concert in Kansas City, or Louisville or Sacramento ... *Bohéme* at the Metropolitan ... six more concerts in six widely separated cities and a frantic dash back to New York for a performance of *Faust* or *Mefistofele* with Chaliapin, with a spring from the opera house to the Pennsylvania Station to catch the midnight Limited for Indianapolis or Detroit or Denver for still another concert. ...

Boo invariably went with me on those tours; and my maid, of course. There was also Frank La Forge, my accompanist, and usually some young tenor or baritone — one year we had a cellist — whom I engaged to appear on the program with me.

Working out a smooth combination of concert dates, train schedules, performances at the Metropolitan, and more train connections to get to the next city on the concert tour was a task for a chess champion. I think poor Boo's dreams were haunted by timetables and telegrams and the constant fear of missing the last possible train to the next one-night stand.

We had more than one agonizing moment over that. As happened when we finished the concert in Louisville too late to catch the train for our next concert in a city some six hundred miles away. And that concert had been guaranteed for three thousand dollars!

What to do?

Nothing, but to hire a special train and follow after the missed Limited as swiftly as possible.

Then, there was the time we were due at Emporia, Kansas, and the train was late. A wreck lay ahead of us.

I sat on the edge of my chair, with an eye on my watch.

Frank La Forge tapped nervously a ghost accompaniment on the panelled drawing-room wall.

Time went on.

I thought of the audience driving up to the high-school

auditorium, as many of them did come to those concerts, from farms and ranches, twenty, thirty miles off.

'We'll have to telegraph that we can't make it,' said Frank.

The concert was set for eight o'clock. My watch now said ten minutes before eight. And Emporia forty-seven miles away!

I saw Boo reach in her bag for the pad of telegraph blanks.

But something told me to wait. Ten minutes. If, by eight o'clock no miracle had happened, then I would telegraph.

Five minutes to eight.

Three minutes to eight.

One minute before the watch hand touched the hour, came a rap at the door. The conductor thrust in his head.

'Thought I'd tell you, we're going to move right away.'

Suddenly the grind of wheels beneath us proved the truth of his words.

'We'll get you folks to Emporia tonight.'

Miracles do happen!

'Send that wire, Boo,' I ordered, 'Only say that I'm coming. I'll be there, on the stage at half-past nine, if the audience will wait for me.'

They did wait, bless them!

The concert manager told us afterward that they had cheered when he read them my wire. Someone had good-naturedly sat down at the piano and played, not concert arias, but songs that everybody in the audience knew and could sing, and did.

I heard them singing when I drove up to the door of the school.

Boo pulled off my coat — I had dressed on the train — I walked out on the platform and finished that song with them!

There was the awful moment when, after boarding the train at midnight in St. Louis to reach St. Joseph for a concert the next night, I woke up in the morning, looked out, and saw we were standing still in a whirling blizzard.

I rang for my maid.

'Where are we?'

'We've never left St. Louis, Madame.'

Fortunately, the blizzard had not taken down the telegraph wires. I sent word to the St. Joseph manager of our predicament and suggested postponing the concert to the next evening — Sunday. Word came back that this would be satisfactory. Later in the day the storm cleared, and the railroad got us to St. Joseph, and to the deferred concert.

But that accident had an amusing aftermath. A clergyman in St. Joseph wrote a letter to the newspapers protesting against the sin of holding a concert on Sunday. Someone sent me a copy of the paper. I wrote in reply, which also was published, that I too enjoyed one day of rest out of the seven. But between my singing at a concert and the singing at the reverend objector's church service I couldn't see there was any difference to the Lord. Unless He had a true musical ear.

In which case, I thought it likely, he'd prefer my concert.

It wasn't just the railroad connections that presented us with problems during those tours. Sometimes it was the hotels.

We arrived one morning, four of us, plus my maid and a small mountain range of luggage, at a hotel in a small Southern city. We stood in the lobby while the townsfolk gathered on the sidewalk outside and stared in through the plate-glass windows, as into an aquarium, at these queer, exotic creatures.

I asked to be shown the two rooms with bath that had been engaged for Madame Alda and her secretary. The gangling clerk behind the counter showed no flicker of interest.

'There ain't no rooms with a bath in this hotel.'

'Sorry.' I turned away. 'Then it must be some other hotel.'

'There ain't no other hotel in this town.'

That settled one half of the question, anyway.

'Let me see what rooms you have,' I proposed.

He whistled to a grinning darky bellboy, gave him a key, and the procession, led by the spirit of Al Jolson, went up the stairs.

They had been carpeted sometime before Fort Sumter was fired on; and since that event no one, I judged, had given them much thought, or as much sweeping.

'Dis yere's our best room, ma'am.'

The bellboy opened the door.

I stood on the threshold and surveyed the hotel's best. I heard Boo, beside me, gasp. I dared not look at my maid.

Shades of the Waldorf and the Ritz and the Lido's Excelsior! But, also, shades of the primitive inns in South America where my grandmother had found lodging for herself and her babies . . .

'All right, boy,' I said. 'This is it. But first, pull all the covers off the bed. Thank God, I always take along my own bed linen. Rip up the carpet, scrub the floor and the walls and every bit of the furniture. Then let me know, and I'll step into the room.'

He stammered and backed away from such a command.

The clerk, produced on the scene by Boo, looked dazed, but finally got the main idea. I saw the first breadth of dirty carpet yanked from its moorings, the first of the scrub women arrive with pails.

'We'll have a picnic in the fields while the housecleaning goes on,' I decided.

And we did.

Those prolonged concert tours gave me a first-hand knowledge of America. There was a kindness and ready friendliness about the audiences in those packed high-school auditoriums and Masonic halls and parish houses that flowed out to one the minute one came on the platform. It was impossible to feel like a stranger. And when I went back to many of the same towns the next year and the year after that, and still again after that, it was like coming back to old friends, who would come and speak to me after the concert was over, and tell me they remembered this song or that one that I had sung for them two or three years before.

Occasionally, on those tours, I was entertained at private homes, though usually I preferred the greater freedom and independence that I could have in a hotel. Still, there were friends, scattered over the country, where I made short visits en route.

And about one of those visits I have a story to tell.

One spring, at the end of my tour I was scheduled to sing two concerts in the same Mid-Western city, two days apart. In the interim between the concerts, I was entertained at the really magnificent home of a great industrialist whose factories made the wealth of the city. He and his wife were charming to me, and we became friends. The friendship has lasted many years. That it has, I think, is due largely to my ability to think swiftly in an emergency that might otherwise be disastrous.

This is what happened:

After the second concert, I took the night train for New York. Three days later I sailed for France. Going aboard the ship I saw no one I knew. I was terribly tired and went at once to my cabin to rest many hours before I came out on deck.

On the first morning that I was sitting in my steamer chair enjoying the perennially amusing spectacle of promenading humanity, I saw coming down the deck the gentleman who had been my host a few days before. He was walking and conversing intimately with a very handsome woman who was a complete stranger to me.

Abreast of my chair, the gentleman's eye fell on me, a slight smile appeared at the corners of his mouth.

'Madame Alda!' he exclaimed. 'How good to see you again! May I present my wife?'

I smiled. The strange lady, who was so unlike the wife who had been my hostess not a week before, and I shook hands.

So began a pleasant shipboard acquaintance. The lady was charming. I admired the industrialist's taste no less than his effrontery. When we docked at Cherbourg we said good-bye with regrets on both sides, I am sure. I have met the industrialist many times since then, but neither he nor I have ever referred to that ship's crossing, or to the temporary Mrs. G—— (that, naturally, is *not* the initial) who crossed with him.

AT FIRST, singing in concerts, I made my program of classical songs — Schubert, Brahms, Debussy, Strauss, whose 'Morgen,' to my way of thinking, is one of the most beautiful songs ever written.

Other artists, like Alma Gluck, who was doing a good deal of concertizing at that time, included in their programs songs that seemed to me trivial and not beautiful in themselves. I suppose I was highbrow. I know I turned up my nose when John McCormack said to me one day:

'Listen, Alda, do you want to know a song that would go over big if you'd sing it? "The Bells of St. Mary's."'

Well, he was right. Later on I did sing 'The Bells' for a gramophone company. The popularity of that record outreached that of any of my records except those I made with Caruso. And when I began to sing less highbrow songs at my concerts, like 'The Land of the Sky Blue Water,' which Charles Wakefield Cadman wrote for me, and which quickly became popular all over America, I think people liked the programs better too.

One of the young singers I took with me on several of my concert tours was Lawrence Tibbett. Frank La Forge brought Tibbett to me, to hear him sing. I thought him likeable, and his voice, which was a good church voice, seemed promising. I told him to study and come back and sing for me again after six months. That time when he came and sang for me, his voice was improved. I asked Gatti to give him an audition at the Metropolitan. But Gatti was not impressed. In his judgment Tibbett was not good enough for the Metropolitan.

I still thought, however, that Tibbett had something, and I encouraged him to go on studying in the expectation of having another audition later on. Meanwhile I took him with me on one of my concert tours, I helped him all I could, and later on, just as I hoped would happen, Gatti heard him again and engaged him for the opera company at seventy-five dollars a week.

Tibbett sang small, unimportant rôles. At the same time I engaged him to sing on my concert tours, paying him two hundred dollars weekly for four concerts. I remember we were off on tour in the Mid-West when I had a telegram from Gatti:

Do you think Tibbett could sing Ford?

This question, I realized, was in prospect of a coming performance of *Falstaff*, in which I was to sing Nannetta, Scotti the title rôle, and Pini-Corsi the part of Ford. Pini-Corsi was ill and would be unable to appear.

Here was Lawrence Tibbett's chance.

'Of course he can,' I wired back to Gatti. And immediately I set to work to coach Lawrence in the part. We came back from the concert tour for a rehearsal.

That rehearsal.... There was no denying it, Tibbett was terrible. He was aware of how ill-prepared he was to sing the rôle. He was nervous, and he sensed the criticism of the other artists. Several of them, I remember, stood at one side of the stage and made frank and uncomplimentary comments on Tibbett's efforts as a singer and an actor. Fortunately for his composure, the remarks were in Italian, which he did not understand.

I understood them. I went over to the group.

'Oh, give the boy a chance,' I protested. 'He'll learn. He'll be all right...'

And in English, to Tibbett: 'That's fine. Go ahead. You're all right. You can do it.'

The night of the performance came. And that night, owing to one of those extraordinary things that sometimes happen, Tibbett stepped into nation-wide publicity.

For some unexplainable reason, after the Second Act of *Falstaff*, in which Ford has a long and beautiful aria to sing, Scotti elected to take the curtain calls alone. The audience quickly resented this. There were loud, repeated calls for 'Ford.' And when Tibbett finally appeared before the curtain, the house gave him warm applause and cheers.

The next morning's newspapers published accounts of the enthusiastic welcome the Metropolitan's audience gave Mr. Tibbett. Immediately telegrams began to pour in to me from concert managers all over the country: 'Is this the same Tibbett who is singing on your concert program?' I replied that it was.

Nor had I any idea that Tibbett had any other plans than to fulfill the contract he had signed with me, until a few days later when the company went over to Philadelphia to give another performance of *Falstaff*. On the train a messenger-boy brought me a huge box of flowers. They were from Lawrence Tibbett. He had written on his card:

A very slight remembrance for your many kindnesses

Lawrence Tibbett

I was touched, and pleased, of course. But later that same day Didur came to my dressing-room to tell me:

'Tibbett says he is not going back on tour with you. He says why should he do so, now that he can make a thousand dollars a night, after all the publicity he has had out of the *Falstaff* incident.'

There the matter rested. I just went out and found another singer to take Tibbett's place on my program.

If I have spoken little of my married life during these busy, crowded years, it is because, I suppose, one's mind goes back more willingly to successes than to failure.

I was not happy in my marriage. Perhaps that unhappiness was a spur to my ambition, and therefore served me in my career as an artist. Perhaps the determination to make a career for myself in the teeth of the opposition I encountered when I first came to America prevented my finding success in marriage.

I do not profess to know.

But as the years went on the differences in age and in temperament between Gatti and myself did not lessen. They increased.

His sullen obstinacy, his preserving toward the rest of the world a gloomy silence whenever he was offended about something, grew on him as he grew older. In the first years of our marriage I had tried to combat this. First with an inconsequential gaiety; later by more direct means. Once, I remember, after going through such a mood for several weeks, I decided to give him a dose of his own medicine.

When he came into my bedroom one morning to tell me something, I did not speak to him. He made a few attempts to draw me into conversation, then he shrugged his shoulders and went off to the opera house. At lunch I remained silent and aloof. At dinner, I showed no more vivaciousness than the bowl of fruit in the centre of the table.

Campbell, our butler, served us in solicitous silence.

It was like a soundless movie, with all the captions left out.

The reel went on the next day. And the next. After nearly a week of this sepulchral silence, Gatti's curiosity outweighed his obstinacy.

'What is the matter?' he demanded.

I shook my head, still refusing to speak to him.

'But tell me,' he entreated. 'Why don't you speak to me? I can't stand this . . .'

BANG. I exploded then and there.

'You can't stand this? Then how do you think I stand it when you go on for weeks without speaking to *me*? Or telling me what the trouble is?'

For a time after that he was better. Then the old habit fastened down on him again. When it did, I made no further effort to conquer what was evidently too strong for him, and for me. I recalled what his mother told me about his moodiness as a boy, and how the fits of melancholy silence would come on him and hold him prisoner for weeks on end.

All this time we were both living at top speed, lives that were crowded to the brim with all sorts of activities and responsibilities. Under this pressure it was inevitable that two temperaments emotionally so different should clash.

'You're a woman of great value, and you have marvellous qualities,' he would say to me. 'You have a heart of gold. But,' — there always seemed to be a 'but' — 'you don't stop to think. You let yourself fly into a temper for the slightest reason. *Che peccato!*'

And I, perhaps because I was subtly aware of the truth of this summary, and yet was constitutionally unable to react otherwise in an atmosphere of chilliness and criticism and reserve, would flare up in self-defence, and condemnation of him.

Such scenes were bad enough at home. But at the opera house, where many of them occurred in my dressing-room just before a performance, they were infinitely worse. After such a scene I would go on the stage with every nerve in my body quivering. I could feel the muscles in my throat tighten up. I would hear my own voice, and the sound of it did not sound like me.

I am not blaming Gatti, or even myself. Though there were times, naturally enough, when I did both. But I have seen so many marriages, I have listened to the stories of so many private lives, that I have come to know how very delicate and sensitive and subject to change is the tie between men and women; how much it demands of both for nourishment and growth.

For years before there was an actual separation between us — and that happened several years before we were formally divorced — Gatti and I were living lives as separate as two human beings who eat, sleep, and receive their mail under the same roof, and whose careers lie in the same field, and even in the same opera company, can live. My comings and goings, my amusements and interests, my friends, did not seem to interest my husband.

I left him to his own.

Only, whilst we were in New York, we would go to certain formal dinners and receptions together. And every summer, after the War, we went to Europe.

I never took another apartment in Paris. But usually, after taking a cure somewhere, I went to the Lido. Jane San Faustino still came every summer to the Excelsior, and Annina Morosini still presided over the gorgeous old palace on the Grand Canal.

But the Kaiser's portrait was gone from its old place on the wall of her boudoir.

Annina's parties were still marvellous. I remember one fancy-dress ball she gave, that brought the old golden Venice of the *Cinquecento* to life for a night. The Morosini footmen, in picturesque livery, stood at the steps of the palace to help the guests from their gondolas as they arrived. The music of guitars and violins floated over the rose-hung garden walls. I wore my gold-brocade Desdemona costume, and a cap of pearls on my hair. And danced all night, until dawn. Then I went in a gondola with the Marchese Casatti to the *piazza* before St. Mark's and watched the first pearly pink light of the sunrise wake the old church out of sleep.

While the pigeons fluttered down about me by the fountain, the Marchese roused a sleepy waiter at one of the cafés, who brought us coffee and crusty bread which the pigeons shared with us. Workmen and a few of the pious on their way to early Mass stopped and stared at us, and rubbed their eyes.

Before 1914, few Americans knew the Lido. The few who went there were the artists, or the cosmopolites who belonged as much to Europe as to America. In those years there was no International Set such as we have today. But in the summers after the War all sorts of Americans began turning up at the Excelsior. You saw them strolling on the sands, or playing bridge in the gay *cabanas*. You heard them talking about Hollywood and Palm Beach and Wall Street and President Harding, and prosperity. They fairly exuded prosperity. And, after the manner of Americans, they fairly took the place.

Whenever I read somewhere how Elsa Maxwell practically made the Lido, I feel a chuckle start deep down inside of me. Remembering many things; some of which I'll tell.

I was in Paris. One day, going into the Ritz to lunch with Admiral 'Andy' Graves, I ran into the solid square bulk that is Elsa.

'Hello, Alda, darling.' She kissed me resoundingly. 'What are you doing these days?'

I told her, ending with 'The day after tomorrow I'm going to Venice.'

'Venice!' Elsa rolled her eyes. She was getting into one of her extravagantly sentimental moods. I could see it coming. Venice ... moonlight ... guitar music ... gondolas ...

'How lucky you are!'

'Why not come along with me?' I said impulsively. 'Come with me as my guest and see if you don't think the Lido is the most perfect place you've ever seen, anywhere.'

That is the true story of how Elsa Maxwell 'discovered' the Lido.

Does anyone know exactly when or how Elsa Maxwell dawned on New York's horizon? Or when she inherited the cap and bells as society's jester that had once belonged to Harry

Lehr? I came to know her during those jumbled war years, when various causes and drives and charities brought together a garbled assortment of people. Along with other things, Elsa wrote songs. One of them, 'Help the Navy Here Over There,' we sang at that Navy Benefit Concert at the Metropolitan. Another song, called 'The Singer,' Elsa dedicated to me. Frank La Forge and I fixed it up a bit, and I sang it on my concert programs all through one season. It was sentimental, but it was one of those songs that people will drop a tear over, and love for the emotion it arouses in them. All about a singer who thought she was pretty good until she heard a little bird warbling in a tree. Then she cried:

'Dear God! How small a singer am I!'

And, presumably, never sang again.

But to come back to Elsa and me and the Lido. I was right about one thing; she did love it. The crowds, the international celebrities, the ex-royalties and aspiring archdukes, the Hollywood queens and the English duchesses. The gossip, the scandal, the atmosphere of a gay, daring, naughty world. With her remarkable flair for knowing exactly the right people to know, and getting to know them, Elsa was in her element.

I think it was that summer that, one morning, I looked over my wardrobe wondering what I should wear on the beach. My eye fell on a suit of Chinese silk pajamas that I had bought in San Francisco. I put them on, with an enormous cartwheel straw beach hat, and went down to my *cabana*. I didn't know it then, but I started something — the Lido beach-pajama vogue. The London illustrated papers carried photographs of Madame Alda in pajamas. Within a week dozens of silk-pajamaed figures were to be seen on the sands.

I never saw Elsa in pajamas. But I have a snapshot which I took of her and Miss Isnaga, the sister of the Duchess of Manchester, in bathing-suits so circumspect they might have been designed as costumes in a comic revue.

I started something — the Lido beach pajama vogue

Alda with Irene Castle

AFTER all, who wasn't at the Lido in those years? There were always plenty of opera folk; John McCormack, glad to escape the damp of his adored Ireland for the baking sunshine and the warm lagoons. Italo Montemezzi, the author of *L'Amore dei Tre Re*, the finest opera to be written in my time. Montemezzi had married an American girl, Katharine Leith. They spent their honeymoon at the Lido. They were tremendously in love, and quite refreshingly and occasionally embarrassingly frank about it. Their suite adjoined my own. Perhaps I'd forgotten the etiquette that should surround newly-married lovers. I know I barged in on them several times when my presence was neither desired nor desirable. Their first son, named Marco in memory of his parents' Venetian honeymoon, has red hair.

'Just the color of yours, Alda,' Montemezzi pointed out to me the first time I saw the baby. 'That's because you *would* keep popping in on Katharine and me...'

Usually Dorothy Caruso was at the Lido too, with little Gloria, whom I adored and with whom I built the most impressive sand castles. The child grew steadily more and more to resemble her father.

Once a gramophone company for whom Caruso made many records conceived the idea that a record sung by Caruso's daughter would be very popular. Gloria's voice was just the sweet, tuneful pipe that belongs to children and birds. She was willing to make the record, and she asked me if I would go with her.

Together we went down to Camden. Just as her father and I went on that sleety day when he fitted me to my first pair of rubbers. At the laboratory Gloria took her place before the recording instrument. I stood with my arm around her, and with her hand in mine.

She began to sing that old Christmas carol for children:
'Little Lord Jesus...'

My eyes filled with tears.

Halfway through the verse comes a high note. Just before it Gloria began to tremble. Her voice quavered. I gave her a quick hug and a big kiss. The fear was lost in a little laugh, and she took a breath and landed on the top note like a bird.

'Bravo!'

SPRING, 1926.

And Buenos Aires once again.

I stood at the ship's rail as we went up the harbor, and watched the clear sunlight play on the magnificent white buildings. It was a new city since I sang there the last time. Toscanini had wanted me to return for an engagement at the Buenos Aires Opera House whilst he was there in 1912. But when I told this to Gatti he looked like a thundercloud and said, positively, 'No.'

Now, driving up the splendid Avenida de Maya, between the opposing rows of Grand Hotels, I felt, as I always do feel when I go places, excited and adventurous and young and gay.

Here was I, engaged to sing a season in the Argentine capital when it was *en fête* for the coming of no less a personage than H.R.H. Edward, Prince of Wales. His ship, the *Renown*, was expected any day. Already the flag of Argentina and the Union Jack were fluttering from many of the buildings.

The opera I was engaged to create in Buenos Aires was *La Cena della Beffe*. Umberto Giordano composed it around *The Jest*, which the Barrymores played so successfully on Broadway a season or two before. It had its première at the Metropolitan in January 1926 with Gigli, Titta Ruffa, Didur, and me, and with Serafin conducting. Now we were to sing it for the first time in South America.

After all, this is the story of me. Of Frances Alda, the woman.

What means most to me today is not the success of *La Cena della Beffe* in Buenos Aires, but the good times I had there.

Especially after the Prince came.

My cosmopolitan citizenship stood me in good stead. As the wife of Gatti-Casazza I travelled with an Italian passport, and the Italian embassy in Buenos Aires was a most hospitable home to me. As a member of the Metropolitan Opera Company in New York, the American embassy and the American colony in Buenos Aires claimed me for their own. But I had been born an Englishwoman. When I visited South America the first time it was as a British subject. And Britons never forget their own. Sir Beelby and Lady Alston, at the British embassy, entertained me frequently.

The embassy was H.R.H.'s official residence. Every day during his visit I was asked to lunch or tea, or to dinner. To play tennis, or to dance.

Golf with Edward VII at Marienbad twenty years ago, the fox-trot and cocktails with his grandson.

On the night of the first performance of *La Cena della Beffe* the Prince gave a ball. His engagements would keep him, I knew, from coming to the opera. But just before I left for the opera house to dress for the performance, a servant from the British embassy delivered a package for me. Inside the wrapping was a photograph of H.R.H. in naval uniform.

Across it he had written:

> *Not forgotten! Good luck for*
> *the performance tonight.*
> EDWARD, P.

When the performance was over I found that the Prince had sent his car to take me from the opera house to the ball.

A few days later the *Renown* was scheduled to sail. On the last day of Edward's stay in Buenos Aires I was asked to lunch at the embassy to say '*Bon voyage.*' When the time came for him to go to the ship we all stood in the drawing-room while he shook hands with each of us in turn, and said some courteous word of appreciation and farewell.

I think no one who was there that day was not touched by the wistful quality of his youth and his dignity.

'Good-bye.'

'Good-bye, sir.'

'*Bon voyage!*'

The farewells were all said. He stood on the threshold, then turned for a final word. It was addressed to me:

'Remember, Alda, when you come to London, you must come to see Mamma.'

Not 'Her Majesty,' but 'Mamma.'

It was, in its way, an accolade.

PART
VII

CASA MIA

*"Mid pleasures and palaces though we
may roam,
Be it ever so humble, there's no place
like home.'*

VII

THE house looked eastward over the bay.

Its shining, diamond-paned windows caught the sunrise, whilst the pearly mists still blanketed the colonial steeples and gabled roofs and dark, old wharves of Port Washington on the opposite shore.

The house's other side stretched two slightly curving arms toward the road, like the welcoming gesture of a warm and generous woman. Ivy overgrew the stucco and timbered walls. Tall trees shaded the level lawns. A hedge hid a useful kitchen garden. A slight depression in the turf cried out to be transformed into a rose garden.

'It's mine,' I said to the startled renting agent, as the car rolled up the driveway.

'How much is it? When can I sign the deeds? How soon can I move in?'

My house.

It couldn't possibly have any other name than just that. 'Casa Mia.'

For a long time the desire for a home of my own had been growing stronger and more insistent. Not an apartment, but a house in the country; though not too far from town. I wanted the feel of my own land under my feet. I wanted to walk under tall trees I could call my own. I wanted a garden brimmed and overflowing with roses; yellow roses, chiefly. I wanted a neat, thrifty *potager*, with rows of parsley and chives and mint, and clumps of grey-leafed lavender; beside all the pot-herbs and soup seasonings. How I adore a garden like that!

Whenever I am in Paris and go out to Lady Mendl's Villa Trianon at Versailles to one of her famous Sunday luncheons, I always steal time from the party to go for a stroll along the paths of her kitchen-garden, and sniff the good, pungent smells.

Moreover, in my own garden I wanted quantities of marigolds and double-flowered hollyhocks. And, in October, lavish masses of bronze and yellow chrysanthemums.

Of course, in those vague, delightful plans that I made whenever the desire for a home of my own was on me, there was a house, a long, rambling, informal house, such as one finds tucked into a fold of the Sussex downs. A house that was really livable, with lots of windows framing views. I've never been able to endure not to be able to look out and away from myself and my immediate surroundings.

A house with every room in it big enough to hold a piano if I wanted one there.

There was no use, I knew, listing such requirements as these and handing the list to the real-estate agents. They would probably have thought me quite mad, and altogether the prima donna. To them I talked about taxes and acreage and land values and roof tiles and plumbing. But all the while, inside, I was looking for a dream to come true. And now it had. I had found it.

It wasn't mine yet, of course, as far as actually owning the title deeds in my name. But in another sense, it was mine from the minute the car turned in at the gates; the minute I saw the house and the broad expanse of bay beyond its terraces. From the minute I stepped out of the car and thought:

'How good it's going to be to come home to this.'

And having bought it, with the title deeds in my pocket, I embarked on the wildest spending debauch of my whole career. Not even those first six weeks in London and Paris with Alby, and with my share of our legacy of ten thousand pounds burning a hole in my pocket, could equal it. I ordered in carpenters and masons and architects and builders. I revelled in blueprints and propositions to turn the whole house inside out and upside down. Spurred on by my passion for closets and places to put things away in, and for having everything put away tidily and beautifully, I began to tap walls here and there for possible extra space for cupboards. I woke in the night and reached for the pencil and paper that were always on my bedside table in those days, and drew diagrams of what could be done by raising the roof over one wing, knocking out all the partitions, cutting new windows to open on a terrace and a garden that I had visioned planted with lilacs of every sort ...

Actually, I bought Casa Mia before I sailed to Buenos Aires — as I have told in the previous chapter. Whilst I was there and for the remainder of the tour, the thought of my house was ever in my mind. My luggage grew heavier and bulkier and more numerous as I bought more and more beautiful things to take home with me.

From Buenos Aires, I sailed for Australia to make a concert tour there and in New Zealand.

The ship docked at Sydney. There, on the pier to meet me, was Alby. It was our first meeting since he had said good-bye to me in Paris when I started to study with Madame Marchesi. He knew me before I recognized my brother in the tall, handsome blonde man who came up the ship's gangplank ...

'Francie!'

One look into his eyes, they were still that marvellous violet color; one look at his features, so like my mother's ...

'Alby!'

Twenty-three years rolled up like a curtain and found us standing there, much as we had stood in the lawyer's office on that eventful day when he handed us the cheque for ten thousand pounds.

Ten thousand pounds worth of adventures!

My share of them in far ports and among people many of whom the world calls famous. Some of the adventures gay, exciting, successful, others with a tinge of bitterness. But all of them sincerely and honestly my own, the direct consequence of my own nature, with its loves, its hates, its desires, its fears, its hopes and ambitions.

To some eyes Alby's adventures might seem less spectacular, more circumscribed, even humdrum. What could a physician have in his life of other people's aches and pains and diseases, and his own pills and powders, to set beside the experiences of a prima donna?

It was Alby himself who, all unknowing, answered that question as we drove from the ship's pier to the hotel.

'You've done what you set out to do, Francie; and I've done with my life what I wanted to do. I suppose, in a way, we've both been successes.'

'To do with your life what you wanted to do ...'

My brother's words were often in my mind during those weeks whilst Australia welcomed and fêted me. Whenever I sang people seemed to remember that my mother had been one of their singers, and that Grandfather had brought the first Italian opera company that ever came to Australia. From Sydney I went to Melbourne, where Alby, married now and a father, lived. Every day, whilst I was there, he would snatch an hour or two from his patients and hospital appointments to spend with me. I remember we used to walk in the Botanical Gardens, for Alby loves Nature as ardently as I do. And we would talk ....

One day we drove out to St. Kilda. Grandmother's house there had been sold long before, but the present owners welcomed us and let us walk through those well-remembered rooms, and see again the familiar patterns the sunlight made on the walls and floors, and catch a faint whiff of lavender that still haunted the room that was my grandmother's.

'To do with your life what you wanted to do ...'

Once there was a little girl carried into this house for the first time in her grandfather's arms. Behind her stretched a long sea voyage and a strange land and Death. Before her waited Life. Someone took her from her grandfather and set her in a high chair and brought her a bowl of bread and milk.

'Are you hungry, dear? Do you want something to eat?'

'I want to sing ...'

A fat little girl in a shapeless, plain, white linen frock and cotton stockings, weeping stormily for the loss of a blue velvet princess gown and a blue velvet hat with a curling feather. A little girl stoutly protesting:

'How can I ever be an opera singer if you won't let me *sing?*'

A little girl seizing her first moment of complete freedom to buy six dozen pairs of heretofore forbidden silk stockings, and declaring that never again, as long as she lived, would she wear anything else but silk; and that the finest and best. A little girl playing Mozart in the moonlight while Death stole softly into the next room . . .

'To do with your life what you wanted to do . . .'

Yes, Alby was right. I had done that.

Is it true that something of us lingers forever in the house and in the rooms where we have met life and tried to understand it? It seemed as though something of my grandmother was still present in that house at St. Kilda. Something that spoke to me with my grandmother's directness and fine, practical judgment:

'To sing, to be an artist, is not enough. You must also live completely, as a woman.'

What had my grandmother learned about living during those years when she and her husband toured the world, making music in strange, foreign cities, and for audiences who spoke all the tongues of Babel? Aside from the conveniences of modern travel, my experiences on my prolonged concert tours and the engagements at operas from Warsaw to the Metropolitan paralleled hers. What she had gained from her nomad adventures she had brought to this house at St. Kilda which was her 'Journey's End.' Here she had gathered the harvest of her years. Here she had made of it a feast for herself and for others. Myself, one of them.

In the house where my first remembered years began, I had a vision of Casa Mia, the new house that was waiting for me on the other side of the world, and what I wanted my life there to hold for me and for those to whom I opened its doors.

I SAID good-bye to Alby and his wife and their adorable, chubby children. I went on to New Zealand.

It was my first visit to my birthplace. And I loved it the minute I set foot on its shore. It was as English as the phrase 'Yes, modom,' coming from respectful lips between a pair of muttonchop whiskers. Everywhere were beautifully spotless towns and villages, each clustered about a stone church, that might have been transported intact out of Dorsetshire or Kent. Christchurch, where I was born, had a river flowing through the centre of the town, bordered by huge willows, and a magnificent university.

I felt a surge of pride that I was of the same blood as the men and women who had created this.

My father's family, the Davieses, had become rich and powerful in the three or four generations since they came as pioneers to the island. My father was dead. I was sorry, for I had long since regretted the hasty pride that made me destroy without a reply the letter he wrote me when word of my grandmother's death reached him. He had wanted me then to come to Christchurch to live with him and his second wife. But I had been brought up by my mother's family, and I suppose it was only natural that I should have reflected their attitude toward my father and the reasons that led my young mother to divorce him.

Today, when half the young people one meets are children of divorced parents, I often remember how that division between my father and mother and the sense of wrong associated with it influenced me in making one of the most important decisions of my life.

Still, I came to New Zealand not as a stranger. I had a letter to the leader of the House of Commons, and by way of that letter came one of the travel experiences that will always stand out in my memory. This was a visit to the Maori villages, where I heard the music of the primitive New Zealanders, and saw their dances.

All my life has been lived among peoples whose civilization is accounted very old and conventionalized. I have never felt any appeal in crudities and unsophistication. But in those beautiful Maoris, the handsomest people on earth, flowed something so natural and untaught as to be truly primitive. And yet so balanced, so smooth, so gentle that it was perfect art. It moves in all their movements. It speaks in the music of their voices and their plaintive instruments.

One of the Maori songs haunted me for days.

Finally I wrote it down. When the first of my series of radio broadcasts began, I used a bar of that song to introduce each of my weekly programs on the air.

NEW YORK once more, and Casa Mia.

The architects and the workmen had accomplished what I gave them to do. There was my house, fresh and expectant, waiting for its furnishings and for my life to begin in it.

Many of the changes I had made in the rooms were designed for the advantage of the lovely old pieces of furniture that Count Trotti had collected for me so long ago, and which I had brought to America under the noses of the War Lords. These took their places in Casa Mia as though they had been intended for the house from the first.

In the whole house, next to my bedroom (which is long, with windows on three sides and a fireplace under an old Provençal mantel; which has a carpet of soft fawn color and curtains of old silk the color of pale sunshine, and a dressing-table and bed draperies of *rosaline* lace that I bought whilst I was singing at La Monnaie; and on the bed a spread made of *fond de bonnet*, using more than a hundred old Breton caps, put together with stitches as fine and as beautiful as the lace itself), the room that I love best is the boudoir.

It is on the first floor, a few steps from the front door. The walls are a pale, dull green against which the old needlepoint on the chairs loses none of the delicacy of its coloring. The windows look eastward over the Bay, and others on the south side of the room open on plantings of the lilacs that I love.

Against that south window stands my piano. It is the nearest thing to having it in the garden that I could achieve.

In the corner beside the fireplace is the little yellow-painted, seventeenth-century spinet that Toscanini loves to play upon whenever he visits me. How many times he has tried to wheedle me into selling it to him!

I had wanted one for years. Perhaps to replace in my heart the little piano which had once been Verdi's, and which I never did succeed in getting out of the Casazza Palace in Ferrara. And where did I ultimately find it? In New York, of all places! I had been to a concert at Carnegie Hall. Driving away, in the crowded traffic of Fifty-Seventh Street, my car was halted outside a shop that sells musical instruments.

There in the shop window stood the spinet.

Hastily I scrambled out of the car and through the honking traffic jam. I went into the shop. The proprietor, a gentle elderly man with the childlike gaze that is so often the indication of a great love of music, came forward.

I had eyes only for the spinet. Its yellow surface was painted over with garlands of roses and lovers' knots and fat cupids. The old ivory of the keys teased me to pull off my gloves and to play upon them.

'I want to buy it,' I said bluntly.

'It is not for sale.'

I argued. But he was adamant. He had found the spinet somewhere in Europe. It was his most prized possession. He placed it in the window only to attract passers-by to his shop, which sold modern instruments and volumes of music, old and new.

I looked along the shelves that held these volumes. One or two I took down, and pored over. We talked about them.

'But you know a great deal about such things,' he said.

'I've been collecting them for years.'

'Indeed. I ought to know your name. Your face is so very familiar to me ...'

'I am Frances Alda.'

'Madame Alda ...'

Well, it turned out exactly the way Hollywood would have staged it. He was an ardent opera-goer. He knew *Manon* and *Bohème* and *Faust* almost as completely as I knew them. We talked operas and old music, and finally his eye came round to rest on the spinet.

'You would like to have it, wouldn't you?' he said wistfully.

'Very, very much.'

'Well, then, it's yours. I give it to you for the pleasure you have given me so many times at the Metropolitan.'

In the end, at my insistence, he accepted a cheque for the amount he had paid for the spinet when he bought it in Europe. But he wouldn't take a penny more.

To me, the spinet has always been the gift he intended it to be.

THE lease on the apartment on Fifty-Eighth Street was up. I did not renew it. Gatti had moved to the Hotel Plaza, and when I came back from my tour in time for the opening of the 1926–1927 season at the Metropolitan, Casa Mia was ready to welcome me. I loved my house. I spent all the time there that I could, driving into New York for appointments and rehearsals and for performances at the opera house. Then driving back again over the Queensborough Bridge, strung with lights. Great Neck is only twenty-four miles from New York.

On the days when I was singing at the Metropolitan I would leave Casa Mia about five in the afternoon, to be in my dressing-room at the opera house by six. Usually Gatti would come backstage for a talk with me before the performance — usually to pour out to me a recital of his trials with the other artists, conductors, stage directors, and box-holders.

The separation between Gatti and myself, which for years had been one of temperament and tastes, was now actual. He had begged me not to let anyone know that we had separated. Naturally, since our separation was our own affair and secret, there would be invitations addressed to us that we should have to accept together. Too, there would be times when I enter tained at Casa Mia when I should want to have Gatti there.

We were agreed in believing that a man and a woman who had been married but who no longer wished to continue the married relationship could be friends. We had a tacit agreement that both of us should go our separate ways, provided always that those ways did not interfere with or hurt the other.

If this agreement had been kept, I should never have divorced Gatti-Casazza. But as the months went on a number of things happened that brought us to a point where a divorce offered the only solution. The reasons and blames are purely personal. For some time before I came to the decision I was being bombarded with anonymous letters and with newspaper clippings concerning certain associations of my husband's.

I AM going to divorce you.'
    The heavy eyelids drooped over Gatti's eyes. The full lips, grey-bearded now, stiffened.

'You wouldn't do that?'

'You don't know me, Giulio, if you think that. I've made up my mind.'

What impressed me most was the sense of relief I experienced the minute the ultimatum had been given.

H OW will this affect your position at the Met.?' my friends
asked when my decision became known.

I replied that I could not see why it should affect it at all.
After all, I was engaged as an artist, not as the wife of the
Metropolitan's Director. But I remembered something Gatti
had said to me once in a moment of anger:

'If you ever divorce me, you may be sure of this — you'll
never sing at the Metropolitan again.'

Would he make good that threat now?

I did not think so. But asking myself that question roused
another query in my mind. Did I want to go on singing at the
Metropolitan?

I loved the opera house and its audience. I loved and was
proud of my career there. And I was at the height of that career.
Of course I wanted to stay on, and go on singing.

But to go on under the direction of my divorced husband and
in the same company with Rosina Galli, whom everybody said
Gatti would soon marry?

The obstacles and unpleasantnesses that such a situation inevitably must present became every day more apparent. I was
in a position where I could not stay on at the Met. and keep my
self-respect.

A member of the company came to me one day and told me
that Gatti was reputed to have said to someone that when my
contract ran out at the end of the year it would not be re-
newed. Nothing was to be said to me in advance, and nothing
was to be said to the public. If this plan were carried out I
should not be allowed even the opportunity of making a formal
Farewell to the audience that had been mine for so long.

Promptly I sat down and telephoned to Otto Kahn. The result of that conversation was that the Metropolitan offered me,
and I accepted, a new contract for one year — my last year at
the opera house.

I sang *Martha* that season, a great many times. And *Manon*

Lescaut, two operas that had become identified with me in the minds of the public. *Martha* and *Mefistofele* and *Othello* have not been given at the Metropolitan since I left its stage.

I made my Farewell in *Manon Lescaut,* with Gigli. It was an opera I had sung scores of times. The rôle suited me. I loved it even more than Massenet's *Manon,* in which I made my operatic début in Paris.

On the night of the Farewell, when I arrived at the opera house, I found the floor of my dressing-room strewn deep with fresh rose petals. There stood Celia, her face one huge smile, and fat tears running down her broad cheeks.

'Madama! *Oh, madama....*'

'None of that,' I scolded vigorously in Italian. 'How am I going to sing my best tonight if you get me started crying? And how am I going to go on the stage unless you stop blubbering and kissing my hand, and start to dress me? You let one tear drop on that rose-brocade costume, Celia, and I'll box your ears.'

The tears dried up as by magic. Over Celia's face came that look of protective understanding I knew so well.

'*Madama e nervosa,*' she said soothingly. 'Never mind. Be calm. Celia will attend to everything.'

From that moment on, the evening became a medley of lights, music, applause, kisses, flowers, more kisses, telegrams, telephone calls, tears, still more kisses, friends and fellow artists crowding into my dressing-room, gifts ...

Of these last, the one that will always mean the most to me is the illuminated scroll that hangs beside my writing desk at Casa Mia. It is a testimonial of the affection and farewell good wishes of the Metropolitan's stage hands.

A farewell testimonial from the Metropolitan's stage hands

A WOMAN with your vitality can't stop her career at its height, and while she is still a young woman, and sit down on the side lines.'

'I've never yet sat on the side lines,' I retorted. 'And I have no intention of doing so now.'

'But what will you do?'

'Radio,' I said.

In the years whilst I had been singing to four thousand people crowded into an opera house, science had invented a means by which a singer could sing to four million persons at a time. The four million interested me. Those concert tours had their effect on my thinking. I felt that I knew America, and I wanted to sing to the whole country.

Here was a way of doing it.

Whilst I was still under contract at the Metropolitan, I had made a number of broadcasts. For years the Metropolitan had an agreement with the Victor Talking Machine Company, whereby the Met.'s artists were permitted to make records for that company. The Victor paid the Metropolitan twenty-five thousand dollars a year for this exclusive privilege. When Atwater Kent began his famous series of Sunday Night Concerts, I was asked to sing at one of the broadcasts. Gatti said 'No,' and Otto Kahn said 'No.' But I contended that as there was no mention of radio in my contract with the Metropolitan I could accept Mr. Kent's offer. And I did.

Naturally that started something among the other artists. 'If Alda can go on the air, why so can the rest of us.'

It ended in Atwater Kent's paying the Metropolitan twenty-five thousand dollars yearly for the right to engage the artists for his broadcasts.

Of all the audiences I ever faced, the microphone gave me the greatest thrill. It wasn't a curious round black hole on the end of a pipe that I was singing to. It was uncounted thousands of human beings. Who were they? Where were they?

Eight P.M. in New York meant 6 P.M. in the vast Middle West. Supper-tables being laid. Women stopping in the act of cutting bread and butter to listen to the adventures of Manon Lescaut and Mimi. Five o'clock in California. Men and women drinking tea and Prohibition cocktails, halting their talk to hear Tosca's '*Vissi d'arte.*' That was how I visioned it when I planned my first broadcasts.

I arranged to give six of Puccini's operas: *Butterfly, Le Villi, Manon Lescaut, Tosca, Bohème, Turandot.* It was the first time the operas of Puccini had ever been put on the air.

I had a sponsor, the American Radiator Company. Between the acts of the opera an announcer took the 'mike,' and made some well-chosen remarks about the products of the company. On the first night, whilst we were giving *Butterfly*, the announcer waxed enthusiastic about the advantages of modern plumbing in the home.

The humor of that caught me.

'If there had been modern plumbing, there would have been no *Butterfly*,' I retorted.

There was a sudden look of consternation on the faces round me which did not vanish until an electrician whispered that that remark, at least, had not gone on the air.

Driving in town to the first of these broadcasts I said to myself:

'Well, Alda, you'll get no applause tonight. No curtain calls. Just the satisfaction that comes of knowing within yourself that you've done the best you're capable of doing.'

That was before I found out that a radio artist's applause comes by mail. Several mornings after the first broadcast I looked out the window at Casa Mia and saw the Great Neck postman coming up the drive literally bowed under a sack of mail.

'Good heavens!' I said to Boo. 'Is it Christmas or Valentine's Day, or something?'

None of these. It was just music-loving America taking its pen in hand.

Some of the thousands of letters that poured in until we were nearly desperate at the sight of so much paper and ink came from old friends who had come to many of my concerts in various cities and who wrote welcoming me 'on the air.' Some were from people hearing me for the first time. Many asked me to sing special favorite songs of their own. Those letters taught me that there is a bond that unites all music-lovers, deeper and stronger than any that exists between those who love and appreciate any of the other forms of art. I think it springs from the fact that to appreciate music one has to have a special hearing and feeling sense. Those who possess this know that they have something not shared by all the world. Something esoteric, that sets them apart.

There were so many letters requesting songs that when I planned my broadcasts for the next season — that year I was sponsored by Bosco Coffee — and for the two years following that when I sang for the Waldorf-Astoria Hotel from my own suite in its Towers, I made them concerts in which I sang the songs my audience requested of me.

Songs of every kind — ballads, hymns, operatic arias, classical songs, old-time melodies. . . .

A good musical program is never created by chance. It requires real artistry to know what to give and which numbers to put together. Not every artist has this gift, which is really that of the impresario. Toscanini, for instance, doesn't know how to build up a program. He invariably includes too many and too varied numbers. In planning my programs I made up my mind that I would be my own announcer. And that I would tell a story about each song that I sang. After all, I argued, I'm not the only person in the world who likes to know about things. People love information, if it isn't given too prosily, or as though you were trying to teach them for their own good.

I believe I was the first artist who did this at her broadcasts. 'Tell me what songs you want, and I'll sing them,' I offered. How the radio audience took me up on that.

The letters asked again and again for 'The Last Rose of Summer,' and 'Home Sweet Home,' and the negro lullaby 'Mighty Lak a Rose.' But by far the most requests were for the famous *Ave Marias*.

There was something exhilarating in this close personal contact with one's audience. It touched me more than any applause or bouquets or curtain calls had ever done. And touching me, I know I sang all the better for it. I had a habit of ending each of the broadcasts with 'Good-night. And God bless you!'

Nearly every letter that came to me ended: 'And God bless *you!*'

One day, I recall, a letter came from a young man in a small town in western Pennsylvania. He told me that he was going to be married on the evening and at the same hour as my weekly broadcast. He had arranged to have the radio turned on in the room where the ceremony would be held, and he wanted to know if I wouldn't sing 'O Promise Me' especially for him and his bride.

I have often wondered at just what point of the marriage service my voice broke in, for of course I sang the song he asked for.

BROKEN HEARTS MENDED

LOST REPUTATIONS RECOVERED

BLASTED HOPES RESTORED

FRANCES ALDA

SINGS FOR YOU TONIGHT

COME IN

This sign, pasted up beside the door of the Bowery Mission, gave me a start when my eye fell on it.

A crowd of battered-looking men stood about the steps of the house. They read the poster, then turned and stared at me getting out of the car to go in. The comments were outspoken:

'Big woman, ain't she!'

'I like a green dress.'

'Come on, boys. Let's take it in.'

The mission hall was packed to its four walls. The Bowery Mission was celebrating the fiftieth anniversary of its founding. This was the special occasion for the concert.

BROKEN HEARTS MENDED — that was a large order to hand anyone to fill. But if any of the promises on the poster were kept that night, it was the songs, not the singer, that accomplished it. On my way out, after it was all over, I overheard a bit of dialogue that made me laugh all the way home to Great Neck:

'When she sang "The Last Rose of Summer," and her voice went up and up, I thought for sure she was going to crack. But, gosh, she didn't. She sang just as good for us as she sang for those rich folks at the opera house.'

'You said it, boy. And can that woman make a noise!'

HAS anyone guessed it?

I was having a wonderful time.

Just as I had hoped and expected, the welcoming gesture I had felt my house make toward me on the first day I set eyes on it was drawing to it a great many guests. Old friends, and new ones. They came for picnic suppers on the beach; to swim, to dance on the roof of the beach house, to lunch and to dine and stay the night.

Often they came to talk about themselves, among them:

Barbara Hutton, a sweet darling child (even though she would persist in eating absolutely nothing and drinking quantities of black coffee for the sake of her figure). She was in the throes of her first serious love affair, before Alexis Mdvani appeared on the horizon. And like most first love affairs it was unhappy. Her family did not approve of the young man. One of her protecting relatives had him shadowed by detectives whilst Babs was in Europe, then when she returned, presented her with the record of his comings and goings. Unfortunately there were things in it that looked pretty black.

Well, of course, a thing like that isn't easy to get over.

Mary Pickford, whom I had known as the most ecstatically happy of married actresses, now broken-hearted by the state of affairs between her and Douglas Fairbanks.

Charlie Chaplin, to spend a week-end. At lunch, on the first day, he suddenly rose from the table and began to act in silent pantomime one of the scenes from his picture *The Gold Rush*. To the uproarious delight of all the other guests and the entire lack of self-control of the butler, who let fall a tray and dribbled the gravy over me.

During that visit Charlie and I went fishing off the end of my boat dock.

'Bet you a dollar you don't catch a fish, Alda.'

'Bet you a dollar I do.'

'Bet you a dollar for every fish you catch.'

'Taken.'

Two hours later my string was eighty-three flapping fish. Charlie called off all bets, and reached for his chequebook.

I knew, what he didn't, and I saw no need to tell him, that the flounder were running.

I think it was Charlie Chaplin who said to me that day: 'Why don't you go into pictures, Alda?'

'Me? I've been. And I've come out again.'

And I told them the story. A picture company offered me twenty-five thousand dollars to make for them three short pictures. I accepted the offer. Following instructions, I drove out to the lot on Long Island where the films were to be made.

One was a patriotic picture in which I appeared as the Spirit of America or Liberty or something else, and sang 'The Star-Spangled Banner.' For years that reel used to come on in motion-picture theatres on the Fourth of July, and if I happened to be there I would suddenly find myself on the screen, looking enormous, and very unhappy as the sound machine gave forth my voice singing the national anthem. The second film was a story that took place in a convent. I was supposed to play the part of the Mother Superior, and lead my procession of nuns along the cloisters. In this I was supposed to sing the 'Ave Maria' from *Othello*.

The orders were that we were to be on the lot for rehearsal early in the morning. I was punctual. I made up for the part. About noon we began to rehearse it. And we rehearsed, and rehearsed. Presently the camera men came out and began to 'shoot.' They shot us this way, and they shot us that way. Then we did it all over again, differently, and they shot us again. Several times. After that, when it was after five o'clock in the afternoon, someone had the bright idea of doing it all over again a shade differently.

I rose up from my *prie-dieu* and jerked the veil and coif from my head.

'If this picture gets made any more ways it won't have me in it,' I declared. 'I'm going home. And I'm not coming back. I've been through too many years of rehearsals at the opera house to stand any more of this.'

OF THE opera folk, Dorothy Caruso came often to Casa Mia, whenever she was in this country. And Scotti and de Segurola.

Jeritza came once, I remember. She asked me if I would give her some lessons in singing. I shook my head.

'No. You and I are friends now. But if I started to teach you we wouldn't be friends. Let's leave it at that.'

The season of 1929–1930, which was the first season after I left the Metropolitan, opened with a production of *Manon Lescaut*. Bori sang the title rôle that I had sung so many times.

On the day after that opening, something happened. Is there an American alive who doesn't remember that twenty-ninth of October? When the crash of Wall Street resounded all over the world? If Patti and Caruso and Nordica and Chaliapin and Melba had suddenly been billed to appear all together at the Metropolitan, would the news have caused more than a flicker of interest?

I doubt it. Not when the foundations of our world were shaking.

True, it was not until a year or so later that the Depression into which the Crash hurled us menaced the fate of New York's opera house. When it did, I had a telephone call one evening from David Sarnoff, who had just been made a director of the Metropolitan.

'What are you doing tonight, Alda?'

'Resting.'

'Will you do something for me? Come over to my house. The directors of the Metropolitan are dining with me, and we'd like to ask you something.'

What they asked me was what I, were I one of their board, would vote to do as regards the immediate future of the opera house.

'I'd close it,' I said promptly. 'Shut it down tight till times are better, and society can come back to it. Then open it. You'll find when the Four Hundred are in their boxes, the Four Thousand will be clamoring to get in.'

I still believe they would have been money in pocket if they had followed the advice they asked me to give. Nothing worse, to my way of thinking, could have happened to the Metropolitan than to place it in the position of a charity patient, in need of help. It was robbed of its prestige, just as more recently the Presidency has been robbed of its prestige.

To have the singers begging funds for it deprived the Metropolitan of half its glamour in the eyes of the public. And the public of America goes to the opera as much, or more, for the glamour and glitter of the show, and all that they believe it stands for, as they go for the music which is heard there.

But in those months after the Crash I confess I wasn't thinking much about the state of grand opera in America. Along with most other Americans, I was thinking about *me*.

When I left the Met., I had the comfortable assurance that I had earned and saved and made a fortune, the income from which would give me the sort of life I wanted to live. It's a life that is fairly expensive. I've never known how to be economical and be happy at the same time. But with securities no longer secure, and dividends taking wings every month, what could I expect in a year or two? I cut down expenses right and left. I put up the Rolls. I 'managed' with three servants in Casa Mia instead of ten.

And when, in the summer of 1932, Ganna Walska came out to Casa Mia and asked me if I would agree to give her lessons in singing, I said that I would.

Ganna Walska is one of the figures who, in our time, has become almost a legend. She came originally from Poland, where her origin is lost in a maze of extraordinary stories. Her first appearance in New York was in *Mlle. Nitouche*, which was put on at the New Theatre. There was only one performance, the reviews of which were so bad that the piece was never repeated. In New York Walska met Otto Kahn, who became interested in her. It was he, I have been told, who sent her to his physician, a Doctor Frankel, whom Walska married ten days or so after her first professional visit to his office. It was while she was Doctor Frankel's wife that her friendship with Harold McCormack began. Not long after, Frankel died and Ganna sailed for Europe. McCormack was on the same boat. So was Alec Cochran and another friend of his and of McCormack's, Dick Crane. Before the ship docked at Cherbourg Cochran was as much in love with Ganna Walska as McCormack was. On the other side McCormack went to see his wife, Edith Rockefeller McCormack, who was in Switzerland, leaving Ganna in Paris. On his return a few days later, he went to her suite at the Ritz and was told by her maid that she had gone to take her singing lesson. McCormack followed to the house of the teacher, M. Monteux (the same Monteux who conducted the performance of *The Blue Bird* at the Metropolitan). There he found Ganna and Alec Cochran.

'Oh, Harold,' Ganna welcomed him. 'I want you to meet my husband.' With a wave of her hand she indicated Alec.

The marriage lasted five or six weeks, during which Cochran bought for Ganna Walska a beautiful house on the rue de Lisbon. Then there was trouble. During it, Cochran shut up the house, locking Ganna outside. But she knocked up the concierge and made him let her in, claiming the protection of the French law which forbids a husband to evict a wife from his property. Ultimately the house was sold and McCormack bought it and gave it to Ganna, whom, after Cochran divorced her, he married.

That, too, was a short-lived union.

Once, whilst she was in New York, Ganna had come and asked me to give her lessons. I had refused.

'If you want my honest advice,' I told her, 'learn to cook. You'll never be a singer.'

But apparently there is no dissuading Ganna Walska from her life-long ambition to become a prima donna. The second time she came to me, in the spring of 1932, she put her request in terms of dollars and cents: Would I sail with her to France, stay six weeks with her at her château, give her a lesson a day, and, for this, accept ten thousand dollars?

I looked wistfully about me; Ganna had driven out to Casa

Mia to have her talk with me. I thought about the peaceful, green and blue summers there, with the Bay under my windows to dive into every morning. I thought about my friends whose houses at Sands Point and elsewhere on the Island were gay, amusing places to drive to or motorboat to. But also, I thought about that ten thousand dollars. And about my alarmingly decreasing income.

'All right,' I told Walska. 'I'll come. Not with you; I'll have to see about renting the house if I can, or at least closing it. I'll join you in Paris and go out to the château and stay with you for six weeks, and give you a lesson every day.'

As the day for sailing drew near, and my trunks, packed and strapped, stood waiting for the van to take them to the pier, I grew more and more dubious about how the plan would work out. I am an individualist. (Has the reader guessed it?) Would it be possible for me to cast aside my individuality for six weeks and play the rôle of guest and teacher? Would my patience hold out? And my temper? And my tact?

I have never been noted for any great supply of the first two of these. Experience has trained me in the third. But would it stand six weeks of strain without an explosion of some sort?

As I say, I had my doubts.

I had more doubts when I saw the château, which was old enough to antedate the kind of plumbing the American Radiator Company would have approved, and which had successfully resisted any efforts to bring it up to date in that direction. Its windows looked sadly out across untidy lawns and shrubberies that made my fingers itch for a pair of gardening shears, and a drive in which weeds were more apparent than gravel. An odd assortment of servants whisked in and out around corners and up and down the crooked stairs. Its mistress had filled the place with the exotic, untidy, confused atmosphere of Poland, which Poles seem to carry with them wherever they go.

Ganna herself seemed to spend most of her time in bed; a great, carved, tumbled bed, the sheets of which were embroidered with crimson cherries and green leaves. Here she slept, ate, read novels, and commanded her household. Every day, toward noon, she would get out of it and come downstairs in her blue pajamas for a lesson with me. Then, the lesson over, she would trail back upstairs to the embroidered cherries and the paper novels and the coffee cups and platters of fruit and buttery *croissants*.

I did my level best in those lessons to teach Ganna Walska to sing. That was my part of the bargain. Between lessons I might fume at the loneliness, the physical discomfort, the appalling hit-or-missness of the household, but while we were at work I became a martinet, *à la Maman Marchesi*. I demonstrated, I repeated, I praised wherever I honestly could praise, I scolded. Old phrases and commands and comments and illustrations came back to my mind from those months when I studied under that great old lady who had more prima donnas to her credit than fingers to her two hands.

But work as I did, I could not teach Ganna Walska to sing.

'No, *No*, No!' I'd say to her. 'Not like that. You're singing like five million pigs.'

And she would just smile.

And do the same thing all over again.

On Sundays I would run away. Sometimes to Paris. Often to Versailles, to Lady Mendl's Villa Trianon, where the Sunday luncheon party was sure to be amusing and clever and refreshing. At one of those luncheons I found myself sitting next to a good-looking young man.

'You don't know me, Madame Alda,' he said, 'but I remember you very well. You and I once appeared on the same stage together.'

It didn't seem possible. I was certain he wasn't a singer.

'Where was that?' I asked him.

'In Chicago. Back in 1910. You came on from New York to sing a performance of *Rigoletto*. There was a big blizzard and the train was late, and everybody at the rehearsal waited and waited for you to get there. Finally, when you did come, you looked at them all and said: "Listen, this is how I sing Gilda. First I do this, then I do that. I ccme on here. I go off there. Now you all know all about it. There's no need of rehearsing any more. Everybody can go home." You waved your hand and left.'

I laughed, remembering the incident. Still, I couldn't place the speaker.

'And what were you doing there?'

'I wore red velvet trousers and coat, and I was one of the boys who held back the stage curtain.'

'And now you are?'

'I'm Mainbocher,' he said quite simply.

Mainbocher ... the American dressmaker who is the English Molyneux's rival, as the leading couturier of Paris today. Mainbocher, who dressed the Duchess of Windsor so effectively ... has come a long way from that post as curtain boy in the Chicago Opera House.

After a gay, entertaining Sunday I would go back to Ganna's château and the lessons again. Once, during the time I was there, Ganna gave a big party in Paris. Princess Helen, the mother of the Duchess of Kent, and a number of other old friends of mine were there. I was sitting with the Princess and the Maharajah of Kapourthala when Ganna came up to our table.

'Oh, Princess,' she said, 'I see you know my singing teacher.'

BANG, went my patience and my temper.

'I may, for my sins, be trying to teach you to sing,' I said shortly. 'But I am NOT your singing teacher. Remember that. I am Madame Alda.'

THOSE six weeks teaching Ganna Walska proved to be worth a great deal more than ten thousand dollars to me. Because they taught me something about myself.

It was something I had never suspected before. Something which, if you had accused me of it, would have made me laugh, and retort: 'Impossible.' It was this: I really like to teach.

A discovery revolutionary to all one's previous ideas about oneself needed thinking about. I thought about it all the way home, lying in my deck chair, and remembering, as a sort of undercurrent to my thinking, the scores of other crossings I had made with Gatti, when we had as one of our objects going to Munich, or Parma, or London to hear this or that new singer, who might be worth importing for the Metropolitan.

Imported singers . . .

Why? When there are more beautiful voices in America than in any country in the world.

The answer was pat on my tongue the minute the question was formed. Because though America has so many 'voices,' there are also in this country more bad and dangerous singing teachers than you will find anywhere else on earth. Out of every hundred persons who teach singing today, I would put the average as two who really know how to sing, or know how to train a pupil to sing.

I have known dozens of young American women, with perfectly exquisite natural voices, some of whom arrived at a fleeting fame in the Metropolitan, only to have their stardom wane because of their lack of correct vocal technique.

They no longer sing in public at all.

They are the victims of bad singing teachers.

It is a crying shame that such conditions should be permitted to exist in a country that requires physicians and dentists and other professional men and women to pass an examination and apply for a license before allowing them to practise on the public. Why should there not be a law decreeing that any man or woman who professes to teach the art of singing should at least have studied the art? Why should not a singing teacher be required to pass an examination on his fitness to handle so delicate an instrument as the human voice, before he is allowed to advertise for pupils whose money he pockets and whose voices, too often, he injures past redemption?

To teach singing the teacher must be able to illustrate what he wants the pupil to do. How else can he teach? All teaching is illustration and imitation. The teacher of the piano shows you how to hold your wrist, how to finger by doing it himself. How then can one teach another to sing unless one *is* a singer?

I was present once at a singing lesson. I heard the teacher say to the pupil:

'Look out of the window. You see that tall building across the street? Well, put your voice up on the top of that.'

Rubbish.

Of course what the man was trying to develop in the pupil was the precious 'head voice.' Only he didn't know how to teach this. And, being a man, he could not illustrate what he wanted his female pupil to achieve.

Again and again I am asked about this teacher, or that one, whose claim to the title consists in his having once been connected with the Metropolitan Opera House. The connection may be that the man was at one time one of the *corps répétiteurs* — one of the accompanists who teach the small artists their rôles. It may be that he rang the bell for the curtain to go up and down. It may be that he was a physician who happened to be called in once in an emergency to treat a famous singer. And on the basis of this connection, he sets himself up as a teacher of singing.

Put down as baldly as this, I know these stories seem ridiculous.

But they are true. The instances I have mentioned are actual facts.

One of these teachers taught a woman pupil who later came to me and told me the story, to sing '*Donna e mobile.*' Perhaps under the impression that Verdi had written it for a soprano voice. Another teacher who has had quite a vogue in New York advertised his ability on the basis that he had been associated with the great de Reszké. Those who knew the facts knew that the association had been that of a secretary-valet to the singer. Of course he heard his master practise, and having a quick ear, he picked up a good deal.

But enough to qualify as a teacher of the art of singing? Hardly.

This would be humorous were it not that earnest young artists put themselves and their future careers in the hands of charlatans such as these.

'If I study with So-and-So, he says he can get me into the Metropolitan,' I have been told of this teacher or of that one.

Does he?

Perhaps.

But can he?

That's another story.

No singer requires the offices of any particular teacher who claims to have 'pull' to get him, or her, an audition at the Metropolitan. The director of every great opera house is always eager to hear new voices, and to welcome enthusiastically any voice that is really beautiful, and is beautifully produced. I know this certainly was true of Gatti-Casazza. It is no less true of the present very competent director, Edward Johnson.

If no one is sterner than I on teachers who are unfit to train voices, no one is readier than I to encourage and praise a teacher who can really be trusted.

When Frank La Forge, who was my accompanist for so many years, decided to begin to coach, I wrote him expressing my confidence in his ability, and my hopes for his success. Evidently the letter pleased him, for he replied:

Sunday night at Casa Mia

Casa Mia on Great Neck, Long Island

MY DEAR FRIEND:

You cannot know how much your endorsement has meant to me, for I respect your opinion more than any other person's, and always wanted to make good with you.

This is a sketch of what you have often said, and I think it is noble and great of you to tell the world about it. Even though you had never done that, the knowledge that you approve of my work gives me a satisfaction that nothing else ever could.

Thank you for everything, and may your tour be a great pleasure and rest to you. You deserve all that is good.

With deepest gratitude, admiration, and affection,

Devotedly,

FRANK

To teach the art of singing requires that the teacher shall not only train the voice, but be able to teach the singer how to preserve the voice for years and years.

When I heard Adelina Patti at that marvellous concert at the Trocadéro she was seventy-two years old. And her singing was so exquisite that I went home and cried my eyes out because I thought I could never learn to sing so well. When I heard Melba as Mimi, she was at least sixty-two. Calvé, when I heard her, was in her sixties, and still a great prima donna. Most of those who read these pages know the marvel of Schumann-Heink, who was still singing toward the eighties.

The reason why these great artists were able to do this was not just because they were great artists. It was because they knew, because they had been taught, how to sing correctly.

All singing revolves around the intercostal muscles, those that the sports writers refer to as the solar plexus. When you see a singer, either a man or a woman, who is getting red in the face, whose neck muscles stand out like cords, pushing, pushing the tones, then you may be perfectly certain that the strident sounds that you are hearing are due to the terribly bad method of production.

Usually it is fright that makes a singer's throat tighten up. Fright, caused by nerves. To sing correctly the muscles of the face, the throat, and the neck must be completely relaxed. The only muscles that must be taut are those of the stomach. In other words, your bellows.

Watch a canary sing. How is it possible, you say, for that tiny feathered creature to have such tremendous breath control, and with such volume? I have watched my canary by the hour trill and trill. I have tried to keep in time with him. But I am completely out of breath while the bird is still singing. That is because he sings spontaneously, without effort and without strain. He has by Nature's gift the art that the singer must learn.

Marchesi, as I have told so many times in this story, laid great emphasis on the use of the head voice. '*Toujours la voix de tête*,' she would say, over and over again. She wrote it as a postscript to nearly all her letters to her pupils. She always illustrated this herself, at the same time insisting that it was impossible for a male teacher to produce the head tones properly. Marchesi, herself, steadfastly refused to teach male applicants.

She never let a pupil sing above F in anything but the head voice. The upper part of the voice was conserved with infinite care to avoid early breakdown. As a result, when her pupils sang top notes, they did so with the feeling that there was something in reserve. The singer who exhausts herself on the top notes is neither artistic nor effective. Moreover, she is ruining her voice.

Most girls overexercise their voices during the years while the voice is immature. That is the gravest temptation that affects American girls. They all want to sing, not to study. And singing, apparently, they want to scream. Marchesi was stern about this. She advised daily lessons of twenty minutes each, and no more. But her pupils were assembled in a class, and each pupil, though she actually sang no more than the twenty minutes Marchesi granted her, heard the lessons of the other pupils in the class, and benefited by the criticism and instruction.

Marchesi's exercises were little more than scales, sung very slowly. Single, sustained tones, repeated time and time again, until her critical ear was entirely satisfied. Then came arpeggios. After these came a more complicated technical drill to prepare the pupil for floritura work in the more florid operas. But at the base of all were the simplest kind of exercises. By these methods Marchesi produced great prima donnas — Melba, Calvé, Eames, Sybil Sanderson — the California girl for whom Massenet wrote *Thaïs*.

Marchesi taught me in the same way, and I know no other method of voice training.

She used to say, and I can see her black eyes snapping as she said it, that more voices collapsed from overpractice, and more careers collapsed from underwork, than from any other causes. All through my career as a singer I studied regularly two hours every morning. True, I seldom sang, full voice, more than twenty minutes of that time. But for the rest of the study period I would sing over, softly, the new rôle I was working on, or the songs for my concert program.

Daily study and practice and exercises, and unremitting care, not of the voice only, but of the general health. All these are needed to keep a voice in perfect condition.

And good food.

Not overeating. We have left behind us the days when the public expected all opera singers to be fat. Audiences today are more critical of a singer's appearance than they used to be. They demand not only that the singer shall sing well, but that she shall look lovely and be an actress, too.

No more beefy Isoldes and pudgy Carmens and bovine Violettas. Who wouldn't rather look at a slim and virginal Elsa than at one who bulges unromantically?

Just the same, severe dieting can seriously affect the voice. I thought of this recently when Ponselle sang Carmen. My old friend Albert Carré in Paris had taught her the rôle. She sang it beautifully. And she looked a lovely, slim, graceful gypsy.

After the performance I went backstage to congratulate her.

'Look at me, Alda!' she cried, twirling round before me. 'I've taken off pounds and pounds.'

'But look what you are doing to your voice,' I retorted. 'You're singing Carmen beautifully. But to do so you have pushed your voice down. When a high soprano does that, what rôles are left to her? Only Carmen and Delilah. No, thank you, I'd rather keep my voice than my figure.' I would, too. And I have.

IF THERE is any short, easy, gilded way of becoming a great singer I never heard of it. In New York I know half a dozen society women, amateur singers, who will tell you blandly how much better they are than the artists engaged at the Metropolitan. Once I sat through an opera in a box with one of these women, and heard her criticism of the singing of a great and finished artist who was the star of that performance. All the lady's remarks revealed to me, a professional singer, was how very much she did *not* know about the art of singing. But I don't doubt several other persons in the box were impressed.

These amateurs figure at the charity concerts. A few of them lately have made their way into night clubs, where their success depends not on their ability as singers but on a certain flair for publicity which they have.

There is Cobina Wright.

I remember one day going into the Ritz in Paris. There sat Admiral 'Andy' Graves and Colonel Groome. They made me join them. Presently Andy said:

'Alda, will you do something for Esther?'

Esther was Esther Cobb; now Cobina Wright.

'What?' I demanded. 'And why?'

He told me that Esther very much wanted a chance to make a career as a singer. She needed someone to coach her and get her started. Would I do it?

The long and the short of it was that Esther went back on my boat to New York. I gave her one of the rooms of my suite. I tried to teach her, and she came a good many times to the apartment; this was before Gatti and I were separated. But what I found was what I have found of more than half the amateur singers who come to me for help, Esther did not want to work.

Like all amateurs who remain amateurs forever, Esther was looking for an easy way round the obstacles that can only be overcome by hours of regular study and concentration.

This attitude belongs to the individual, not to a class. I meet it, where Heaven knows I should not have to meet it, in the girls who are training to be professional singers, and who know perfectly well that they have got to support themselves. Even the demands of a career do not make them serious. They all want to sing, but not to study. I'd say that was the distinguishing mark of the American girl today.

It is the greatest obstacle in the way of our having fine American singers.

As I say, this failing runs through all classes. On the other side there are society women who have in addition to lovely voices the zeal for study and work. Such a one is Mrs. James P. Donahue, one of the heiresses to the enormous Woolworth fortunes. She is a pupil of mine. If Jessie Donahue were not enormously rich, if she had to make her way in the world, she could achieve tremendous success as a singer. Not only has she one of the loveliest soprano voices I ever heard — very high and sweet and clear, but the quality in her singing and the gift for interpretation which are natural to her are what many singers have to study to attain.

O UT of these reflections, and this startling discovery that I enjoyed teaching, a brand-new career has come to me.

A career as absorbing, as demanding, as adventurous in its way as my stage life has been.

I started on it the same year that Gatti resigned from the Metropolitan, in 1934. He and Rosina Galli had married some time before he left.

The last time I was abroad I stayed a few days with the Toscaninis, whose home is on an island in the lake. In one of their boats we sailed past the rococco villa where my former husband lives what must be for a man of his experience and tastes a very dreary existence.

I felt sorry for Gatti, having today so much in my own life that is rich and active and creative.

On the heels of those shipboard reflections, after my six weeks spent in teaching Ganna Walska, came the inspiration which had developed into my present career.

It was this:

I would set out to discover for the American people who were my audience, and of whom I now was one, some new and beautiful voices. And I would pass on to these young singers what Marchesi taught me about the art of singing.

Mind you, I have never had any intention of being a 'singing teacher.' I thought of my career as that of a pioneer, an explorer. I do not, will not, take any pupil who comes along who offers me a fat round sum for lessons. But, as Marchesi did, I hear voices and select those that seem to me promising and worth training. The girls who come to me come from every walk in life. A few are rich men's wives or daughters. But the majority are girls from poor homes, or with no homes at all. Girls who will have to support themselves. Lacking the money for a musical education, these girls would otherwise never have their voices developed. Or hope to go further than a part in a night-club chorus.

For these girls, if their voices are really so good, and they themselves are sufficiently intelligent to study, I have a system of scholarships.

When I first got my idea of discovering and training singers for America, I talked it over with four or five very rich men and women who have long been friends of mine, and who love music. The idea was wildly idealistic, of course. But I've always found that the capitalists and so-called hard-headed business men are the greatest idealists in the world. Apparently my idea struck these friends of mine as rather magnificent. For immediately they began to come forward with suggestions, very businesslike suggestions; and then with requests to be allowed to help and have a share in what I was going to do.

It works this way:

A girl comes to me, or someone brings her, and I hear her sing. Or, I hold an audition and a number of applicants come and I hear them, one after another. Having heard them I decide whether they have voices worth training; or whether the best advice I can give them is what I advised Ganna Walska: 'Learn to cook. You'll never be a singer.'

If I accept a girl as a pupil, she signs a contract with me. She must promise not to sing in public without my permission. She cannot take a job, or do any work that will take her attention and strength from her musical studies. If she is a 'society' girl, I expect her when she becomes my pupil to put her lessons and her hours of study ahead of all social engagements. I expect her to go home from parties and to bed at a reasonable hour; not to smoke, or drink or gad about to excess.

You can't do those things and learn to sing at the same time.

If the girl is poor — and most of them are — then I arrange for her to have a scholarship.

'That is how you can help,' I said to those rich men and

women who fell in love with my idea. 'When I discover a promising singer you can make it possible for her to have at least two years of study with me. You can make her an allowance for living expenses, in a good club like the Three Arts, and for her clothes; for lessons in Italian and French. And later on, if she promises to become an opera singer, lessons in *mise en scène*.'

This is not charity.

The contract calls for the repayment of the scholarship money to the donors after the girl begins to earn her living as a singer.

And does it work?

Recently, one of the girls who has been studying with me just a year was offered an engagement to sing Aïda in Cincinnati, next summer. One or two will probably go before long to Hollywood. Their voices are lovely and they sing well, but they have not the volume needed for operatic work. In pictures this lack does not matter, as the voice is mechanically amplified. (Knowing this, I laughed the other day when someone told me about a singing teacher whose claim to fame was an ability to teach pupils to sing for the radio and the screen. To sing for the radio or for the movies is no different from singing for a friend in your own music room, and requires no special training or technique.)

A year and a half ago Mary Garden brought a girl to me. She is a Canadian, but she was singing in a chorus of six girls at a night club in New York. Singing bass. The manager of the club wasn't too pleased with her. She seemed to him to lack that something that makes a night-club singer 'go over' with the patrons. But someone brought the girl to Mary, and Mary, having heard her, bundled her into a taxi and brought her to me, at my apartment at the Waldorf.

'I want you to hear her, Alda,' said Mary. 'She's got a gorgeous voice. Gorgeous. Contralto.'

I sat down at the piano and played one of the songs the girl brought with her. Mary held her *élan vital* in leash long enough to listen whilst the girl sang ...

She sang atrociously. She pushed her voice, and she breathed in the wrong places. She strained until the cords of her neck stood out.

But even so there was no disguising the fact that the voice itself, if only she could learn to produce it, was superbly beautiful.

Tears were in Mary Garden's eyes. The bracelets on her arms clinked and jingled with her ecstatic waving of her hands.

'Listen to that, Alda. Listen to it. It's marvellous. I'll make her the greatest Delilah, the greatest....'

'Delilah, my eye!' I brought my two hands down on the keys in a conclusive chord. 'That girl's no mezzo-soprano. She's not a contralto. I don't care what she's been singing. That voice is a high, high soprano. She'll sing Aïda, marvellously. She'll sing Tosca, and Traviata.'

I hadn't bothered with the girl's name until now.

'Listen, my child,' I said to her. 'You'll start right away, to-day. You don't go back to the night club. You pin up your hair in a neat schoolgirl bun. You scrub the rouge and the lipstick and the powder from your face. You go out and buy yourself a lamb chop and spinach and a fresh green salad for lunch. And at three o'clock be back here for a lesson. After that we'll settle all the other things that have to be done.'

Will she really become a great opera singer?

That depends on her. On her capacity for study, for learning, and on something that is the backbone of every career. On the stage or in any of the other arts or professions. Marchesi called it a capacity for work. Anyway, it's a driving force; a hunger and thirst after knowledge of the art that one dedicates oneself to.

Has this girl got it?

Frankly, I do not know.

If she has, she will undoubtedly be a great singer some day. If she has not it won't be for any lack on my part in trying to rouse it in her, and in the other pupils who have scholarships.

Last summer, whilst I was at Narragansett, I rented a house near the club where I stayed, and put four of the girls to live there so that they should not miss their daily lessons and practice periods. In between, they had the sea and the beach and the sunshine and fresh air and proper food and good times that did not interfere with work.

Sometimes one or two of them are out at Casa Mia with me — learning the thousand and one things, besides singing, that a singer has to know if she is to be a success. How to come into a room. How to meet people of various nationalities and ranks. How to carry herself and speak and even how to dress, and — not least important of all — how *not* to make up her face.

'Alda, you're a regular Simon Legree with those girls,' one of my friends said to me the other day.

We were in my bedroom, which is directly over the long salon. Below us, Mary Garden's 'find' was practising scales. I had one ear for my friend's conversation, the other was on the sounds that proceeded from the room below.

Those sounds were flat.

I stamped my foot hard on the floor.

The voice found the middle of the note and stayed there.

'No, I'm not hard on them,' I refuted my friend's accusation. 'Only remember this: I have a passion for perfection. And an eye and an ear for details ... OUCH! Flat again ...'

I ripped the slipper from my foot and banged its high heel down on the floor directly above where the piano stands in the salon. The scales stopped. There was a second's pause; then the voice took them up again. This time, perfectly. I smiled.

'Hear that,' I said. 'Each note like a drop of clear water.'

That's what I mean by liking to teach. I was as deeply satisfied with those perfect scales as if I'd been singing them myself.

THERE isn't any ending to this story, in which every day may introduce a new chapter.

Here at Casa Mia there are guests coming to spend the week-end. The Toscaninis and my good friend and lawyer Jack Curtin, Alfred and 'Rene Sloan, David Sarnoff, and others. We are going to have ham steaks, two inches thick, parboiled in milk, spread with brown sugar, and then broiled over a charcoal fire. Ray Vir Den and I will broil them in the dining-room fireplace.

You, who have read this book, can say what you like about my virtues and my faults. But let anyone presume to criticize my cooking . . .

And at dinner and afterward there will be talk — gay, amusing, and informative talk. The sort that I love best. Talk of politics and business and of places and people and events. And still later there will be music in the long, lemon-yellow drawing-room. Toscanini will play, divinely. And with him to accompany me, I shall sing once more — and for the last time in these pages — Mimi's wistful 'Farewell.'

'*Senti, Aldina,*' Toscanini will surely say. 'You are happy?'

And I shall look around the softly lighted room, at the dear familiar chairs and tables and *bibelots* that made that astounding journey across the sea, at these friends who have been friends for years and then, perhaps, out through the windows to the moonlit garden.

There's a frost in the air.

Today, I shall remember, three cases of tulips and daffodils came by express. They are waiting for Joe, the gardener, and me to plant them tomorrow; the daffodils in golden drifts about the fountain in front of the house door; the tulips in a gay, trailing ribbon along the edge of the lawn on the Bay side.

And out of the fulness of my heart I shall answer Toscanini: 'Happy? Yes.'

THE END